# MUMMIES, CATACOMBS
# AND
# MAMMOTH CAVE

By
ANGELO I. GEORGE

H.M.I. Press

Mummies, Catacombs and Mammoth Cave
Second Edition

Library of Congress Control Number:  2013912941

ISBN  978-0-9713038-3-6  (pbk)


Published by
H. M. I. Press
P.O. Box 5426
Louisville, Kentucky 40255

# DEDICATION

To the memory of my parents

Constantino Angelo George, for giving me the time to pursue a life below ground; and to Clara Margaret Isham George for introducing me to fossils, geology, and Mammoth Cave.

Wood engraving from JulesVerne, *Voyage au Centre de la Terre*, 1867, Riou illustrated edition.

Mammoth Dome is one of the largest underground
voids in Mammoth Cave. Wood engraving from *Harper's
Weekly,* October 28, 1876.

# TABLE OF CONTENTS

# PREFACE

*When alarm subsided, and the sentiment of dismay and surprise permitted further research and enquiry, the figures were found to be Indian mummies, preserved by the art of embalming to great preservation and perfection of state!*

Thomas Ashe (1808)

The greatest cave is Mammoth Cave. Early in the settlement of Kentucky, the cave was discovered in 1798 to have rich deposits of saltpeter, the prime ingredient needed to make black gunpowder. By 1816, the cave was world famous because of the Indian mummies supposed to have been found in the far reaches in the cave. From then on, no other cave would ever eclipse the mammoth of all caves. It is one of the seven natural wonders of North America, the longest cave in the world, and possesses a rich history spanning over 3000 years of human involvement.

Stories that made Mammoth Cave great initially occurred between 1810 and 1816. In just seven years, these accounts in large part became staple traditions for the second oldest commercial cave in America. In time, the source of these traditions became lost. Some of them occurred in nearby caves and were transplanted to Mammoth.

The saltpeter miners during their excavations in neighboring Short Cave accidently encountered Indian burials. They were found in stone box tombs buried in the dirt of the cave floor that had since been covered over with hundreds of tons of rock. These were no ordinary burials, nor were the human remains mere skeletons. They had found Indian mummies preserved to a high degree of completeness. Each of the mummies was interred with a great amount of personal clothing and jewelry. The rich assortment of artifacts and the way they were buried led the discoverers to suspect these were no ordinary people. They must have been high ranking people or kings and queens to be buried and mummified in such fashion.

These American Indian mummies were not embalmed, had not been preserved with exotic spices and chemicals, nor were they wrapped in bandages. They became naturally mummified by the dry soil and atmospheric conditions in caves. Human artifacts of this nature are still exceptionally rare; and their mode of burial was a great mystery to their discovers.

At least two of the mummies were destroyed by the superstitious miners. The other three or four found residence in museums. One of them, referred to as Fawn Hoof, would launch Mammoth Cave to world wide recognition. In time, all the mummies from Short Cave were said to have been found in the far distant reaches of Mammoth Cave. Late in the century (1875), Little Al was discovered in a side passage of Salts Cave. In the shadow of the early twentieth century, another mummy, called Lost John, was discovered in 1935 under a boulder in Mammoth Cave. These were not burials, but are the result of the earliest known fatal accidents in North American caves.

Short Cave, Salts Cave, and Mammoth Cave were not the only caves to produce Indian mummies. Big Bone Cave in east central Tennessee, probably produced six or more mummies. Two of them were in part collected and displayed in museums.

There was a Catacomb of mummies found near Lexington, Kentucky. That tradition recalls a cave that contained hundreds of Indian mummies. Other catacombs were found in Park City, Bloomfield, Litchfield, and Hart County, Kentucky; and one each in Ohio and Tennessee.

The lore associated with catacomb mummies became inter-twined with those from the mummy caves in Kentucky and Tennessee. Embellishment in time displaced the Indian in favor of Egyptian mummies placed here by trans-Atlantic voyagers from the Old World. Against this backdrop, I first met Lost John in Mammoth Cave.

My grandmother, Mayme Grace Monroe (1899-1975) grew up near Mammoth Cave in a place called Jennie on Toohey Ridge. In my early youth she recited many exciting stories about the cave, her father's help with building the Mammoth Cave railroad, and the mummy that once lived in the cave. With no field of reference, I experienced a shock about 1952 upon seeing Lost John without his bandages, and wondered were they were. I was told the man in the cave was not like the Egyptian mummies I had seen in the museum of the Louisville Free Public Library or the Field Museum in Chicago. Lost John became a mute friend of dreams and we often met in the cave years later. He remains in my memory as a caver friend who came to Mammoth Cave and stayed.

Only Horace C. Hovey, Harold Meloy, and the author actually sat down to work out the convoluted history of these mummies. Hovey's *Celebrated American Caverns* in 1882 provided the groundwork from which all of the contemporary Mammoth Cave investigations sprang. Meloy's book, *Mummies of Mammoth Cave*, was published in 1968 and revised in 1971. My own work, *Mummies of Short Cave and the Great Catacomb Mystery*, came out in 1985. All of these books are out of print.

From time to time, I looked at the *Mummies of Short Cave and the Great Catacomb Mystery* with an eye toward revision. Since 1985, much new material had been collected on the Catacomb and its relationship to Mammoth Cave. Some of this was published in anthology form in *Prehistoric Mummies from the Mammoth Cave Area, Foundations and Concepts* in 1990. What was lacking was an all encompassing view of the people involved over a wide geographic area and the way it shaped their perception of Indian mummies. This book brings together all of the Tennessee and Kentucky mummy discoveries and their impact on the development of archaeological investigation in the Midwest.

Louisville, Kentucky
July 1, 1994

# PREFACE TO THE SECOND EDITION

*Mummies, Catacombs and Mammoth Cave* has been in print for nineteen years. During that time, new information has been discovered to better clarify events, dates, and people involved. This information was incorporated into the text to help flesh out more detail about the discoveries of mummies from the Mammoth Cave area.

Several individuals shared their insight on Short Cave, Long Cave and Salts Cave, especially, Stanley Sides, M.D., Dr. Patty Jo Watson, and Mr. Norman Warnell. Their input has been of great value and helped place events and people in a proper perspective. My wife, Diana Emerson George typeset the book, rendered illustrations for clarity, and guided publication.

Louisville, Kentucky
July 14, 2013

# ACKNOWLEDGMENT

Much thanks is extended to the following individuals who shared their knowledge on the life and exploits of Thomas Ashe: Dr. J. Winston Coleman, Jr.; Eugene H. Conner, M.D.; Mr. Harold Meloy, authority on the mummies from the Mammoth Cave region for his help and generous comments on the manuscript during its early preparation. Dr. James F. Quinlan for critical comments on portions of the manuscript. Additional documentation was furnished by: Mr. Roy E. Goodman, and Ms. Beth Carroll-Horrocks Reference Librarian of the American Philosophical Society; Mr. Harold Meloy; William R. Halliday, M.D.; Stanley Sides, M.D.; Dr. Gary O'Dell; Mr. Marion O. Smith; Mr. William W. Torode; Dr. Roger Sperka; Dr. Stuart S. Sprague; Dr. George M. Crothers; and Mr. Gordon L. Smith. The American Antiquarian Society for permission to quote from unpublished correspondences in their manuscript collections. The University of Louisville Medical Library offered the services of their rare book room and manuscript files. The The Earl Gregg Swem Library, College of William and Mary, Manuscript Department, provided for view significant William and Peyton Short correspondences. Mammoth Cave National Park and the Cave Research Foundation is acknowledged for their field support and library assistance. Mr. Laurence R. McCarty provided assistance while in the field. He also proofread and offered suggestions for the improvement of the manuscript prior to publication. Mrs. Diana Emerson George offered editorial suggestions, type set the manuscript, and supervised the publication of the book.

Mr. James Holberg, Curator of Manuscripts, The Filson Club, was of invaluable service in providing insight into William Clark. He also provided for view, significant correspondence of Charles Wilkins, Samuel Brown, and the Short family.

Mr. Marion O. Smith supplied hard-to-find historical cave references, helped to sort out antique place names, and generally acted as a sounding board during the development research on this project. Mr. Philip J. DiBlasi, archaeologist, University of Louisville, for getting me excited to do more mummy research. He also provided technical suggestions for the improvement of the manuscript. Dr. Patty Jo Watson offered comments on Mammoth Cave area archaeology.

"The dark and bloody ground" in John Filson's *Kentucke*, is often pictured as representative of Indian and pioneer conflicts. Wood engraving from *Ballou's Pictorial Drawing-Room Companion*, November 29, 1856.

CHAPTER ONE

# INTRODUCTION

*I furnished the lovers of nature with a variety of interesting
information; and to the lovers of antiquity I presented objects of
absolute astonishment.*

Thomas Ashe (1815)

It's the adventure that counts! Wild wilderness, the smell of green grass
along the waters edge, the spray of white water rapids from shooting the
Falls of the Ohio, and far outposts of civilization: Cincinnati, Louisville,
and Natchez. These pioneer towns were rough and tumble rendezvous of
river boatmen and their portage of cargo. It was a time of gritty sun baked
necks, dark deeds, and Bowie knives. With a little patience for mischief,
a person could get into a lot of trouble in any one of those places. The
towns and byways were populated by rugged individualists of pioneer
resourcefulness and hospitality. Travelers, peddlers, and journeymen were
put up in rural homesteads, treated as family, and sent on their way in the
morning. In return, the traveler brought the news of the day to his often
illiterate host. The voyager was royally accepted in the best of homes,
especially if he was a foreigner. This was the world that Thomas Ashe
(1770-1835) traveled in 1806.

The river system was the easiest way to reach the interior of America.
Ashe witnessed the changing frontier scenes from the deck of a flatboat.
Some of the vistas that caught his eye were the Indian mounds at
Marietta and Cincinnati, Ohio, Port William (Carrolton, Kentucky), and
the two outstanding natural features on the Ohio River: The Falls at
Louisville, and Cave-In-Rock. These features would figure prominently in
the travelogue that he would compose a year later in England. *Travels
in America* is a novel of unexcelled high adventure worthy of any boast
Mike Fink (c. 1770-1823) could ever dream a decade later. Ashe's motive
was "fame and glory." He was a "gonzo" writer of travel fiction in which
the action and adventure revolved around him and was due in part to his
interaction with events.

Early 1806 wood engraving of the map of North America. From *Geography Made Easy*, by Jedidiah Morse, (Thomas and Andrew, Boston, 1807).

Between the years 1808 and 1816, news of an astounding nature swept through eastern North America and spread all the way to the European continent. American Indian mummies were discovered in the caves of Kentucky and Tennessee.[1] Ordinarily these events would not have attracted much attention, but the mummies were preserved so well that they were thought to have been embalmed in a style similar to Egyptian mummies! Word of these rarest of antiquities produced a tremendous amount of excitement in the popular press and scientific journals. The general public became eager to see these wonders and gladly paid cash money for a chance view of petrified human remains from a long forgotten past.[2]

Who would have thought that caves, especially dry caves, could house the mummified remains of the American Indian? An Irishman, Captain Thomas Ashe, Esq., first recorded the pioneers discovery of mummies from one of these Kentucky caves. He published the report as a "true" story in his new book of *Travels in America, Performed in 1806*.[3] In time, the cave with its "thousands" of mummies became known as the Lexington Catacomb.

Ashe's book was published in England in 1808 and reprinted the following year in America. It became an instant success for a number of reasons, especially Americans' thirst to read about themselves and to experience the wilds and marvels of "the west." The travel book helped to popularize Indian mummy burials in caves and to polarize the discovery, lore, and mythology of all North American mummy burials. His stories were of such improbable substance that most investigators turned their attention to exploring more fruitful ground. The journal is attractively written in a correspondence style of *belles-lettres,* containing various geographical facts, adventures, frontier stories, and quite a few fabrications and extensions of the truth. His book is composed in a self serving style that is more cavalier, easy to read, and at the same time, captivates one's imagination with frontier views across eastern North America. The book is written using an Elizabethan cadence style, with phrases and quotes similar to those employed by Free and Accepted Masons. His journey was confined to the major waterways of the Alleghany, Monongahela, Ohio, and Mississippi rivers. The book had a strong impact on the reading public and as a result, received wide circulation, reprinting, and criticism. It is important because it is "one of the earliest judgments passed on American life."[4]

Archaeological discoveries from Indian mounds were other matters considered in his book. The identity of the people who built them was a complete mystery. Even the present Indians could not recall from what tribe they were built. The mounds had been there a long time; huge oak trees, hundreds of years old stood on these structures. Some of the mounds were obviously the graves of the people who built them. Others were empty

TRAVELS

IN

AMERICA,

PERFORMED IN 1806,

For the Purpose of exploring the

RIVERS

ALLEGHANY, MONONGAHELA, OHIO, AND
MISSISSIPPI,

AND

Ascertaining the Produce and condition

OF

THEIR BANKS AND VICINITY.

By THOMAS ASHE, Esq.

London: Printed.
Newburyport—re-printed for Wm. SAWYER & CO.
By E. M. Blunt, State-Street.
1808.

Title page to Thomas Ashe's *Travels in America.*

and had the shape of walled fortifications inclosing a mound or two. All sorts of ideas were offered to explain their occurrence and architecture. These features were said to have been built by the Mound Builders.

Consistently throughout *Travels*, Ashe tries to show a cultural and historical connection from the Mound Builders to the classical Greek, Roman, and Egyptian civilizations. He strongly suggests the Egyptians along with legions of other European nations, colonized North America in antediluvian time, before the great flood of Noah! A concept embraced by many naturalists during the Speculative Period in archaeology (1661-1847).

Perhaps while in Cincinnati or Natchez, Ashe acquired the discovery story of a catacomb of Indian mummies. The locale was supposed to be in a cave near Lexington, Kentucky. Diligent search of newspapers in the early 1800s does not reveal the existence of this catacomb of mummies. The first reference to authentic Indian mummies in caves does not occur until 1810, and that one was from Tennessee.

According to Ashe, the catacomb or cave containing the Indian mummies is located "adjacent to the town of Lexington," Kentucky; and has for more than 200 years received a good share of scientific and historical attention.[5] Today, the catacomb is a staple tradition connected with the early pioneer settlement of Lexington, a story well known even though its original author and the circumstances surrounding its discovery have been forgotten. The Lexington Catacomb is a true mystery in search of a place and time of origin. It is a "who-dun-it" of grave robbers, bone thieves, failures, opportunists, and showmen.

Without doubt, the setting for the Lexington Catacomb with its stock of Indian mummies is one of the major high points in the travelogue. It is an incredible story of pioneer adventure and discovery. Ashe's swashbuckling account shrouded the authenticity of future Native American mummies for years to come.

The Lexington Catacomb story consists of the following narrative from Ashe's *Travels*.[6] There are numerous renditions and alterations of Ashe's original story. Popular and scientific writers very often construct their own synopses of the account and in doing so, have provided much additional color, often detracting and adding to Ashe's original statements.

Lexington stands on the site of an old Indian town, which must have been of great extent and magnificence, as is amply evinced by the wide range of its circumvallatory works, and the great quantity of ground it once occupied. Time and the more destructive ravage of man have nearly levelled these remains of former greatness with the dust, and would possibly allow them to sink into an entire oblivion, were they not connected with a

ANCIENT WORK,
*FAYETTE CO. KENTUCKY.*

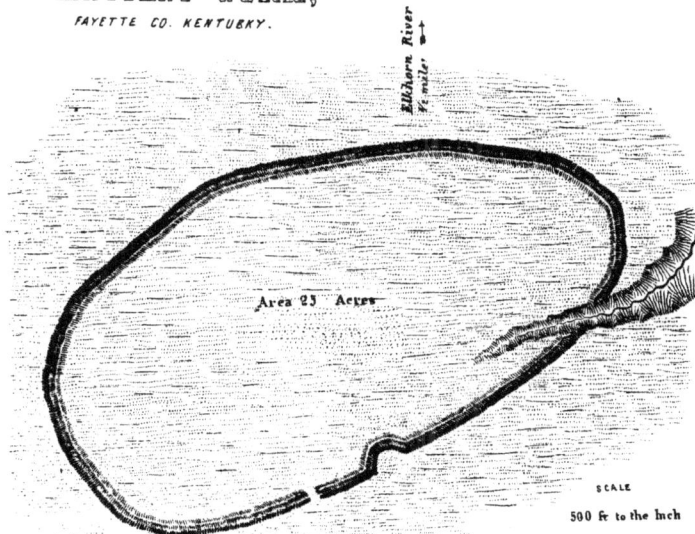

Survey of ancient earthworks near Lexington, Kentucky, by Constatine S. Rafinesque. Wood engraving in E. G. Squire and E. H. Davis, *Ancient Monuments of the Mississippi Valley*, 1848.

catacomb, formed in the bowels of the limestone rock, about fifteen feet below the surface of the earth, and laying adjacent to the town of Lexington! This grand object, so novel and extraordinary in America, was discovered about twenty years ago by some of the first settlers, whose curiosity was excited by something remarkable in the character of stones which struck their attention while hunting in the woods. They removed these stones, and came to others of singular workmanship; the removal of which laid open the mouth of a cave – deep, gloomy, and terrific. With augmented numbers, and provided with cordage and light, they descended, and entered without obstruction a spacious apartment; the sides and extreme ends were formed into nitches [sic] and compartments, and occupied by figures representing men! When alarm subsided, and the sentiment of dismay and surprise permitted further research and enquiry, the figures were found to be Indian mummies, preserved by the art of embalming to great preservation and perfection of state!

Unfortunately for antiquity, science, and every thing else held sacred by the illumined and learned, this inestimable discovery was made at a period when a bloody and inveterate warfare was carried on between the Indians and the whites, and the power of the former was displayed in so formidable a manner, that the latter were filled with terror and a spirit of revenge, which

5

manifested itself both on contemptible and important occasions. Animated by this worthless and detestable spirit, the discoverers of the catacomb delighted to wreak their vengeance even on the Indian dead. They dragged the mummies to the day, tore the bandages open, kicked the bodies into dust, and made a general bonfire of the most ancient remains antiquity could boast: of remains respected by many hundred revolving years, held sacred by time, and unsusceptible of corruption, if not visited by profane and violating hands!

What these despoilers did not accomplish, their followers in the course of time took care to effect. I have explored the catacomb, and can bear testimony to the industry and determination of the curious who resort to it to efface every mark of workmanship, and to destroy every evidence of its intention or original design! – The angles and ornaments of the nitches [sic] are mutilated; all projections and protuberances are struck off; every mummy removed, and so many fires have been made in the place, either to warm the visitors or to burn up the remains, that the shades, dispositions, and aspects, have been tortured into essential difference and change.

The descent is gradually inclined, without a rapid or flight of stairs. – The width four feet, the height seven. – The passage but six feet long, is a proportion larger, and the catacomb extends one hundred paces by thirty-five. It is about eighteen feet high; the roof represents an irregular vault, and the floor an oblong

Indians attack pioneer forts and homesteads in Kentucky. Lithograph from Martha G. Purcell, *Stories of Old Kentucky*, 1915.

square nearly level. From the nitches [sic] and shelvings on the sides, it might be conjectured, that the catacomb could contain in appropriate situations about two thousand mummies. I could never learn the exact quantity it did contain, the answer to my enquiries being "Oh! they burned up and destroyed hundreds." Nor could I arrive at any knowledge of the fashion, manner, and apparel of the mummies in general, or receive any other information than that "they were well lapped up, appeared sound and red, and consumed in the fire with a rapidity that baffled all observation and description."

Not content with such general and traditionary remarks, I employed several hands, and brought to light forty or fifty baskets of rubbish gleaned throughout the vault, both from the sides and from the floor. The dust of the heap was so light, impalpable and pungent, that it rose into the atmosphere and affected the senses so much as to cause effusion of the eyes and sneezing, to a troublesome degree. I still proceeded on a minute investigation, and separated from the general mass, several pieces of human limbs, fragments of bodies, solid, sound, and apparently capable of eternal duration! With much violence they broke into parts, but emitted no dust, or shewed any inclination to putrization. The impalpable powder arose from the bands and ligatures with which they were bound, the pungency of which denoted their composition to be vegetable matter.

In a cold state the subjects had no smell whatever, but when submitted to the action of fire they consumed with great violence, emitted no smoke, and diffused an agreeable effluviae which scented the air, but with no particular flagrance to which it could be assimilated.

How the bodies were embalmed, how long preserved; by what nation, and from what people descended, no ideas can be formed, nor any calculation made, but what must result from speculative fancy and wild conjecture. For my part, I am lost in the deepest ignorance. My readings affords me no knowledge; my travels no light. I have neither read, heard nor know of any of the North American Indians who formed catacombs for their dead, or who were acquainted with the art of preservation by embalming. The Egyptians, according to Herodotus, had three methods of embalming; but Diodorus observes that the ancient Egyptians had a fourth method, of far greater superiority. That manner is not mentioned by Diodorus, it has been extinct three thousand years, and yet I cannot think it presumptuous to conceive that the Indians were acquainted with it, or with a mode of equal virtue and effect.

The Kentuckyans [sic] assert in the very words of the Greek that the features of the face and the form and appearance of the whole body were so well preserved, that they must have been the exact representations of the living subject. The Indians could not have had the art of embalming in the methods made known by Herodotus, because they never could have had the necessary

7

materials – as evidence let us review the three systems, to which, in Egypt, different prices were attached. In the most esteemed method, they extracted the brains by the nose with a crooked iron, and then poured in drugs: afterwards they opened the body, took out the bowels, washed the inside with palm wine, and having rubbed into it pounded perfumes, filled the cavity with myrrh, cassia, and other spices, and then sewed it up. After this they washed the body with nitre, then let it lie seventy days; and having washed it again, bound it up in folds of linnen, besmearing it over with gums which they used instead of glue. The relations then took home the body, and enclosing it in the wooden figure of a man, placed it in the catacombs. Another method of embalming was, injecting turpentine of cedar with a pipe into the body, without cutting it: they then salted it for seventy days, and afterwards drew out the pipe, which brought along with it the intestines. The nitre dried up the flesh leaving nothing but skin and bones. The third way was only cleansing the inside with salt and water, and salting it for seventy days.

The first three methods could not have been employed by the Indians for want of palm wine, myrrh, cassia, and other perfumes. The second could not be that practised by them, as it tended to waste the flesh and preserve the mere skin and bones – and the third is inadmissible, from its incapacity to resist the unremitting destruction and ravages of time.

Discovery of human remains in caves was an event of profound importance. Wood engraving from *Famous Catacombs and Caves*, 1886.

An argument may be adduced to favor an opinion of the remote antiquity of the Indian mummies, from the entire and complete consumption of their bandages, wrappers, and bands – which on the Egyptian mummies continue to this day in higher preservation than the body they envelop. There is a mummy in an English collection of curiosities, brought from Egypt by the French, and taken from them by one of our privateers, which is remarkable for containing only the head and part of the thigh and leg bones wrapped in folds of fine linnen to the consistence of three inches thick. The linnen in some parts was as white and perfect as new, and on the legs there was some appearance of the flesh still remaining, although, from a moderate calculation, it must have been embalmed upwards of two thousand years. It may then again be repeated, that the Indian mummies are of higher antiquity then the Egyptian, as the bandages are consumed on the one though not on the other; except, as I had occasion to remark, that the Indian ligatures were of a substance more susceptible of decay than the Egyptian. But this is a subject of too great magnitude,variety and diffusion, for my purpose. I submit the fact for the consideration of a better judgment and an able pen, and conclude by informing you that I restored every article to the catacomb – save some specimens retained as objects of the first curiosity, and blocking up the entry with huge stones which orginally closed it up, left the spot with the strongest emotions of veneration and displeasure: veneration for so sublime a monument of antiquity, and displeasure against the men whose barbarous and brutal hands reduced it to such a state of waste and desolation.

No other catacomb is known in the State, though barrows abound in various directions.[7]

Thomas Ashe is the last person to visit the great catacomb of Fayette County, Kentucky. Its true location has been lost since 1806.

Reading the actual account for the first time in the Filson Club library on West Breckenridge Street, I broke out in a cold sweat, accompanied with goose pimples, and a resounding "what a story!" Sitting amongst the greatest repository of Kentucky history, her aged portraits, the Filson map of *Kentucke*, and the varnish of dust that made the Filson Club what it used to be; caused a whorl of pioneer imagery to blend into this catacomb discovery. Surrounded in this atmosphere, the cold sweat would not go away as the story took on new meaning. I did not know it then, but I had experienced the very same feeling of awe and wonder felt by readers when the book was first issued in 1808! On a grand scale, it was my first research encounter with "fantastic archaeology" on a Kentucky subject.

Stephen Williams would characterize the subject of "fantastic archaeology" as suspect cultural discoveries associated with a high level of strangeness in the field. The discipline is characterized as "those alternative views of the past that use data and interpretations that will not stand close scrutiny."[8] Ashe's story becomes fantastic archaeology through his use of event hyperbole and artistic licence to make a good story better. With Ashe as the only witness inside the Catacomb, a lack of traceable documentation before his visit, and a strong air for a hoax, lends credence to this concept employed by Williams.

Ashe was an accomplished fireside traveler who really did make a journey to America. He traveled inland along the major waterways, went back home to England, and a year later, sat down in his study and composed his travelogue. He is not to be confused with other "fireside travelers" such as Daniel Defoe (1660-1731), who never left home, yet wrote exciting adventures and New World discoveries.[9]

The American edition of *Travels* caused an immediate sensation. Harsh reviews enhanced the entertainment and sale value of the book from the author who "felt no love for Americans."[10] American cultural backwardness was offset against exotic views of variegated frontier scenes, wild animals, mysterious earthworks, thousands of mummies, Egyptian hieroglyphics on the walls of dark caves, and a whole cortége of rude backwoods pioneers. These images enthralled early readers with vision of fantasy and wonder. The same kind of substance without the vitriol would be effectively used three decades later in *Davy Crockett's Almanacks*. Both elicited a certain amount of guffaws and knee slapping.

*Travels in America* is a lampoon of straight faced satire of geographical Americana, cultural morals, coupled with the foibles of inland travel. Ashe as comedian, employs his own brand of vitriolic dead pan social commentary. Americans didn't realize *Travels* was a joke book about America written for a specialty market in Great Britain. Elements of a good joke require a series of simple premises known to everyone. The premise is then added to by using an air of hyperbole, thereby spinning the subject matter beyond credible reason. Done with a straight face, makes a good story all the more funny. American and British reviewers were not laughing for they took the book as gospel according to Ashe and crucified him for his action.

# CHAPTER TWO

# CHARACTER AND REPUTATION OF THOMAS ASHE

*Wonderful he is to be sure, for he tells tales that are wonderful,*
*but which are as far from the truth, as the earth is from the sun's*
*center.*

Zadok Cramer (1814)

Thomas Ashe represents the quintessential adventurer who crafted his achievements from over two hundred years of North American travelogues, history, and geography. He was fortunate enough to write and publish three volumes of *Memoirs and Confessions of Captain Ashe* in 1815.[1] The autobiography promised to reveal his full checkered life; but in reality, perpetuates a Don Quixotean fantasy that forms the basic signature of his many publications. Using his autobiography as a "truthful source," allows one to fall into his trap. There are no reliable sources to draw substance other than his works. Published biographical sketches of Ashe are all taken from this autobiography.[2] There are no accurate accounts assembled from primary or secondary sources. The following profile from his *Memoirs* is submitted with a full measure of caution.

In Ireland, he received a military commission from the 83rd Regiment of Foot which was immediately disbanded. Eugene H. Conner tried without success to establish Ashe's military service record.[3] Early in Ashe's adult life he seduced a young woman in Bordeaux, France. Honor being what it was in those days, the woman's enraged brother fought a duel with him. Her brother was almost fatally wounded during the exchange. This landed Ashe in prison for a short time to contemplate his shortcomings, or shall I say, errors in judgement. His duelling partner lived and Ashe was released from jail. An idle life in learning the wine merchant trade caused his father to disinherit him for life.

Later, he found himself in financial debt (a condition he seemed always to court), and migrated (fled) to Switzerland. Tiring of Swiss hospitality or some other thin excuse, Ashe launched his first voyage to North America in the spring of 1799.[4] While in America, he established himself as a gentleman farmer in the backwoods of Pennsylvania. In Washington City, he became editor of the *National Intelligencer* and was succeeded by Stephen Pickney. During his stay in the seat of government, he was befriended by Thomas Jefferson, only to later fall into disfavor.[5] He migrated back to England in perhaps the year 1804. The Irishman amassed and lost many fortunes, dabbled in natural science, became a successful museum exhibitor, gentleman of sterling qualities, and world traveler.

He modeled his personality character on an idealized counterpart, the famous French explorer and exaggerative geographer, Michel-Guillaume Saint Jean de Crèvecoeur (1735-1813). Ashe "borrowed" his military service and rank of Captain, pretended to be a gentleman farmer in America, explorer, adventurer, and writer of fabulous encounters in America and elsewhere. Ashe's manufactured life shows many parallels with Crèvecoeur, whose inventive mind, popularity, and skill as a writer eclipsed even Ashe's. Much of the American portion of the autobiography is a rewritten plagiarized outlined rendition from St. Jean de Crèvecoeur's book, *Letters from an American Farmer*, an immensely popular work in France and in America.[6] The rest is in the style of Jean-Jacques Rousseau's (1712-1778) *Les Confessions*. The detail of the autobiography is taken from structural encounters found in a three part fantasy novel *Histoire de Gil Blas de Santillane*, written between the years 1715 and 1735 by Alain René Le Sage (1668-1747). Rousseau's fictional life treatment was augmented with accomplishments of Crèvecoeur, and then coupled with the likable rascal Gil Blas. Rewritten exploits of Gil Blas formed basic anecdotes in Ashe's life and adventures. Here, as with Gil Blas, he encountered low lifes and crowned heads of Europe. The best works from these authors suited the engineered character of Thomas Ashe, who later in life was "granted free passage to Botany Bay, but missed the ship!"[7]

In keeping with the tragic novels of the Romantic Movement, Ashe's *Memoirs* is a vale of tears and woe, revealing he was the most victimized individual on the face of this earth. He never recants or admits any wrong-doing – Simon Pure he is, and tells completely different stories about the people who became his victims. His *Memoirs* would make good afternoon television soap opera material, needing little alteration! If Ashe were living today, he could find active employment writing copy for scandal

Pioneer tavern life centered on a place locals could meet, cuss and discuss the events of the day, and enjoy mutual company. Wood engraving from *The Century Illustrated Monthly Magazine*, 1901.

sheet tabloids, similar to the ones he contributed to during his lifetime in England.

Based upon primary first and second hand accounts of Ashe's presence in America, a character profile starts to materialize. Ashe was tried and fried in the local press, castigated in taverns, and his skin hung out to dry in the scientific literature. Thomas Ashe was a career criminal, con artist, cheat, embezzler, blackmailer, deadbeat, dilettante in natural science, plagiarist, hypocrite, forger, impersonator, egotist, defamer of American patriotism, bone thief, grave robber, pot hunter, and soldier of fortune (other persons' fortunes). Ashe preyed on people's gullibility or their desire to acquire instant wealth. In essence, Thomas Ashe was a larcenous bunco artist who researched his marks before making his kill. Could a person be all these things and still sleep well? It was easy! The social deviate Ashe absolved himself of all of these charges. Not guilty. Obviously his marks were talking about someone else.

The actual character and reputation of Thomas Ashe is quite derogatory. He is a dirty rotten scoundrel of the first order, just the kind of villain one could love to hate and every mystery book needs one. This is why

Ashe tailor-made his life as a metaphor of Gil Blas. It was this love-hate relationship that made him famous in a likeable infamous sort of way. Of the references used in the compilation of this research, only Archer B. Hulbert compliments Ashe's integrity by saying he was "...erratic and opinionated but honest...."[8] Critics (his only friends), said he was one of the lowest vermin ever to have landed in America. Calling Ashe a "rat" and a "liar" were probably some of the kindest things said about him and his writings. These were badges of distinction worn with a certain amount of pride. Apparently, it worked, for Ashe kept writing the same kind of books for the rest of his life. With a winning smile and a certain amount of bravado, Ashe brought new meaning to the phrase "trust me."

The sonorous litany of Ashe's critics is long, but this overview should suffice. Archaeologists Bennett H. Young in 1910 and William D. Funkhouser and William S. Webb in 1932, said Ashe had "...a vivid imagination and a very slight respect for veracity."[9] Kentucky historians on the other hand were not so kind. Robert Peter in 1882, would retort that Ashe was a "notorious traveler."[10] J. Stoddard Johnson, in 1889, mentions Ashe was "the slanderer of our country."[11] Kentucky's most illustrious geologist, Willard R. Jillson, came right out and said, "Captain Ashe was a liar and literary thief."[12] Floyd L. McCollum in an unpublished masters thesis on *Bones from Kentucky Caves*, retorted that Ashe was, "...an unworthy Irish globe tramp and notorious liar."[13] Otto A. Rothert, perhaps best known as the author of the spelean-history classic, *The Outlaws of Cave-In-Rock*; submitted the following:

> The critics in Ashe's day, and ever since, declared that the writer of *Travels* was a literary thief, bone thief, and infamous prevaricator and ridiculed his work on the ground that it was filled with incredible stories grafted onto authentic incidents and actual facts. This general condemnation gave the new book a wide circulation for a few years.[14]

Criticism of Ashe's new book often appeared in leading periodicals and newspapers of the day. One of the first and often considered the best, appeared in *The Port Folio* of February 1809.[15] Charles Caldwell, M.D., said as Ashe proceeded to the:

> "wilderness of the West" where he meets with adventures as numerous as those of the "Knight of the Woeful Countenance," and hardly less miraculous than those of the most renowned Baron Munchausen.[16]

He ends his review of *Travels* with:

> we cannot take leave of Mr. Ashe, without expressing our entire contempt both of himself and his book. He appears to us, and we speak on no slender authority, to be one of those European *malcontents*, who either to escape from the wholesome discipline of their government, or allured by the love of change, and the prospects of successful adventure, emigrate to us with the most delusive expectations, which being disappointed, return home to redeem their patriotism, and assuage their mortification by the most illiberal, rancorous, and malignant abuse of our country, and its institutions.
>
> The work contains nothing to instruct, and little to amuse any description of readers, and that little is produced at the expense of the author's candor and veracity.[17]

As to Ashe's ability as a reliable and creditable natural scientist, Caldwell says, "after appropriating a few weeks, thus actively, to the investigations of *American Antiquities*, in which short interval, it must be confessed, that he *saw* and *did* more, than all the people of the country from its earliest settlement to the present hour."[18] The reviewer relates experiences of Ashe's adventure and tries to track down original sources – only to end in failure. It was fine for Ashe to write of a New World philosopher's stone, pre-deluvial sculpture, or even alligators that produce a roar like thunder. All of these were passed down to the reading public.

At first in looking into the character and reputation of Thomas Ashe, I considered that perhaps there may have been much cultural bias toward him from Americans. He certainly raised their ire. His English counterparts followed in similar form and denounced his work. *The Edinburgh Review, or Critical Journal* critiques the new 1809, three volume edition of *Travels*. This anonymous reviewer spared no descriptive adjectives in panning the work. For example: "But it would be endless to notice all his ravings on these subjects. He never begins to speculate, without plunging at once into the depths of absurdity. Like 'bold Arball' in the Duciad, he makes 'a furious dive,' and sinks far below all the other sons of dullness."[19]

It was not just American vanity over Ashe's malignant treatment of her national heritage, people, and institutions. Critics on both sides of the Atlantic felt justified in their censorious attitude toward the Irishman.

Other English travelers, especially John Melish (1771-1822) and Christian Schultz would follow Ashe's route through the west. They were cognizant of Ashe's *Travels* and were surprised Americans were not as bad as pictured by Ashe. Schultz was quick to point out that Ashe never made his trip to America and had plagiarized extensively from Zadok Cramer's (1773-1831?) *The Navigator*, a guidebook to the interior rivers.[20]

Between 1809 and 1811, another Englishman, John Bradbury traveled over many of the same frontier routes, observed the people of the land, and felt their reaction to Ashe's recently published book. With a self serving tongue almost as sharp as Ashe's, he says of the book and its reaction on the American people:

> had I not witnessed the just indignation it has excited in that country, and also found that Ashe had been received and treated with the greatest kindness by the very people whom he has so grossly libelled....I think it a duty to myself and my country to state, that his description of the American people, and the accusations he makes against them, are void of foundation. If Mr. Ashe saw any instance to warrant his observations, he must have kept the worst of company.[21]

By 1814, Zadok Cramer, editor of *The Navigator*, became particularly upset when he learned that Ashe had modeled *Travels* from his 1806 edition.[22] Ashe had plagiarized whole pages from Cramer's river guidebook, along with various geographical and historical facts. He delivers a severe tongue-lashing: "a well-known and much celebrated character of Europe has taken liberties with this book, which, had he done the like to a butcher's stall, they would have brought him to the gallows, long ere this."[23] With humanity in his heart, Cramer forgives the Irishman for his plagiarism.[24] About the literary quality and accuracy of *Travels*, Cramer exhorts that Ashe, "...comes out fair and square as an original author, and a great and wonderful traveller. Wonderful he is to be sure, for he tells tales that are wonderful, but which are as far from the truth, as the earth is from the sun's center."[25] *Travels* proved so popular that it was republished seven or eight times.

The dean of Kentucky history, Thomas D. Clark, reports that Ashe was critical of American culture, considered Kentuckians "the fallen people," and the "notorious Irishman" was the "great libeler of Kentucky."[26] And "whatever the indiscretions of Thomas Ashe, his descriptions of the land are little short of being poetic."[27] Reuben G. Thwaites, in reviewing some works of early travelers, was of the opinion that Ashe had flights of fancy in his descriptions.[28] As Ashe pushed into the wilds of the west, he "sought the marvelous, and found it."[29] *Travels* according to Thwaites, is easily "among the best of the early journals, although abounding in exaggerations."[30]

The essayist, short story writer, humorous, biographer, and historian, Washington Irving (1783-1859) produced his *English Writers on America* in 1819. He gave five basic reasons for English writers biased scatological treatment of Americans and their institutions. Percy G. Adams capsulated Irving's thoughts as containing:

jealousy, the lack of comfortable inns and carriages; the fact that only the worst class of English travelers did the writing; disappointed avarice because of ill success in business; and their own antidemocratic environment.[31]

Ashe was only thirty five years old when he made the trip that would become his *Travels*. I don't think Ashe was any of the things he said about himself. His personality was so weak that he hid behind a mask in order to conceal his true inner self; an actor's role he played to the hilt with all the trappings and accoutrements of the best stage performer. He used several pseudonyms while traveling in America; in Europe he was known as Captain Light Dragoons, Olivia Moreland, and T. A.[32] I do not think the name Thomas Ashe is a pen name. I would think a person with as sordid a "past" as his needed this kind of insulation to live in respectable society. Not so, back home in England, he became an even greater shameless blackguard and lived to a ripe old age of sixty-five.

To be sure, it took some spirited element of adventure to undertake an inland journey. Once the traveler departed Philadelphia, few creature comforts awaited him. The steamboat, locomotive, well maintained roads, and a structured lodging system had not been introduced in the western country, let alone a practical reality. These inventions and institutions were a long time in coming. Any kind of inland travel whether on water or by land was a hardship undertaking. Awful road conditions and the seasonal uncertainties of water travel presented the only way to get from one place to another. In certain parts of the country outbreaks of yellow fever and malaria awaited travelers as they made haste to get through the infected area. Highwaymen and river pirates were other dangers. Local people and the occasional European visitor took it in stride by accepting the rigors associated with the journey.[33]

The old country adage, "you can't get there from here," had real meaning in 1806 when Ashe traveled across America. This is amplified by Daniel Drake (1785-1852) who knew the travel conditions of the period. He says:

> getting from one part of the country to another, I say, was a very different affair from what it now is (except when the river is frozen over), for one may now [in 1845] breakfast in Mayslick [Kentucky] and sup in Broadway [Cincinnati, Ohio]. In the first place, the roads were most of the way only "bridle paths," and even difficult to follow, for at their ramifications or "forks" there were no finger-boards, and not many living fingers to point the true way to the puzzled traveller. In the second place, between Mayslick and Cin., there were no taverns. Third, and lastly, as the said *via nova deserta, obscura*, was, also, *montosa et rugossissima*, the travel along it was slow and wearisome.[34]

17

Now you can imagine why Ashe rarely strayed inland. The only places we definitely know he stepped ashore are in Pittsburgh, Cincinnati, Louisville, Natchez, and New Orleans. All are river cities. There is only one piece of collateral documentation for a side trip away from the banks of the river. The salt maker Mr. Ballingal at the Blue Licks, Nicholas County, Kentucky, recalled having breakfast with the Irishman.[35] It is not known how Ballingal identified him from other travelers, especially knowing Ashe was using a pseudonym during his travels. This is the furthest known inland transit made by Ashe into Kentucky.

These subsequent inland voyages were manufactured from existing travelogues and histories, subjects of which his predecessors had also made fine use in constructing their *voyages extraordinaires*.[36] The hardships associated with back country travel, although great, served as a means to acquire the wealth of other people's money. Ashe could not and would not accept anything less. He did this without remorse or conscience and he never looked back.

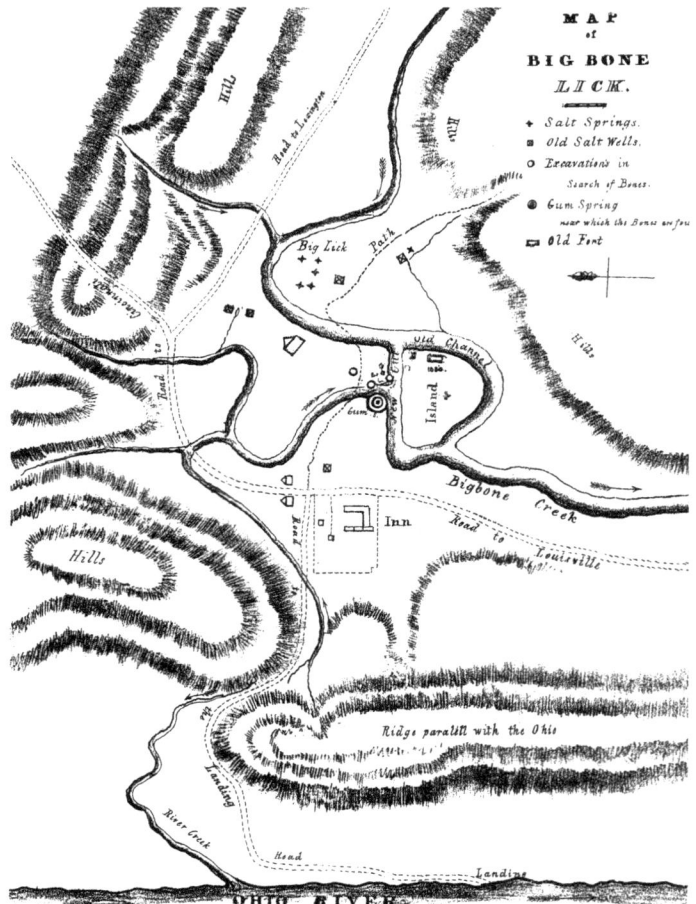

Map of Big Bone Lick in Boone County, Kentucky. From a wood engraving in the *The Monthly American Journal of Geology and Natural Science*, 1831.

CHAPTER THREE

# THOMAS ASHE
# AND THE BIG BONE CAPER

*Why do you rob banks?*

*Because that's where the money is.*

Willie Sutton
(Philosopher and thief)

The collection of Pleistocene vertebrates and Indian artifacts was an active pursuit of the intelligencia in Colonial and pioneer America. Bones and artifacts of this nature were exceptionally rare, esteemed to possess great value, and worthy of additional study and preservation. These lofty goals were well founded as private individuals and public institutions vied for possession. As the urban society pushed west, evidence of these remains was being destroyed at an alarming rate. The number of lost vertebrate fossils, mounds, graves, artifacts, and other vestiges associated with the Indian culture can not now be estimated.

Having introduced our villain, it's now time to bring on a cast of characters whose main goal seems to be greed and intellectual aggrandizement.

Thus enters Thomas Ashe's victim, William Goforth, M.D. (1766-1817) of Cincinnati, Ohio.[1] Dr. Goforth had labored in 1802 and then for four weeks beginning near the first of May 1803 with Mr. Reeder at Big Bone Lick in Boone County, Kentucky.[2] Their quest was the excavation of large Pleistocene Mammoth bones, long buried in the muck and sediments of this old salt lick. Using at times from six to eight laborers, they excavated numerous bones of the Mammoth, Mastodon, Musk ox, Elk and Megalonyx or ground sloth.

Two excavations were made, the largest one was eleven feet deep and thirty feet on a square side. Mr. Reeder excavated a small pit that produced large bones too.[3] Goforth divided his collection into two groups. The first group was shipped back to Cincinnati. Apparently the larger bones were left at the lick for future transport to Cincinnati.

According to Goforth, the bones were excavated at great personal expense and labor, associated with mounting frustration with the absent land owner. Sometime between 1804 or 1805, five tons of bones were shipped up the river to Dr. Andrew Richardson (Goforth's agent) at Pittsburgh, Pennsylvania.

This collection of Pleistocene vertebrates

Demonstration of salt making during the Salt Festival, Big Bone State Park, Kentucky.

represented the largest find of its day and learned institutions were perceived as eager to acquire ownership. The collection was earmarked for eventual sale to either Peale's Museum or to the American Philosophical Society.[4] For a time, Thomas Jefferson (1743-1826) found the purchase price unacceptable and turned down the offer on behalf of the Society.[5] Charles Wilson Peale (1741-1827) had his own complete Mammoth and other Pleistocene vertebrates on display in his Philadelphia Museum and did not need any more.[6] Finding a willing buyer became a source of frustration to Goforth and his agent Dr. Richardson.

Thomas Ashe arrived in America circa mid-1805 with forged letters of introduction as Thomas D'Arville.[7] It was during this early unrecorded segment of *Travels* when Ashe discovered the Goforth collection in Pittsburgh. He conducted a character profile on Goforth and found he was uniquely fond of Frenchmen, French ways, and France. A true Francophile was Goforth. In fact, most of the western inhabitants found it advantageous to be pro-French and anti-British. England was beginning to control the shipping lanes against one of Americas' chief trading partners, France. England and France were at war and the former was trying to embargo supplies to the latter. This cut revenues due American clients who had no personal recourse with a growing adversary. Merchant marines sailing for French held ports had their boats and cargo seized, and sailors impressed onto British vessels. The kidnapping of American sailors was a constant source of irritation to the President, Congress, and citizens.

Parading as a British traveler was not the sort of thing Ashe thought he could use to win friends and influence people. He used a disguise to hide his true identity and intentions.[8] Ashe assumed the personage of Monsieur Thomas D'Arville, a French scientist, educator, and dandy of some continental note. He presented his credentials to Dr. Benjamin S. Barton (1766-1815) of Philadelphia, who, seeing the paper work was in order, issued new letters of introduction that would open doors for D'Arville (Ashe) to the intellectual community.[9] It should be noted that at this time there was, in fact, a famous French geographer and cartographer by the name of Jean Baptiste Bourguignon Anville. Possibly Ashe wanted his American friends to make a mistaken identification of him as one of D'Anville's relations.

D'Arville (Ashe) arrived in Cincinnati complete with forged letters of introduction, a real letter of introduction from Barton, (the nation's preeminent naturalist), and French etiquette, accent, language, and the manners of the new post-revolution nobility. While in Cincinnati and Louisville, he set up a school to teach French. He had announced a similar plan while in Pittsburgh to Zadok Cramer.[10] He befriended Dr. Goforth with his gratuitous charm, and patronized descriptions of his exploits, adventures, and discoveries.

After D'Arville (Ashe) gained the confidence of Dr. Goforth, the good doctor described his paleontological collections from Big Bone Lick. As their conversations and meetings continued over the next few weeks, it was clear Goforth was in the business of trying to make a high profit from the bones. He knew as early as 1803 the bones would command a higher price in Europe than in America.[11] D'Arville (Ashe), no doubt, reinforced Goforth's original ideas of their net worth. Goforth entered into a written contract with M. D'Arville, whereby the Frenchman would act as his new sales agent.[12] Though a European sale was most desirable, the goal was to sell the bones in New Orleans and have D'Arville (Ashe) return with the profits.

Goforth was fond of any scheme that would make him quick money. He had been bilked on more than one occasion with speculations in bogus mineral mines and other harebrained investments that never paid off.[13] Selling off the bones was a way to cover old losses and gain a cash reserve. Goforth was too trusting of the sincerity of promoters with a bag full of pyrite (fools' gold) over the perceived potential for big returns. It was against this backdrop that Goforth lost most of his personal wealth. Today, we would sadly say he was easy, so very easy a mark, that it was like taking candy away from a baby. This is exactly what Ashe achieved, he took the bones and ran. Execution of the Big Bone caper was not an easy task, for it required almost a year to complete.

To pick up the bones, D'Arville (Ashe) departed Cincinnati and journeyed down the Ohio and Mississippi rivers en route to Pittsburgh by way of New Orleans. For the time period, this mode of travel although

Large river going flatboats were a means to transport heavy cargo. Wood engraving from *Wonders of the World*, 1877.

not the fastest, was perhaps less tiring than an uncertain overland trip on horse back.

By February, he had reached Philadelphia and an overland journey to Pittsburgh commenced. Arriving in town, Ashe presented his credentials to Dr. Richardson as Goforth's new fossil bone agent. Bad weather and the frozen Ohio River prevented his return river journey until early spring. When the ice did melt on the upper Ohio River, Ashe was on his way with five tons of bones safely secured to the deck of a flatboat. The Philadelphia landfall is the point in *Travels* where Ashe starts his American adventure story. Critics and reviewers have often wondered what Ashe meant by the "purpose of his visit." The "purpose" had materialized — Ashe was in flight with a cargo of bones, which, once sold to the proper individual, would reap a handsome profit. Once again he could enjoy the ranks of the rich and famous.

According to *Travels*, Ashe arrived in Cincinnati in July 1806.[14] There he renewed acquaintance with Dr. Goforth, and by August, D'Arville (Ashe) was shooting the rapids at the Falls of the Ohio. By October, he was in Natchez and then sometime in November, landed in New Orleans.

Cramped quarters aboard flatboats often mixed crew, passengers and cargo shared common deck space. Barrels of gunpowder and bags of saltpeter are shown in this wood engraving from *The Family Magazine*, 1840.

His travel chronology does not hold water. Eye witnesses placed him in Natchez on or about the 24th of August, 1806.[15] After exhibiting his bone collection, he loaded them up on that day and continued his flatboat trip to New Orleans, a distance of 313 river miles. A flatboat journey with rest stops could probably reach its destination in less than five or six days.

You just don't disappear with five tons of bones! Someone will find you! In the early 1800s, con men could easily pass from one town to another without detection. Communication was slow with uncertain dispatched mail undergoing the same hardships as Ashe experienced. Time was on Ashe's side and he used it to his advantage to ship his booty out of the country. Yet, he could not resist the avarice of displaying his collection to the public and attracting potential buyers at safe harbors far from Cincinnati.

By and by there were efforts to intercept Ashe and purchase some of the bones. So great a prize did they represent to American vertebrate paleontology that Thomas Jefferson learned of their availability and issued request letters for their whereabouts. One of these reached New Orleans and his old friend Samuel Brown, M.D. (1769-1830).[16] Brown was part owner of one of the largest saltpeter mines in Kentucky, Great Saltpetre Cave. He had made valuable paleontological finds in his own cave, especially the skull of a flat nosed peccary (the first of its kind) and a *Megalonyx jeffersonii* ground sloth in 1805. He was the paramount naturalist living in the west and as such was the best judge of their value and purchase.

Word of the bone exhibit had already reached New Orleans. Brown raced from this place to Natchez to view the collection. Unfortunately, he arrived a few hours too late on the 24th of August. Ashe, now using the alias of Mr. Irvills had departed with the bones for New Orleans. Brown immediately sent word to his brother James (1766-1845) in New Orleans, with instructions to view the bones and interest their friend, wealthy businessman Daniel Clark, in purchasing some of them for the American Philosophical Society.[17]

During the Natchez exposition, Ashe told everyone he had dug them up on the Missouri River. No nonsense Col. John Stuart (1749-1823) cornered Ashe on the ownership of the bones. Where upon Ashe confessed he had purchased them from Dr. Goforth for $100.00.[18]

Arriving in New Orleans, Ashe was now asking $10,000.00 for the collection and was offended with counter offers from a company of Frenchmen for $2500.00. Until now, it is clear Ashe was trying to sell the bones to perhaps satisfy his contract with Dr. Goforth, even though Goforth's name was not mentioned. I do not know if James Brown and Daniel Clark ever intercepted Ashe. If they did, it is clear Ashe would not sell any of the bones. Not willing to split up the collection, it was either purchase the lot at the set price or none at all.

Seemingly unaware of Jefferson's plans, Goforth became more suspicious that something was amiss with his collection and especially the profits from the sale. He wrote Jefferson on December 1, 1806, that:

> the bones I collected were unfortunately entrusted to the care of
> a person who descended the Mississippi with them some months
> since; whether he proceeded to Europe with them I am ignorant,
> as from accident, or some other cause, I have received no account
> either of him or them.[19]

With no word from his sales agent, Goforth starts to face the fact that M. D'Arville had fled the country with the collection.

William Goforth, already experiencing great financial loss, wanted to resume excavation at the Big Bone Lick.[20] But here is the rub — it seems Goforth and Reeder in 1803 were initially trespassing at the lick even though they had initial permission from the tenant occupant. David Ross

(d. 1817) of Richmond, Virginia, the owner of the property refused to give Goforth permission after four weeks of excavation in 1803. Apparently Ross impounded the remaining collection in storage at the lick; Goforth told Meriwether Lewis (1774-1809):

> that he had been interdicted by the Agent of Mr. David Ross of Virginia, (the proprietor of the Lick) from removing these bones, as he was also from the further prosecution of his researches; he is much chagrined at this occurrence, and seems very anxious that some measures should be taken by which to induced Mr. Ross to suffer him to prosecute his enquiries.[21]

Goforth tried to get permission for a new dig and possession of the bones from the last dig, but Ross refused his offer.[22] The Virginia planter wanted the bones and profits for himself! That's understandable. It became a question of who stole the bones from whom. The real victim was David Ross. Thomas Ashe and William Goforth were just common bone thieves.

Beset with speculative business failure upon failure, practically ruined financially, William Goforth moved from Cincinnati to New Orleans between December 1806 and January 1807. The pretext according to his biographical reviewers was he wanted to satisfy his Francophilic desires in New Orleans. I suspect the real reason for his journey was face saving in Cincinnati coupled with a half hearted chance to give chase to M. D'Arville (Ashe). Goforth arrived too late and was left standing at the dock. Profiteering Goforth had been had by one of history's greatest swindlers — the infamous Thomas Ashe!

According to Ashe's *Memoirs*, when he arrived in New Orleans, he tried to sell the bone collection. Faced with an offer of seven thousand dollars for the six tons of bones (notice the weight difference) was a major set back in anticipated profits. Ashe valued the bones at 20,000 pounds Sterling.[23] Offended by such a pitiful offer — probably more so by design — Ashe shipped the whole collection to Liverpool England.

What about the contract with Goforth? Ashe is completely silent on that point of legality. A sea voyage was what Ashe needed, for the climate back in the States was getting too hot. The rhapsodic adventure does not stop here, for Ashe has egotistical aspirations of greatness.

On board ship, Ashe dreams of becoming a great man through the public exhibition of the bones, incognita, etc. He tells a different story over the accumulation of the Goforth collection. Omitting his patron altogether, Ashe said that he bought the bones outright for 1,100 pounds Sterling.[24] A handsome purse, especially since he told Col. Stuart the real price was $100.00. During this sea voyage he finished writing a physical description of the mammoth bones. The book was published in England upon his arrival.[25] I suspect Goforth had drafted up some notes on his bones and Ashe took it with him as part of the documented manifest on the collection. The *Memoirs of Mammoth...and Stupendous Bones* is so detailed, it is remote that Ashe had enough technical knowledge to write it without a good outline. Willard R. Jillson said the pamphlet was:

> a grandiloquent piece of writing, attempting to be scientific but actually a composite piracy of the writings of [Peter] Collinson, [Thomas] Jefferson, [Charles Wilson] Peale, [LeClerc de] Buffon, [William] Hunter, [George] Turner, and others.[26]

He plagiarized these works because their descriptions fit the bones in the Goforth collection. Ashe wrote in his *Memoirs* his future desires and aspirations:

> in forming a plan for the establishment of a museum in London, where the skeletons of my superb incognita were to take the principal lead, because I had also collected in America several cases of non-descript curiosities, petrifactions, organic remains, etc. etc., all of which were eminently adapted to constitute a cabinet of the first distinction in the world.[27]

There is no direct mention of the mummy fragments from the Lexington Catacomb. Perhaps he was being poetic and the "non-descript curiosities, petrifactions" are the mummies in question. I doubt it very much.

On arrival at Liverpool, the Customs House refused to let Ashe unload his cargo, because there was not a good description as to what the crates contained. Ashe says "but it seems there was an error in the Bill of Lading, which could only be corrected by a Bill of View."[28] To Ashe's surprise, he was advised by the Custom House that he needed a security deposit of 500 pounds Sterling for a duty import tax. As is typical throughout his *Memoirs*, a tale of woe ensued.

After what seemed like weeks of negotiation, even providing a Bill of View, Ashe, was, predictably, unable to secure the needed money. The bones and other curiosities were sold by the Customs House to William Bullock, proprietor of the Liverpool Museum for the sum of 200 pounds Sterling.[29] Ashe's plan for a natural history museum fell through. In later years he said he would actually build one, and become quite a success with that venture. Later, he financially over extended himself and wound up in debt, a disposition he had experienced several times before. With the thought of prison in mind and with a new plan, he fled England from an almost certain stay behind bars — this time to new adventures in the diamond fields near Rio de Janeiro.

Through the fog of time several different stories on the disposition of the bones materialized. The only correlation between these and Ashe's account is that Ashe no longer had possession of the fossils.

Another "character" worthy of mention was said to be in New Orleans, when Ashe exhibited his bones to the public.[30] This was Joseph Dorfeuille (1791-1840) whose early years are a blur of contradiction in parentage, nationality, training, and employment as museum exhibitor.[31] In 1823, Dorfeuille purchased the Western Museum of Cincinnati from Daniel Drake and the stockholders. The museum became known as the "Ohio Show-Shop," and its popularity with its automatons, can only be characterized as the Disneyland of its day.[32] Showman Dorfeuille was out to entertain everyone with an assortment of artifacts, freaks, fakes, relics of local murders, wax works, and a house of horrors with trips into the Infernal Regions.

The museum was popular and attracted many patrons, one of whom was the English traveler and Mammoth Cave explorer, William N. Blane.[33] His visit to the museum must have been in 1823. Blane is considered a factual observer and reliable recorder of western events as well as conversations with people he encountered. He was quick to point out any inconsistencies if they did not jibe with perceived reality. Dorfeuille informed Blane:

> that he was at New Orleans, when the bones were brought to that place. There Ashe, getting into some pecuniary embarrassment, pledged them to a Monsieur Saint for several hundred dollars, and then set out for England. Mr. D'Orfeuil [sic] added, that as the seventeen chest of bones were very heavy and bulky, they were deposited in a warehouse, in which they were unfortunately destroyed, during a conflagration that took place soon afterwards.[34]

The Dorfeuille recollection is years after the event, greatly embellished, and inspired in part from Ashe's *Memoirs* with much color from the master Show-Shop salesman of Cincinnati.

At the time of Goforth's death in 1817, his friend since childhood, Daniel Drake, M.D. (1785-1852), said the bones "were immediately taken to Great Britain, sold, in part at least, to the proprietor [William Bullock] of the Liverpool Museum, and the proceeds embezzled."[35] With the exception of embezzlement, the final repository is taken straight out of Ashe's *Memoirs*. A letter from William Bullock (1826) and outlined in Lewis Collins' (1797-1870) undocumented *History of Kentucky* list a number of new repositories for the bones sold by William Bullock to: (1) the Royal College of Surgeons in London; (2) Dr. Blake of Dublin, and Professor Monroe of Edinburgh;

(3) and finally the rest sold at auction in 1819.[36] One of Ashe's victims is Zadok Cramer who was closer to the events reported. He stated that Ashe was exhibiting the bones at the court of London.[37] This rings true to Ashe's gift of showmanship and advance use of his *Stupendous* bone paper to clarion his traveling museum.

The Big Bone caper produced lasting positive side effects. President Thomas Jefferson soothed his old friend David Ross of Virginia, and Jefferson received permission to dig for more bones at the Big Bone Lick. Jefferson supplied his own money and directed General William Clark (1770-1838) to superintend the on-site excavation. Clark had just returned to Washington City from exploring the upper Louisiana Territory with Meriwether Lewis. Theirs was an epic journey of adventure and scientific discovery that was needed to lay claim to the new west. Jefferson commissioned Clark to hire laborers and search the lick for more fossil vertebrates. In 1807, many fossils were found and successfully shipped to Jefferson. "The Mammoth Room" (Blue Room) in the White House became America's first paleontological laboratory with Jefferson becoming the father of North American vertebrate paleontology.[38]

"Into the Unknown." Engraving from Herbert E. Balch, *Wookey Hole, its Caves and Cave Dwellers*, 1914.

28

CHAPTER FOUR

# EARLY INVESTIGATIONS OF THE CATACOMB STORY

*Here was a frail memorial of the mysterious.*

Charles Cassedy (1829)

There were a few early investigations into the validity of Ashe's Catacomb. Yet the majority of the editorial investigations were unsuccessful in clarifying the existence of the Lexington Catacomb.

It was the preferred literary style of *The Port Folio* editor, Oliver Odlschool to select prominent scholars to write review articles of recently published books and important scientific papers. Much of *Travels* contains geographic and natural history subjects; and so, Odlschool needed a well known academic versed in the sciences and arts to render an opinion for the February 1809 issue. He picked Charles Caldwell, M.D. (1772-1853), as the right man with the right temper to assassinate Thomas Ashe on paper.[1] He pulled out all the stops and sank the book with his own unique broadsides of intellectual arrogance.

Caldwell's patience as a reviewer was taxed to some degree, in that only the less startling points of the Catacomb story were mentioned - the mummies were not discussed in any detail. His reaction to the Catacomb is thus:

> of the ruins of this Western Palmyra, that which struck us with the most astonishment is a catacomb of *masterly workmanship,* and *stupendous dimensions.*
> We wish for the sake of those of our readers, whose "gloomy habits of soul," might relish these sepulchral *Tales,* that our limits would allow us to extract the description of "this deep and ample repository of the dead."[2]

*The Edinburgh Review* was not as timid as *The Port Folio* when it came to mummies: "Thus, he discovers, with equal ease and certainty, that some Indian mummies, which are said to have been found at Lexington, are far higher date than the mummy-making eras of Egypt...."[3] Equally harsh reviews appeared in the British *Quarterly Review.*[4]

29

As word of the mummies from a Kentucky cave spread, there was a thin chance that a portion of Ashe's grafted story rested upon an actual event. A recognized authority on American antiquities, Benjamin Smith Barton, M.D. (1766-1815), became interested with the subject.[5] The finding of the Catacomb and associated Indian mummies would answer many questions about the aborigines occupying the west before the present Indians. Barton would be remiss if he did not follow up Ashe's Catacomb story. Laying aside public ridicule and working in an objective fashion, he cut through to the actual questions at hand. Was there really a catacomb of Indian mummies? If so, then where was it located in Kentucky? Who found it and when? What of the grave goods? He apparently realized that much of the story was falsified or at least exaggerated. The residue suggested an authentic site worthy of additional research with discrete enquiries.

Barton repeatedly interviewed a young gentleman from Lexington, then living in Philadelphia (late 1808 or early 1809).[6] Only one Lexington resident was studying medicine under Barton in this time frame, John Todd.[7] What better source to tap for information than a local native with family connections to some of the earliest pioneers in the west. From this gentleman, Barton tried to substantiate portions of the Catacomb allegedly located at Lexington. Todd had read Ashe's account, but could not substantiate any of the events to Barton. The whole thing about a catacomb of mummies underneath Lexington was news to him.

John Todd then wrote a letter to a family member who was a local Lexington politician and one of the earliest pioneers, General Robert Todd.[8] General Todd apparently was just as curious and unknowledgeable as everyone else had been. The letter was first printed in the *Kentucky Reporter* and then republished in the *Kentucky Gazette* on April 18, 1809.[9] John Bradford (1749-1830) supplied an editorial introduction just as anti-intellectual as the one rendered by editor William Worsley for the *Reporter*. The Bradford editorial and Todd letter are partially reprinted below:

> We copy the following extract of a letter from the [*Kentucky*] *Reporter*. The object of the editors of that paper in publishing it, was no doubt to shew what falsehoods are sometimes told by travelers to impose on the world, and....sell their books. Dr. Franklin said fifty years ago, that traveler had a privilege of dealing in the marvelous: and since the fabrications of D[]mberger [D'Alembert] and the nefarious falsehoods of [Isaac] Weld and [Thomas] Moore, the observation has lost none of its force. We confess that we cannot avoid expressing our astonishment that the tale of Mr. Ashe should come introduced to the notice of the people of Kentucky under the auspices of a learned professor of the University of Pennsylvania, in the very metropolis of the

United States. Doctor Barton, is, we understand a man of letters and research, who has published some works upon the antiquities of America, and promises to publish some more. A man like him, one object of whose life it has been to instruct others, should neither suffer himself to be imposed on for a moment by such tales as these, nor yet confess himself to be ignorant of the history and [sit]uation of a part of the United States as well known as the neighborhood of Lexington.

In the bounds and neighborhood of this town are several small mounds, and fortifications; and indeed similar appearances are to be found in various parts of the Western Country; but the subterranean apartment, filled with mummies has never existed but in the imagination and book of Mr. traveller Ashe. His tale therefore relative to the barbarians settled in Lexington, who betrayed such savage fury against these precious relic of antiquity are entirely without foundation. We will add nothing relative to his presentation of the state of society in this country. If his book has procured for the author a reward similar to that obtained by Weld and Moore, who for their a[b]use to America obtained pensions from their government, it would seem not to have been written with an object.

Extract of a letter from [John Todd] a young gentleman of Lexington, at present in Philadelphia, to Gen. Robert Todd.

Since I have been in this place, I have seen a publication of travels made by a Mr. Ashe in America in the year 1806, which, from the novelty of his history and particularly by the account he has given of Kentucky, and the western states, has excited much attention in many portions, and particularly those who feel an interest in natural history; among these letters I have only conversed with Dr. Barton, who has frequently interrogated me as to the authenticity of Mr. Ashe's history, and who is disposed to think it incorrect on many of those subjects. As they relate to periods too far back for the reach of my recollection, I have been unable to satisfy his inquires, but believing that the facts which Mr. Ashe relates must, if not fabrications have fallen within your notice, I am induced by the request of Dr. Barton to address you on this subject, and indeed I feel myself as I am sure you would if you had seen the book, a[s] with that his story if wrong should be at once and as early as possible checked by proper evidence of its falsity; for he has represented the Kentuckians in colours little short of savage barbarity; destitute of feeling, learning, capacity, or even an ordinary share of natural benevolence.

[What then follows is an abstract of Ashe's Catacomb story, rewritten and condensed — this section is deleted.]

This is but a short extract of the account of Mr. Ashe has given of the cave and its embalmed inhabitants and the savage barbarity, and unpolished rudeness of our countrymen even in

31

1806, when he traveled among us. I beg sir, you may write me what you know, have heard or can collect from other old letters in the state concerning this cave and its mummies; and also anything you may hear or know of Mr. Ashe himself. His book is written in a style truly imposing and calculated I conceive, in almost every particular to excite very false and unjust notions of the face of our country and the character of its inhabitants.[10]

Publication of the John Todd letter was the first chance Lexingtonians received notice of their soon to become famous Catacomb. It was also their *first* encounter with Thomas Ashe. He never visited that city, nor had copies of *Travels* been circulated that far west.[11] The Todd letter in the *Kentucky Reporter* and *Kentucky Gazette* created a stir of amazement and outright disbelief that still permeates today. For Barton's efforts, he was given a strong tongue-lashing in the local press for taking up people's valuable time and for exploring frivolous subjects of enquiry. After that, the editors of the local papers were not about to print anymore humbug stories about mummies lodged in catacombs or caves, preferring instead to fan the saber rattling of Henry Clay's War Hawks for military engagement against Great Britain, the "very late" progress of Napoléon on the continent, and who was offering the best local price for saltpeter. The catacomb story seems to have died a noble death. Just when things looked calm, real Indian mummies from saltpeter caves started to turn up at an alarming rate in Tennessee and Kentucky. Dead silence from newspapers in Kentucky.

The only other antebellum authority to consider the Lexington Catacomb was the Reverend Timothy Flint (1780-1840). He had traveled throughout the Midwest and recorded his observations in *Recollections of the Last Ten Years in the Valley of the Mississippi*, edited *The Western Monthly Review*, and published the useful gazetteer *The History and Geography of the Mississippi Valley*. It was in the latter he considered the catacomb of mummies. He says of the Lexington catacomb:

> When this country was first discovered, great numbers of human bodies in a state of entire preservation were found in a cave near Lexington. The pioneers of the settlement in this country did not attach much consequence to skeletons; and none of them remain.[12]

There was no reason to doubt the sincerity of the pioneer tradition, because he had seen one of these Indian mummies from Big Bone Cave, Tennessee, and knew the similarity of Indian burial practices in saltpeter caves.[13] It is through the writings of Flint that we know much about the early history of the Midwest.

# CHAPTER FIVE

# LATER INVESTIGATIONS

*Of the large Subterranean Vault and Catacomb...it is wholly invention, or Munchausen tale, without the least shadow of foundation.*

William Leavy (1873)

The Catacomb and Ashe's observations have hindered efforts to work out early pioneer and prehistoric archaeological history in this part of Kentucky. At most, historians and archaeologists have discredited the book as an unreliable source reference. They often point out the improbable nature of the Catacomb as one of the reasons for not using the book.

Researching archaeological literature for a chapter on the early Indian inhabitants at Lexington, Kentucky, historian George W. Ranck (1841-1901) incorporates the Catacomb tale into his 1872 book. As oral tradition, the account is long forgotten from its original literature source. Variations of the tradition with new embellishments are still recited today. Reading the 1809 *Kentucky Gazette* account, Ranck writes with some caution, "tradition related to this day of an extensive cave existing under the city of Lexington, relieve of its improbable air the statement that a subterranean cemetery of the original inhabitants of this place was discovered nearly a century ago."[1] Ranck's account was an unintentional bombshell with the shrapnel blowing back on him and his *History of Lexington*.

William A. Leavy took great issue with Ranck's description of the Catacomb in his private *Memoir of Lexington and its Vicinity* in 1873.[2] He was a contemporary of the early pioneers and recalled certain events and personages who lived at the time Ashe made his journey to the Western Country. Leavy wanted to counter and correct his perception of Ranck's "blunder." He denounced Ashe's account of the catacomb and its mummies as a lie and a fiction, possessing no substance whatsoever. Through Leavy's recollection and historical knowledge, he attempted to document and authenticate the fallacy of Ashe's story. Unfortunately, Leavy cites no one as his source, relying instead on his memory and his perceptions of the generalized thoughts of the early pioneers. He says that none of the founders of Lexington mention the initial Catacomb, nor is there record in the *Kentucky Gazette* vouching to its real existence. In the last chapter, John Bradford, editor of the *Kentucky Gazette* emphatically stated the substance of the catacomb existed only in Ashe's imagination and no such subterranean cemetery ever existed in Lexington. Leavy echoes similar statements:

> Beside the character of the first settlers and residents so well known ever since the first location of Lexington, which are only a small part enumerated, which are sufficient to give the lie to this tale of the Catacomb.[3]

> Of the large Subterranean Vault and Catacomb spoken of at second hand by Ashe — it is wholly invention, or Munchausen tale, without the least shadow of foundation — inserted probably to help the sale of the book...The Professors in College [Transylvania], as I recollect, were of the opinion that Ashe's book which in 1808 or 1810 was to be seen in the Lexington Library was probably written in a garret in London, by a professed writer.[4]

Leavy's denunciation of Ashe and his Catacomb is more extensive and vociferous than the above quote. Leavy was of the opinion that Ashe never visited Lexington.[5] He is probably right in his suspicions. Descriptions of Lexington in *Travels* are pale in comparison with the richness bestowed on Cincinnati, a place Ashe visited. Geographical information on Lexington could have been easily gleened from gazeteers and travelogues. Ashe used these sources throughout *Travels*.

By 1816, two real Indian mummies would be on display in Lexington. This was the Gapped Tooth Mummy in Clifford's Cabinet and Fawn Hoof, both from Midwest saltpeter caves. It is not known why Leavy did not discuss them in his *Memoir*. The possibility of a hoax may have been too great in his minds eye.

At least one archaeologist, Joseph Jones, M. D., without questioning the source or validity of the Catacomb presents the information in context with mummies found in the caves of Tennessee and Kentucky. He says:

> When Kentucky was first explored, great numbers of human bodies are said to have been found in a state of preservation in a cave near Lexington. As the pioneers did not appear to attach much importance to antiquities, these bodies were not preserved. The bodies found in the saltpetre [Short] cave of Kentucky are said to have been considerably smaller than the men of our times; and their teeth are described as long, white, and sharp, and separated by considerable intervals.[6]

Ranck is cautious about the true existence of the Lexington Catacomb, and he is certain the Catacomb is improbable. The Catacomb was a sore subject with Lexingtonians and they were not about to let anyone dignify the tradition in a history of their town.

From then on it was smooth sailing for the Catacomb tradition. In 1882, chemist and geologist Robert Peter, M.D. (1805-1894), published his *History of Fayette County, Kentucky*. He abstracted Ashe's Catacomb statements "for what it is worth" to the preference of the reader.[7] He realized the jam his old friend Ranck had gotten into when he discussed the Catacomb of mummies. Peter used geology and history to save the moment. Objectively:

> if such a cemetery [Catacomb] ever existed, its locality has remained unknown, though a somewhat similar one is mentioned by Collins as having been discovered in Hart County, Ky., as late as 1826, and the fact that embalmed bodies have been found in several caves in this State is too well known to need reference to authorities.[8]

Critics believed Peter's rationale for he escaped the fate that nailed Ranck. An authentic mummy, Little Al (a.k.a., American Mummy or Little Alice) had recently been discovered in Salts Cave in 1875.[9] The Hart County mummy site is actually a description of Indian skeletons, not mummies.[10] With Little Al and the stable of Short Cave mummies, there was little need to verify the long lost existence of mummies in the Lexington Catacomb. The location of the Catacomb remained as elusive as it did in 1809 when Lexingtonians first heard of their subterranean sarcophagus of mummies.

Mummy tales don't die, they keep coming back with new clothes cut from old cloth. By 1928, archaeologist, William D. Funkhouser and William S. Webb debunked the story in a heavy handed sort of way. They reported:

> Since there is no scientific foundation for such a tradition, we are forced to consider it merely a fanciful tale which has grown much in the telling...the tale is probably nothing more than the figment of a well developed imagination and there are absolutely no facts to support it, but because of its appeal to the fancy and its sensational nature, it always finds ready listeners.[11]

They did pass along the current tradition about "the extensive and magnificent catacombs beneath Lexington and the two thousand mummies, the idols, the spacious compartments and the alters[sic] which these catacombs contained."[12] Their work was of such authority and widespread circulation, it met no challenges to their scientific method. It was biased, submitting opinion masquerading as investigative fact. They made no attempt to investigate the original story, preferring instead to use the current tradition as their vehicle of destruction. Archaeologist Charles D. Hockensmith in 1976, pointed out their short sighted methods and "distortions" of the Catacomb story.[13]

Coming almost full circle in 1987, Don Edwards, news columnist for the *Lexington Herald-Leader*, gives a tongue-in-cheek report on the discovery of the old book, *American Antiquities* by Josiah Priest. It seems there still could be a colony of Egyptian mummies in their Catacomb beneath Main Street. Edwards said the story is "so good that it persisted for two centuries."[14] Priest lives![15]

ANCIENT WORKS
at
MARIETTA.
OHIO.

REFERENCES

a. Parapets.
b. Excavations.
c. Conical mounds.
d. Large covered way.
e. Small covered way.
f. Pond or reservoir.
g. Elevated oblong squares.
h. Elevated square.

Early travelogues often mention the extensive Marietta earthworks in Ohio. Wood engraving from Caleb Atwater, *The Writing of Caleb Atwater*, 1833.

CHAPTER SIX

# THE MOUND BUILDERS AND THE CORE
# OF THE CATACOMB

*Near Lexington are to be seen curious sepulchers, full of human
skeletons....This method of burying appears to be totally different
from that now practiced by the Indians.*

John Filson (1784)

Most historians, scientists, and laymen agreed Ashe invented the
Lexington Catacomb with its repository of Indian mummies. Only
Benjamin S. Barton, Timothy Flint, Joseph Jones, and Robert Peter
realized the core of the tale had some worth for consideration. All failed to
realize or recognize Ashe's story pre-dated any known mummy discovery
to the outside world! The earliest authenticated mummy discovery was
in Tennessee's Copperas (Big Bone) Cave on September 2, 1810. Ashe
described his mummies from his 1806 visit and published it in 1808. Using
Ashe's visit date of 1806 as a pivot point reveals his description is four years
before the Tennessee find and five years before the Short Cave discovery.
Possibly there could have been text changes to *Travels* up to the time of
publication in 1808. Even so, the mummy description is still two and three
years prior to actual known events. Ashe is straight on the mark in his
Indian mummy descriptions, enough so to rule out coincidence. Believable
elements of the story points toward a core of fractured historical events
taking place in the Midwest and within the scope of his travel chronology.

The proof is based on the association of Catacomb mummies to
authenticated mummy burials in saltpeter caves. From tantalizing clues
in *Travels,* there are enough physical comparative data in Ashe's story to
target the kind of cave containing the mummies, the approximate time
period of discovery, nationality of mummies buried, and assorted grave
goods. The key piece of co-documentation needed to verify a mummy
discovery in the 1806 time frame has not been discovered. The report by
Ashe is the first and only reference available at the present time. What
follows is a comparative analysis of the Catacomb story and correlation

with authentic events occurring after the time of Ashe's visit to America in Midwest caves.

Ashe used two major publications in the compilation of the Kentucky portion of *Travels*: (1) John Filson, *The Discovery, Settlement, and Present State of Kentucke*, published in 1784; and (2) Zadok Cramer, *The Navigator*, published in 1806 (there are a number of prior editions).[1] Each of these travel guidebooks was extensively plagiarized, selections of which served as a prototype to form part of the structure of the Catacomb setting. Filson observed and described the "curious sepulchers" of the Mound Builders in the environs of Lexington. Cramer reprints Filson's Mound Builder section in his sketch of Lexington. Filson submits the following:

> Near Lexington are to be seen curious sepulchers, full of human skeletons, which are thus fabricated. First, on the ground are laid large broad stones; on these were placed the bodies, separated from each other by broad stones, covered with others, which served as a basis for the next arrangement of bodies. In this order they are built, without mortar, growing still narrower to the height of a man. This method of burying appears to be totally different from that now practiced by the Indians.[2]

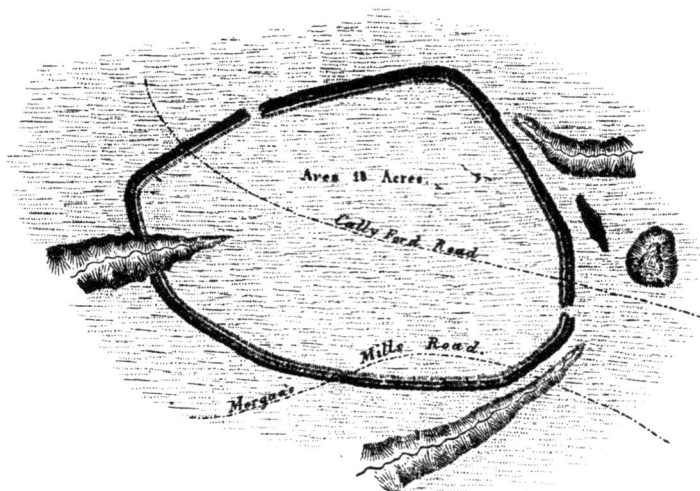

N.° 4.

ANCIENT WORK,

6 M. FROM LEXINGTON FAYETTE CO. KENTUCKY.

SCALE
500 ft to the Inch.

C. Rafinesque del.

Survey of ancient Peter Village earthworks near Lexington, Kentucky, by Constantine S. Rafinesque. Wood engraving in E. G. Squire and E. H. Davis, *Ancient Monuments of the Mississippi Valley*, 1848.

According to the Catacomb story there were initially several hundred embalmed mummies. Filson reported the finding of hundreds of buried Indian skeletons in the mounds at Lexington. In 1920, Geologist Arthur M. Miller (1861-1929) arrived at the same conclusions on Ashe's use of Filson's prototype mound for the Catacomb tale.[3]

From Filson's time onward, the mounds and fortifications were being destroyed by an advancing urban society at Lexington. Filson probably is referring to the large geometric mounds located on North Elkhorn Creek (Mt. Horeb, Peter Village, and Fisher Mounds earthworks) or South Elkhorn Creek (South Fork and Town Fork earthworks). Ashe says, the "...wide range of its circumvallatory works, and the quantity of ground it once occupied. Time, and the more destructive ravages of man have nearly leveled these remains of former greatness...."[4] True in 1806 and a reality today.

As to their age, said Ashe, "...the Indian mummies are of higher antiquity than the Egyptian."[5] As to how the bodies were embalmed, or their length of preservation, or from what race descended, Ashe would only say that he had no idea on the above questions. But he says, "...for my part, I am lost in the deepest ignorance."[6] Ashe researched his material for the story, for he adds in true Masonic form, "my reading affords me no knowledge, my travels no light. I have neither read, heard, nor know of any of the North American Indians who formed catacombs for their dead, or who were acquainted with the art of preservation by embalming."[7] John Hay Farnham echoed these sentiments when he saw Fawn Hoof in Mammoth Cave.[8]

Displaying his prowess in studying antiquities, Ashe allegedly made a visit to the mounds near the mouth of the Kentucky River, in which he says "...must have been the efforts of a people acquainted with some science, and capable of infinite labor; and it is difficult to conceive how they could be constructed without the use of iron tools and the instruments we are compelled to employ in works of much less magnitude and character."[9]

Of the antiquities in the Cincinnati locale, he says, "that the antediluvian Americans were acquainted with the use properties of iron, of the advantage and of which the flood deprived their descendants, and from which it would appear that the same flood swept off every individual from whom that knowledge might be derived."[10] The question over the use of iron tools was a hot topic with antiquarians at this time period, and Ashe is just following their lead.

Ashe, like his contemporaries of the Romantic Movement, made historical comparisons of the Mound Builder (Adena, Hopewell, and Mississippian) culture to modern European civilization. The mounds had to have been built by a superior race of men, skilled in science, culture, metallurgy, and architecture. He went to great lengths throughout *Travels* in an attempt to draw ethno-cultural links between the Mound Builders and classical Greek, Roman, and Egyptian civilizations. Within the Speculative Period of Archaeology, this was no more preposterous than saying the Mound Builders were a white race of men from Asia.[11] Or that they migrated from Africa, resting momentarily in Atlantis, and finally landed on the shores of North America.[12] A twentieth century urban myth variation is our ancestors received knowledge of technology or even their transplanted presence on the face of the earth from humanoids who traveled here in flying saucers. True to form, Ashe was one of those early students of pseudo-ethno-racial origins of man that would in later years spark the imaginations of Josiah Priest, Ignatius Donnelly, James Churchward, and Erich von Däniken. All of their books are gross exercises into the realm of fantastic archaeology.[13]

Just who the Mound Builders were, Ashe had no idea and neither did anyone else during the Speculative Period of Archaeology. But he was sure of one thing, they were not the present Indian culture. A similar thought was shared by contemporary Indians who lived along the upper Ohio Valley. The concept was generally embraced by white settlers who saw the mounds and "knew" the local cultural practices of the present Indians. The pioneers carried the concept one step forward as a simple matter of racial superiority. Only white Indians could precision build the forts and mounds. Hence these white Mound Builders were perceived as descendants of the Picts, Welsh, Aztecs, Egyptians, and even a few of the ten lost tribes of Israel. It never occurred to the early pioneer writers and researchers that the Mound Builders were the direct ancestors of the very American Indians then occupying the Midwest. These Indians were just men, not gods from space, not Welsh, nor Egyptian, just men!

It took over 150 years to work out the cultural-time stratigraphic sequence of the Mound Builders into three distinct cultures. Only with the widespread introduction of Carbon[14] dating in the early 1950's did we start to know for certain the age relationship of the mounds and the people who built them. News of this has traveled very slowly. The Mound Builders have gotten such good press, they are still used today as a single all-encompassing cultural unit for Welsh settlement in the valley of the Ohio.[14] It's as if some of these contemporary white mound builder proponents never got beyond nor even up to the 1848 watershed works of Squire and Davis.[15]

# CHAPTER SEVEN

# CATACOMBS AND SALTPETER CAVES

*They dragged the mummies to the day, tore the bandages open,*
*kicked the bodies into dust, and made a general bonfire of the most*
*ancient remains antiquity could boast.*

Thomas Ashe (1808)

It took certain dry caves with the right environmental conditions to mummify a body. Authenticated mummy sites are found in dry cave passages! It is that simple, although not as simple as one would suspect. Ashe's account of Indian mummies pre-dates any presently known mummy literature or discovery. Since it is certainly a dry cave, then could the Catacomb actually be a saltpeter cave?

Ashe received enough physical information from unnamed individual(s) to single out the kind of cave that could preserve a human body, under what conditions this could occur, and a physical description of a real Indian cave mummy.

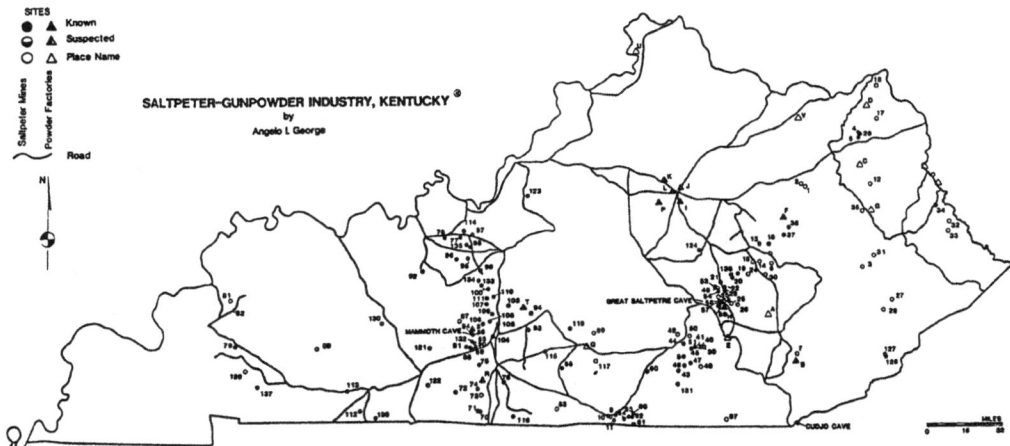

Distribution of saltpeter sites, gunpowder mills and wagon roads. Base map greatly abridged from Luke Munsell *Map of Kentucky*. From Angelo I. George, "Saltpeter and Gunpowder Manufacturing in Kentucky," *The Filson Club History Quarterly*, 1986.

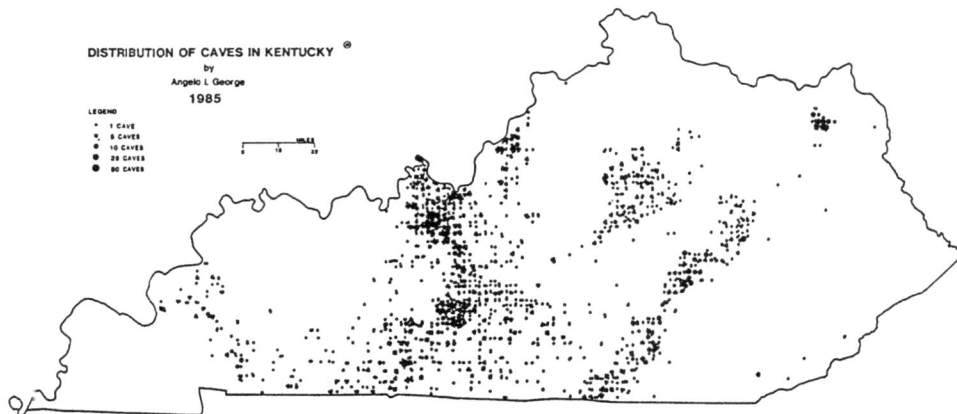

Geographic distribution of cave entrances in Kentucky. From Angelo I. George, "Saltpeter and Gunpowder Manufacturing in Kentucky," *The Filson Club History Quarterly*, 1986.

Any one of the hundreds of caves in and around Lexington could be the Catacomb. It's the "guess the location of the mummy in the shell game." Most of the caves in the Inner Blue Grass Region are wet and damp. They do not meet minimal environmental conditions needed for natural mummification to occur. The driest caves were the ones exploited for saltpeter. My inventory of saltpeter sites in Kentucky produced no known, suspected, or place name localities related to saltpeter mining in the Inner Blue Grass.[1] Saltpeter mine developers were very selective in picking the caves to exploit. Of the 3770 caves catalogued in Kentucky, only 3.53% of the population has some indicated connection with saltpeter activity.[2] This certainly narrows down the population. I am forced to look away from the Inner Blue Grass for a cave that physically resembles the Lexington Catacomb.

The heyday of domestic saltpeter mining is bracketed between 1804-1815. The time period is significant because most of our saltpeter prior to 1804 was being imported from British controlled India. As war raged in Europe (1804-1807), supplies of this important commodity became uncertain to American manufacturers of gunpowder. Thus began a concerted effort to build up the necessary infrastructure to produce saltpeter from caves and rockshelters found in the interior of America.

The time period of 1808-1815 is important from the Jeffersonian *laissez faire* doctrine of internal self sufficiency. The hallmark of this concept was shutting down American dependence on foreign imports. The following edicts were partly successful in stopping trade between Great Britain and her Colonies: The Embargo Act of December 1807, and the Nonintercourse Act of March 1809 did much to drive up the price of saltpeter and to foster the exploitation of numerous saltpeter sites in the Midwest of Kentucky, Missouri, Virginia, and Tennessee. International relations with the Mother Country continued to deteriorate. The War Hawks got their wish when war was declared on June 18, 1812. The manufacturer's price of saltpeter sky-rocketed to five times its peace time level.

The quest for saltpeter riches progressed to such an extent in Dixon Cave, located right next to Mammoth Cave, that over 30,875 tons of breakdown rock was removed from the front half of the cave and stacked in the back half![3] Truly a herculean effort in saltpeter mining. Part of the goal in Dixon Cave was to intercept the clay filled floor of the cave. An objective that never occurred. Removing the breakdown rock peripheral to the cave wall exposed important rock horizons rich in nitrates. These intervals were selectively mined. It was the removal of this breakdown overburden in Mammoth and Short caves that laid bare the nitrate impregnated soils. Most of the significant paleontological and Indian artifacts were chance discovered in these and like caves. Within the 1804-1815 time frame, we would *never* see such copious discoveries of this nature from caves ever again. Nor would we see such a concerted effort to explore hundreds of caves to find the perfect cave to exploit its mineral riches.

Ashe allegedly made a personal visit to the Catacomb and in doing so, tried to substantiate the pioneer account of "hundreds of mummies" in the cave. He contracted several local laborers and they excavated the floor of the cave passage for artifacts. The following quote by Ashe is important because he tells us something about digging in dry caves. Ashe reports that he:

> employed several hands, and brought to light forty or fifty baskets of rubbish gleaned throughout the vault, both from the sides and from the floor. The dust of the heap was so light, impalpable and pungent, that it rose into the atmosphere and affected the senses so much as to cause effusion of the eyes and sneezing, to a troublesome degree.[4]

For Ashe to write the description, he would have had either to experience the above or to have talked with individuals who had or knew of these physiological reactions occurring while digging in dry cave passages. My own experience in just walking through some of the dry saltpeter caves in Kentucky resulted in sneezing and eye watering problems. Digging in dry caves stirs up even more dust to a troublesome degree. Exploration in Big Bone Cave, Tennessee, requires the use of a face mask to filter out dust particles churned up while walking and crawling in the cave. Persons in Ashe's day most likely to have this kind of experience were either saltpeter and copperas miners or persons directly connected with the commercial manufacture, exploitation, and distribution of saltpeter and gunpowder. The Catacomb story points to a dry saltpeter cave, not found in the Inner Blue Grass Region. Saltpeter caves were the only caves purposely excavated during this time period and in the course accidently discovered Indian artifacts, human skeletons, mummies, and fossil vertebrates. We need to look no further than a saltpeter type cave.

There are only four saltpeter cave names associated with mummy burials: Big Bone Cave, Smith Fork Cave, Dutch (sic) River Cave, Tennessee, and Short Cave, Kentucky. Analysis of the geographic description and cave locations to Dutch (sic) River and Smith Fork Cave suggest them to be synonym locations for Big Bone Cave.[5] The reader should be aware of their existence and consideration is directed to Chapter Nine. Big Bone (Copperas) Cave and Short Cave will be handled together for this comparative analysis with the Lexington Catacomb. All authenticated mummy discoveries post date the 1808 publication of Ashe's *Travels*.

One of the candidates for Ashe's prototype model within his travel chronology is Big Bone Cave in present day Van Buren County, Tennessee. Large scale saltpeter mining commenced in 1806.[6] Sometime prior to August 1813, remains of the extinct Pleistocene Megalonyx were found buried in the cave near the entrance to the Maze.[7] Dried cartilage and muscular flesh still adhered to some of the articulated bone surfaces.[8] John D. Clifford of Lexington, Kentucky, acquired ownership of the majority of the fossils and placed them in his cabinet. He also became the owner of the Gapped Tooth Mummy from this same "vast limestone cavern in Tennessee."[9]

Clifford discusses mummies from the "Western Country" (obviously Tennessee and Kentucky), yet makes *no* reference to mummies found in Big Bone Cave.[10] He uses the mummified flesh on his Megalonyx bones to account for the saltpeter earths ability to preserve human specimens under similar circumstances in dry caves. He speaks in generalities, uses "our caves" as a location, and lumps all the mummy sites as one discussion unit. Clifford's discussion led George M. Crothers to believe that mummies of an early date had been found in Big Bone Cave.[11] An analysis of the geography around Copperas Cave, Tennessee, led Angelo I. George to identify the mummy cave as Big Bone Cave.[12] The mining time frame of 1806 is the right time and within the travel chronology of Thomas Ashe.

Short Cave near the famous Mammoth Cave in Edmonson County, Kentucky, is the only known site in this State to produce Indian mummy burials during the saltpeter mining era. Equally so, there are quite a few physical geographical associations between this cave and the Lexington Catacomb.

The validity of Ashe's mummy description is based upon the comparison to known Indian mummy discoveries in the Midwest. Was the mummy of Egyptian or of American Indian origin? We know the Egyptians never made it to North America. The origin of the American Indian was a great mystery to the pioneers and naturalists of this time period. They were greatly puzzled with the great mounds, geometric earthworks, stone box burials in the mounds, and the mummies found in a few caves. The pioneers credited a number of trans Atlantic voyagers as the builders of these great works.

Ashe asserts the Catacomb mummies were all well wrapped. All of the mummies found in Big Bone (Copperas) Cave and Short Cave were wrapped up in multiple coverings. Then Ashe says something truly unexpected: "The Kentuckyans assert in the very words of the Greek that the features of the face and the form and appearance of the whole body were so well preserved, that they must have been the exact representations of the living subjects."[13] And the mummies "...were well *lapped up*, appeared sound and *red*...."[14] How did Ashe or the un-named "Kentuckyans" know what the facial features and the red skin looked like? One must keep in mind that all of Ashe's mummies were well wrapped up as in *true* Egyptian mummies. At least Ashe gives the misdirected impression his mummies were all bound in linen strips. He does not specifically mention linen strips until his discourse on Egyptian mummification practices.[15] When he specifically mentions the encasing material of the Catacomb mummies, he uses such terms as "bandages, wrappers, and bands," "ligatures," or even "well lapped up." Judging from the phraseology used in describing authenticated cave mummies, this matches Ashe's description. The Catacomb mummies "were well *lapped up*" does not necessarily mean linen bandages, but coupled with the wrappers and bands mentioned above suggests a distorted analogous version of a deer skin feathered cape and the multiple canvas-like outer coverings encasing the mummy. These outer coverings were held in place with cords tightly wrapped around the body.

With nothing better to draw from, Ashe gives the impression the mummies were embalmed using a method he could not readily adduce. He dwells on this subject at great length. Take notice of Ebenezer Meriam's (1794-1864) account of garments worn by Fawn Hoof. He says the "outside of the two [deer] skins was a large sheet, which was either wove or knit. This fabric was the inner bark of a tree, which I judged from appearance, to be that of the Linn tree."[16] Moses Fisk would make a similar observation on grave goods associated with the female mummy from Big Bone (Copperas) Cave.[17] Flint says garments worn by the Gapped

Toothed Mummy consisted of "cloth, on which these feathers were woven, was a kind of linen of neat texture, of the same kind with that which is now woven from the fibers of the nettle."[18]

Were the Catacomb mummies also wrapped up in some kind of canvas-like sheet made from the inner bark of the linden tree (*Tilia americana*)? This leads me to suspect that the term linnen (sic) used by Thomas Ashe is a bastardized rural Kentucky dialect for the linden tree. It is easy to understand how the Irishman could have misinterpreted linden for "linnen." In talking with a native Green County Kentuckian who grew up on a farm around the turn of the last century (circa 1900), Elmer C. Vance was asked about the Linden tree. His pronunciation of the name produces a silent *d* and the word sounds like "linnen tree."[19] And so, Ashe was essentially correct, the Catacomb mummies were wrapped up in linen.

The skin tone of the Catacomb mummies was of a red color. Compare this with substantiated mummy skin tone. Fawn Hoof (the mummy) according to Meriam, "...was dark, not black."[20] Farnham reports that her skin tone was "...that of dried tobacco, of a yellowish hue."[21] John Rice viewed the male Scudder and the female Peale's Museum mummy, and concluded "...the color was that of a dull dusky brown. A cake of chocolate scraped will give a pretty just idea of the color."[22] Within the time period that Ashe writes his story, the Native Americans were considered to be red skinned. Ethnological research in later years would show considerable variation in skin tone throughout the Americas.

Ashe produces a lengthy essay on the art of Egyptian embalming practices as passed down from Herodotus and Diodorus. There were four techniques. Three of them Ashe discards for want of the necessary raw spices and herbs needed to cure the body. A fourth method which he did elect was based upon a hitherto unlocated secret Egyptian method recorded by Diodorus. This method covers the practice of mummification without the removal of the internal organs.[23] The other three methods involves the removal of most or all internal organs. These Catacomb Indian mummies were complete human cadavers with all organs! Real cave mummies are also complete human bodies *with all internal organs*! This is a surprising bit of information within Ashe's story that strengthens the idea of an authentic cave mummy.

There are ten points of correlation between Ashe's mummy observational source and what we know about real Indian mummies.

Site characterization points toward a saltpeter cave:

1. Dry cave.
2. Excavation in dry caves churns up dust and causes choking, sneezing, and eye watering.

Catacomb mummy points of correlation with actual mummies:

1. Mummies well wrapped up.
2. Face and external features well preserved.
3. Exact representations of the living subject.
4. Mummies had red skin.
5. Mummies tied up with bandages, wrappers and bands.
6. Linden tree bark thread woven into a fabric similar to fine linen was employed as a covering. Only used on Short and Big Bone mummies.
7. Mummies were complete human beings with all internal organs.
8. The mummies were Indians.

Stripping away the cloak of fantastic archaeology from Ashe's Catacomb tale shows the residue of a real Indian mummy with a high order of probability the site is in a saltpeter cave.

I already know from Ashe's past experiences that he would use authentic events and skillfully graft them into his travel fantasies. In reconstructing the true mummy site of the Catacomb, it will be necessary to tear apart and rearrange the sequence of events in *Travels*. I am forced to make one major assumption, let's say we are already inside the cave, and Ashe's description is the opening of one individual Indian burial crypt (stone box grave) by the saltpeter miners. Notice my rewritten account in brackets inserted with Ashe's statement over the initial discovery of the Catacomb:

> by some of the...[saltpeter miners]..., whose curiosity was excited by something remarkable in the character of [flat] stones which struck their attention [above the top of the stone box grave] while ... [digging for saltpeter]... in [a cave in] the woods. They removed these stones and came to others of singular workmanship [the top of the stone lid]; the removal of which laid open the mouth of a ... [burial crypt]. [And]...a catacomb, formed in the bowels of the limestone rock [in the floor of the cave], about fifteen feet below the surface of the earth....[24]

At first I considered the "fifteen feet below the surface of the earth" to indicate the depth of the cave opening below the level of the surface landscape. But, I think it means the burial depth position of the mummy rather than the literal explanation. The Big Bone Cave mummies were buried under six feet of cave soil.[25] Compare this to Charles Wilkins description of the Short Cave mummy burial position of Fawn Hoof. The surface of the cave floor was "...covered with loose limestone, from four to six feet deep, before you enter the clay impregnated with nitre."[26] The mummy "was found at the depth of about ten feet from the surface of the cave, bedded in clay, strongly impregnated with nitre, placed in a sitting posture, encased in broad stones, standing on their edges, with a flat stone covering the whole."[27] Using Wilkins' stratigraphic profile of from four to six feet of breakdown on top of ten feet of cave soil deposited over the top of the stone box grave. This is from fourteen to sixteen feet total depth. Ashe uses a average depth of fifteen feet. A remarkable coincidence to say the least. Ashe continues his description with:

> the sides and extreme ends [of the catacomb] were formed into niches and compartments, and occupied by figures representing men! When alarm subsided, and the sentiment of dismay and surprise permitted further research and enquiry, the figures were found to be Indian mummies, preserved by the art of embalming to great preservation and perfection of state![28]

The opening of the Short Cave burial crypt is described in detail by Meriam:

> In the digging of saltpetre earth, in the Short Cave, some little distance from the Mammoth Cave, a flat rock was met with by the workman, a little below the surface of the earth in the cave, and about a quarter of a mile from the Cave's mouth, this stone was raised, was about four feet wide and as many long; beneath it was a square excavation about three feet deep, and as many in length and width. In this small nether subterranean chamber, sat in solemn silence, one of the human species, a female, with her wardrobe and ornaments placed by her side.[29]

Evidently the Catacomb mummies were buried with articles of clothing and personal effects; Ashe continues this by saying, "nor could I arrive at any knowledge of the fashion, manner, and apparel of the mummies in general, or receive any other information."[30]

During the ravaging of the Catacomb, the mummies were burned in a general bonfire, both inside and outside the cave; Ashe's account refers to "...so many fires have been made in the place [inside the Catacomb], either to warm the visitors or to burn up the remains, that the shades, dispositions, and aspects, have been tortured into essential difference and change....I could never learn the exact quantity it did contain, the answer to my enquiries being 'Oh! they burned up and destroyed hundreds.'"[31] Ashe has described the cave ceiling as being soot blackened and the floor as covered with numerous ash heaps. This is reminiscent of a true Indian site. Wilkins adds, "this place [Short Cave] had evident marks of having once been the residence of the aborigines of the country, from the quantity of ashes, and the remains of fuel, and torches made from the reed, & c. [cane] which were found in it."[32] Big Bone Cave has "sooty walls and ceilings of the apartments, and exhibited the most dismal and lugubrious [sic] appearance."[33] Large quantities of ashes are also needed for the saltpeter leaching vats. The ash acts as the alkali used in the chemical conversion of calcium nitrate into potassium nitrate (saltpeter). This site would be located close to the evaporation furnaces and outside the cave entrance. Ashe probably is referring to both aboriginal and saltpeter site activity.

The sheer quantity of mummies found in the Lexington Catacomb, numbering into the hundreds, is another example of Ashe's fantastic archaeology. Except for the Smith Fork (Big Bone) site, all of the authentic mummy burials found by the saltpeter miners involved two mummy burials per reported incident. It is highly probable the Catacomb site yielded only two mummies at the time of Ashe's visit. Two mummies sounds a lot better and more credible, although not as dramatic as hundreds!

Still exercising the theatrical, Ashe gives this fractured account: "they dragged the mummies to the day, tore the bandages open, *kicked the bodies into dust* [emphasis added], and made a general bonfire of the most ancient remains antiquity could boast...."[34] Now compare Ashe's statement with John D. Clifford's second hand account obtained from Charles Wilkins on the destruction of the initial Short Cave baby mummy found in 1811: "the corpse appeared as if newly dead but upon exposure to the open atmosphere it in a few hours crumbled into its natural dust."[35] Charles Wilkins adds, "...and that its remains, except the skull, with all its clothing had been thrown into the furnace."[36] Fawn Hoof (a female) was found in late September and possessed a wound near her backbone between two of her ribs and one of her eyes had been injured. One of the 1814 mummies (an adolescent boy) had a skull fracture (occipital bone), possibly produced by a club or rock. The female had a wound hole that passed through her thorax, about the size of a rifle ball!

The two Big Bone Cave mummies found by the copperas miners in 1810, show signs of mutilation by the hands of their discovers. The female "had a slight injury to the right of the head, originating from the awkwardness and inattention of those who discovered and first raised the body, & a traverse cut across the abdomen, of some length."[37] Cassedy established "the feet were partially drawn up, and the hands crossed over the breast."[38] Of the male, Cassedy says "his legs were drawn up, and closely bound in dressed deer skins."[39] And "his frame was entire except the bowels...."[40] When Cassedy and Dr. Bedford re-excavated the male mummy, they found him to have undergone a lot of wear and tear. He says "the male seemed to have undergone a considerable change; owing probably to the former exposure [illegible] to the atmosphere, and was not removed from its bed."[41] Pleasant M. Miller adds the "coffins, in which they were preserved, were not long enough for the whole body; the legs were cut off and laid on their breast."[42] This is also echoed by Haywood, quoting the literature, who like Miller never saw the site.[43] Moses Fisk went to the site after the Cassedy re-excavation and collected the wicker basket of the female mummy. He viewed the female, but made no reference to disarticulation or the missing feet.[44] These wicker coffins were four feet long and the mummies were interred in a vertical seated position.[45] There was no need for disarticulation of the legs. Cassedy in 1829, established the 1810 mummies were damaged in the course of discovery. Wray supports this conclusion by saying the mummies "were found by illiterate labourers, who set no value whatever on their discovery, and who allowed every visitor that wished it, to break off parts either to be totally destroyed on the spot, or taken away."[46] Damage to the mummies constitute an overt act of vandalism. This led to the mistaken notion the mummies were disarticulated prior to burial in the cave. The concept of disarticulation has been embraced by archaeologists up to the present day. Assembled documentation from near the time period of discovery establishes that the miners were responsible for the mutilation. It was not a part of Indian burial customs.

What I have established is an expected mode of operation for the saltpeter miners at Big Bone Cave and Short Cave. Numerous writers stemming from Ashe to the present stress the fact that each mummy upon initial discovery looked as if newly dead — in the case of Short Cave, fright, alarm and dismay spread through the initial discovers. The workmen in Big Bone Cave were frightened by their discovery to such an extent they thought the mummies' ghosts would haunt them. So they reburied them in a shallow grave in the cave passage.

In talking to Harold Meloy in 1975 about the destruction of the Catacomb mummies,[47] he said that all of the Short Cave mummies were mutilated in some fashion. He stressed the opinion that the Short Cave miners, out of fright and superstition, wanted to make sure the discovered bodies in the stone box graves were really dead. They kicked(?), clubbed, stabbed, shot, and cremated the mummy(s) to make sure that the individual found was not a ghost or some other supernatural being from the infernal regions. Ashe says the discoverers of the Catacomb mummies were "filled with terror," and "when alarm subsided, and the sentiment of dismay and surprise" slacked off, they found them to be Indian mummies.[48] Some additional strength to the saltpeter miner superstition theory is given by Farnham: "I forgot to mention to you, that the superstition of some people in the vicinity of the [Mammoth] cave, though perfectly independent of classical or fabulous history, induces them to believe this [Mammoth] cave to be the passage to hell itself."[49] Of Big Bone Cave, Cassedy says the two mummies were reburied by the miners, "under the impression that the *spirits* of deceased persons generally amused themselves by haunting the disturbers of the dead!"[50]

Notice in the Clifford-Ashe account, the mummy(s) were taken outside the cave and exposed to the air. Ashe has his mummies destroyed by a vindictive mob who kicked them "into dust." Miller and Haywood speak of disarticulation of the legs of the male mummy. Cassedy and Wray establish that the miners vandalized the mummies when they found them. Clifford on the other hand says the Short Cave child mummy disintegrated into "its natural dust." Ashe uses a bonfire and Wilkins' miners used a saltpeter evaporation furnace for the cremation sequence. Of all the known mummies found from the Mammoth Cave region, only the 1811 child mummy disintegrated upon exposure to the outside environment. The other mummies under similar circumstances gained weight after several hours in the sun light. The 1810 male Big Bone Cave mummy started to rot. Only after several years and much man-handling did Fawn Hoof and the rest of the Short Cave mummies become brittle and show signs of partial destruction. Essentially the mummies were fairly durable, except for the child mummy and the male Big Bone Cave mummy.

I can only conclude that the original account of Wilkins and Clifford may have been only partially correct, in that the superstitious saltpeter miners lied in order to protect themselves from retribution by their overseer at the Short Cave saltpeter operation. I suspect the 1811 child mummy was mutilated even more upon its initial discovery in the stone box grave. Charles Wilkins was conscientious enough to realize the importance of this discovery to antiquarians. He lamented over the acts of the saltpeter miners on the first mummy. He posted a cash reward for any more mummies that would follow.[51] Only a token mutilation by the saltpeter miners was performed on the next three or four mummies from Short Cave. These alleged ritualistic murders of the mummies occurred only at Big Bone Cave and Short Cave. Miners' superstitions, accompanied by the horror of discovering the unexpected, led to these acts.

There is some indication the saltpeter miners damaged the mummies during or after discovery. Early reports describe wounds on the mummies framed with dried blood. Dried blood could only happen near the time of death or soon after. My question on the wounds and dried blood: Could the cadavers have suffered some accident, been killed, or participated in some ritual sacrifice? The whole forensic nature of the mummy's death needs to be reexamined.

Big Bone Cave comes in a close second as to site characterization, but lacks certain key elements, especially: burial depth, stone box grave (curious rocks), and incineration of the mummies.

Short Cave points of correlation to the Catacomb:

1. Mummies found 15 feet below the surface.
2. Curious rocks over the grave.
3. Possible grave goods.
4. Mummy(s) burned in a bonfire.
5. Mummy(s) kicked about or mutilated.
7. Mummy(s) turned into dust.
8. Blackened ceiling.
9. Ash heaps.

With the amount of comparative evidence assembled, I am forced to consider the core account by Thomas Ashe of his Lexington Catacomb to be descriptive of a true historic site, hinging on the discovery of perhaps two authentic Native American mummies in a saltpeter cave.

Roman catacombs often conjures up pictures of the Lexington Catacomb. Engraving from Thomas W. Knox, *The Underground World*, 1879.

# CHAPTER EIGHT

# GEOGRAPHY OF THE CATACOMB

*The Cave in which the Mummy was found, is not of great extent..."*

Charles Wilkins (1817)

There are geographical similarities between the Lexington Catacomb to: Short Cave, Cave-In-Rock, and Big Bone Cave. Several good early physical descriptions and cave maps will be used as vehicles of comparison.[1] Ashe obtained through his informant enough information to paint a good description of the external and internal geography of the Catacomb. Some of the geography is fabricated (as expected) whereas, other sections in his description of the Catacomb can be accurately correlated with the physical setting in: Cave-In-Rock, Big Bone Cave and Short Cave. The geography of Ashe's Catacomb is thus:

> The descent is gradually inclined, without a rapid or flight of stairs. — The width four feet, the height seven. — The passage but six feet long, is a proportion larger, and the catacomb extends one hundred paces by thirty-five. It is about eighteen feet high; the roof represents an irregular vault, and the floor an oblong square nearly level. From the niches and shelvings on the sides, it might be conjectured, that the catacomb could contain in appropriate situations about two thousand mummies.[2]

Aside from post 1808 folklore, there is no historic documentation from the time period attesting Cave-In-Rock, Illinois, harbored: river pirates, cut-throat killers, and licentious women.[3] River pirates did plunder boats and their crews on the lower Ohio and Mississippi rivers. None of these boat wrecking events nor the pirates involved have ever been connected with the cave as historic fact. The Cave-In-Rock used as a den of thieves starts with Thomas Ashe's description in *Travels*.[4] He produced the groundwork from which its notoriety matured over the next twenty years, incorporated into other travelogues as fact, and has continued to blossom to this day.

Ashe constructed his saga of Cave-In-Rock from a description published in a French Romance novel called *Histoire de Gil Blas de Santillane* by Alain René Le Sage. He generously "borrowed" its extensive interior geography of man-made rooms constructed into treasure chambers, kitchen, horse stable, and living quarters. The cave was occupied by a band of eleven cut-throat highwaymen who used the cave to store their loot and to kill their victims. The Spanish cave of Gil Blas in all of its ramifications was transplanted to the banks of the Ohio River as Cave-In-Rock. Traditions surrounding Eleven Jones Cave, Jefferson County, Kentucky, borrows heavily from the Gil Blas story.

From Ashe's activities on the western frontier; I know he made two trips down the Ohio and Mississippi rivers, there by passing Cave-In-Rock on each occasion. Early editions of Zadok Cramer's *The Navigator* river boatman's guidebook list the cave as a curiosity.[5] Cramer makes no references to river pirates at the cave; yet, points out abundant navigational river hazards to avoid. Surely, the substance of *The Navigator* was to alert boatmen of river dangers. River pirates occupying this notorious place for such a long period should have justifiably been mentioned in the book as a true life threatening navigational hazard. *The Navigator* is completely silent.

From the profusion of cave wall graffiti (even in Ashe's time), it was frequented often by river men desiring a respite from their toil. The cave entrance is an inviting natural feature on the Ohio, and many stopped there to take in its underground beauties and unmatched river scenery from its large entrance. Published travelogues before and after Ashe, reference the cave as a scenic stop on the

The Cave of Gil Blas produced many imitators in the world of cave fiction involving cut-throat killers, treasure chambers, and underground adventures. Wood engraving from *Harper's New Monthly Magazine*, December 1872.

54

river. None of the published travelogues before Ashe mention the cave as a den of river pirates.

Cave-In-Rock is probably the only cave Ashe saw at first hand during his journey. Memory and association from an actual place in the Midwest played a pivotal role in Ashe's Cave-In-Rock and Catacomb descriptions. During the composition of the Catacomb story in *Travels*, Ashe used part of the interior geographic setting of Cave-In-Rock, and incorporated it in the Catacomb narrative. He gives this Cave-In-Rock description:

> I found the cave to measure two hundred feet long.[,] and forty feet high: the entrance forming a semicircular arch of ninety feet at its base, and forty-five in its perpendicular.... The floor is very remarkable; it is level through the whole length of its centre, and rises to the sides in stone grades, in the manner of seats in the pit of a theatre.[6]

From Ashe's point of view, the Catacomb and Cave-In-Rock share similar (but not equal) length, large width (twice as wide in the Catacomb), level floor, and stone grades or shelves along both lengths of the cave wall. Key differences are: the entrance height and width are a whole order smaller for the Catacomb, and approach into each cave have exactly opposite grade slopes. Otto A. Rothert says the floor in Cave-In-Rock "gradually inclines upward toward the rear, and at the extreme end comes within a few feet of the arched ceiling."[7] Clearly, the floor in Cave-In-Rock was not level.

There are compelling geographic similarities between Cave-In-Rock and the Catacomb. To make the Catacomb's geography believable, Ashe used some of the Cave-In-Rock setting, and expanded its dimentions to fit his source description of the real Catacomb. Such an exercise was needed because Ashe never actually saw the Catacomb; and his remembrance was more than a year old when he finally sat down to write his *Travels*. Ashe's proclivity for astounding his readers with larger than life natural features, used the Cave-In-Rock motief to fill in portions of the Catacomb geography. There is a tantalizing residue correlatable to Big Bone Cave and Short Cave. These two caves actually produced Indian mummies, and each have geographic similarities to the Lexington Catacomb.

The oldest Short Cave physical description was written in 1817 and recounts the 1811 visit of Charles Wilkins. The following entrance data is given: "It is of easy access, being about twenty feet wide, and six feet high, at the mouth or entrance. It is enlarged to about fifty feet wide, and ten feet high, almost as soon as you enter it."[8] Wilkins adds that the cave is about three quarters of a mile long. Several other writers of the period say the cave is less than a quarter of a mile long. Ashe's length is about 250

Entrance to Short Cave.

feet long, 88 feet wide and averaging 18 feet high. His entrance height of seven feet is close to the actual six feet high opening, although his width of four feet seems to be error. Or is it?

Ashe might be close to correct with his picture of the entrance opening of seven feet high and four feet wide. The State of Kentucky had an environmental law that required all saltpeter and salt works to be gated. This was needed to keep cattle and livestock from entering the site and injuring themselves. They would eat chemical waste products from the manufacturing process and die of internal bleeding. Commonly, a rock wall was constructed across the entrance opening and fitted with a small wood door or other suitable barrier. After the saltpeter mining era the wall was removed. Later on Short Cave gained new life and was used to grow mushrooms, produce warehouse, commercially exhibited as a tourist attractrion, banquet and music hall.

Interior view of the large trunk cave passage and asphalt driveway in Short Cave. Morning sunlight during late May and June illuminates 300 feet of entrance passage.

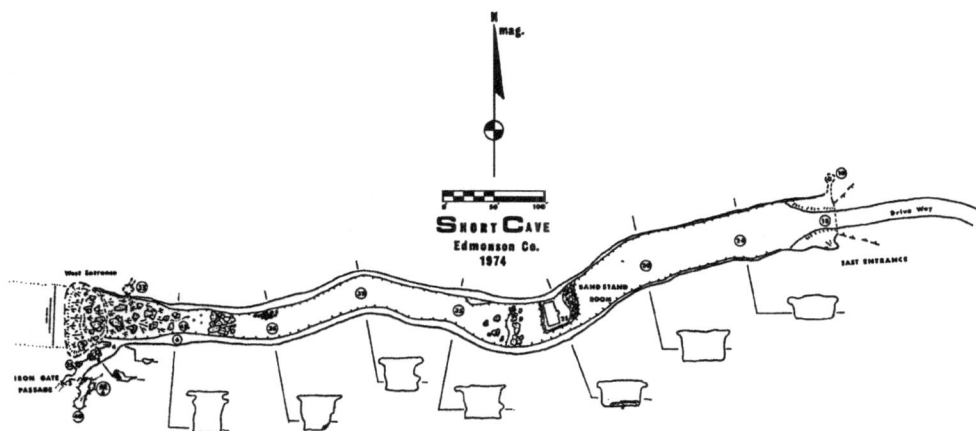

Compass, tripod, and tape survey map of Short Cave. Cartography and drafting by Angelo I. George.

The main entrance is still of easy access and is now floored with an asphalt pavement leading into the cave proper. The entrance passage does open up to ten feet then eighteen feet high. As one proceeds farther into the cave, the height reaches forty five feet. The width of the cave averages about 50 feet.

Henry C. Mercer describes the entrance to Big Bone Cave as "the gloomy hole...was too wet and steep for savage shelter. Water dripping from the low arch fourty-two feet wide and only six feet high."[9]

I suspect Ashe's length of 250 feet is the burial position of his Catacomb mummy from the entrance. This is consistent with how the saltpeter miners went about excavating a cave for saltpeter. They would first work the entrance area and then progress further into the interior of the cave. Mammoth Cave, in Edmonson County, and Great Saltpetre Cave, in Rockcastle County, were mined in this fashion. In considering Ashe's width of 88 feet, it is still within the margin for error of certainty for a 50 foot wide passage. By oil lamp illumination, everything looks bigger in caves, especially large volume trunk passages.

Ashe is cryptic as to what his informant saw in the Lexington Catacomb in terms of physical setting. The large vaulted ceiling in Short Cave matches his picture of an "irregular vault" and the floor is level. The floor was level, even when Wilkins saw the cave in 1811.

One of the murky and pervasive statements by Ashe is the reference to niches and shelves found in his catacomb. This is fine if he is talking about artificial burial niches and shelves as in Roman or Egyptian interment quarters. But, could the niches and shelves mean just what his unknown source is describing, i.e., a niche or shelf that extends the length of each wall in the Catacomb?

Cave-In-Rock and Short Cave do have an elevated niche or shelf on each side of the main trunk passage. The shelf in Cave-In-Rock are stair stepped, ending in a high proto-tube shelf. The shelf in Short Cave is below the ceiling proto-tube. It was part of the old floor of the cave. The paleo-floor was preserved after the old cave stream down cut through this floor, forming a large trunk canyon passage. Cave explorers can walk and stoop the complete 800 foot length of the cave along this shelf. Both sides of the cave can be negotiated in this fashion. Using this understanding, Cave-In-Rock and Short Cave correlates well with Ashe's description of the shelf in the Catacomb. This shelf or proto-tube unit is within easy sight and reach in the main entrance area of each cave. The height of the proto-tube shelf walkway in Short Cave is from 5 to 6 feet high and from 10 to 39 feet above the main cave floor.

The proto-tube shelf, gradual entrance descent, level floor, entrance height and width, distended width once inside, aboriginal site, ash pits, soot blackened ceiling, dusty dry soil, and mummies of the Lexington Catacomb are ten points of geographic and cultural correlation with Short Cave.

Ashe gives a clue to the location of the cave when he says "no other catacomb is known in the State" of Kentucky.[10]

At the beginning of this investigation, I considered the Catacomb to be a separate mummy site. But there are too many chance similarities between the mode of operation of the original discoverers of the Catacomb and the saltpeter miners at Short Cave. Short Cave is the only grotto in Kentucky, where specific documented Indian mummy burials have been found.[11]

I am drawn to the conclusion the Catacomb account as retold by Thomas Ashe is the earliest published historical reference to the unearthing of a real Indian mummy from Short Cave, Edmonson County, Kentucky. There were not two thousand, or even hundreds of mummies, just one or two mummies prior to the discovery of the child mummy in 1811. Ashe being an opportunist for fantastic frontier tales, changed the locale of the mummy site to one with which he was more familiar and within the travel context of his book.

Trying to arrive at the discovery date of the Short Cave Catacomb of mummies is difficult. Thomas Ashe traveled in the Midwest from mid-1805 to late 1806 and *Travels* was published in 1808. The story in *Travels* establishes a discovery date of twenty years ago, which places the event in 1785-1786. His date is definitely too early. Ashe is fond of placing additional zeros or integers of ten when ever there is some kind of count going on. Using hundreds of mummies in the Catacomb is an example of his exponential method of counting. This exaggerated counting method is used throughout *Travels*.

In the saltpeter caves of Kentucky, especially Mammoth Cave (Edmonson County) and Great Saltpetre Cave (Rockcastle County), there is an abundance of early references related to their mining operation. The subsoils in the caves, once leached of their calcium nitrate where then returned to the cave floor and there they were allowed to lie fallow for three years.[12] Thus, renitrification would occur awaiting the next re-excavation by the saltpeter miners. Or so I thought. Minable saltpeter earth in Mammoth Cave was at a premium and could only be gotten to by removing a massive thickness of breakdown. This was only done in a few places. Apparently most of the soils came from Bat Avenue, Audubon Avenue, lower Gothic Avenue, and the passage across from Gothic. A number of small lateral passages down the Main Cave were also exploited. There is no evidence for recycling of lixiviated saltpeter earth in Mammoth Cave. Only in neighboring Dixon Cave is there any evidence for this kind of activity.

Thinking that lixiviated earth was automatically recycled in smaller caves, forced one to consider alternative ideas to keep the work force busy while the saltpeter earth lay fallow in the cave. If so, then more than one saltpeter cave may have been used by the same labor force. A minimum of three caves would be linked in a kind of work cycle based upon the period of working one cave for one year and then moving on to the next, the following year, until the cycle was completed. Nice idea, but I have never been able to discover if this three cave scenario was ever practiced in the saltpeter caves of eastern North America.

The demand for saltpeter was so great leading up to and through the War of 1812, that cost cutting measures were employed. It was more practical to processes as much saltpeter as possible, thereby depleting this renewable resource. Recycling was time consuming and not practiced in the majority of Kentucky saltpeter sites. Present day field investigation into saltpeter mining practices just does not support the conservation concept of universal recycling. Depleted saltpeter resources and New Madrid earthquake devastation of the processing plant in Mammoth Cave were the key reasons it went out of the mining business at the end of 1813 or shortly thereafter. A new business quickly replaced the failed enterprise with the introduction of tourism.

The discovery of the Child and Fawn Hoof in 1811 and the discovery of the Scudder and Peale's Museum mummies in 1814 correlate well with this conceptualized cyclic period of excavation-fallow time frame. Every time there was excavation work in the cave, a group of mummies was dug up. Specifically, these mummies were subsoil stone box graves overlain with tons of breakdown. It may have taken that long to prepare the site for soil excavation. The following rock breakdown work-soil excavation interval for Short Cave is established: 1814, 1811, 1808, 1805, 1802.

The travel context of Ashe's known stay in America is from mid-1805 to late 1806. The Short Cave work period of 1805 falls within or just prior to the time frame of his visit. Because this time period nearly marks the early start of the domestic saltpeter manufacturing industry in America; and it is just a little over twenty years into the future from when Ashe said the mummies were discovered in 1785. The 1805 date is within his chronology of travel in America.

Who was the source of information for Thomas Ashe's Lexington Catacomb? Lexington was the center for gunpowder production and the "home office" for some of the entrepreneurs engaged in the lucrative business of saltpeter mining and speculation. There is enough historical commentary and comparative documented evidence to suggest Ashe never visited Lexington, nor did he set foot in the Barrens of Kentucky. One of the few places where Ashe is locally documented to have stayed is in Cincinnati and another is in Natchez.

John Stuart encountered Ashe in Natchez. Stuart was a knowledgeable associate of the saltpeter entrepreneurs in the Greenbrier Valley, Virginia (now West Virginia).

Stuart was well acquainted with others in the same profession, especially Samuel Brown. Stuart had the grasp and interest in collecting large exotic Pleistocene bones and bringing them to the attention of those who could study them. He could have been a source of communication to Ashe on the environment of saltpeter caves, people active in the industry, and artifacts found in that kind of cave. Stuart would be a long-shot first guess.

Ashe's chief contact in Cincinnati was William Goforth, M.D. Soon after the first mummies were found in Short Cave, Goforth was in a strategic position to receive word of the mummy discovery.[13]

Ashe says, "I have been favored with the friendship and notice of Doctor Goforth, a very skillful physician, and a true lover of learning and science. He has lived in the western world twenty years, and employed the beginning of that period in the study of nature, from which he was turned by the scoffs of the vulgar and the ridicule of fools."[14]

Ashe often refers to Goforth as "my very intelligent friend Dr. Goforth,"[15] and to the late Colonel Israel Ludlow (1765-1804) who:

had the reputation of possessing the learning of a scholar and the manners of a gentleman. Doctor Goforth, who was his particular friend, tells me, that no person was so well versed in the ancient history of his country, (America) that he sought after subjects of antiquity, and data on which to found certain and irrefragable conclusions, with great ardour and zeal, and that had he lived, he would have given the world his fund of interesting research and philosophic enquiries to beat down the absurdity and errors it had been so long cultivating and acquiring.[16]

According to Ashe, Ludlow had investigated mounds and collected Indian artifacts.[17] Certainly, Ludlow should be a prime candidate for consideration. Other than Ashe's statements, little is known about Ludlow's antiquarian interests.

The most plausible source is found in members of the Peyton Short clan who lived near Cincinnati. Ashe generated the acquaintance of Judge John Cleves Symmes (1742-1814), on whose land the town of Cincinnati would be surveyed by land speculators Israel Ludlow, John Filson, and others. With only the account by Ashe, there is no collateral physical record these two ever met. It is not unreasonable to expect an association; especially knowing Ashe's ability to search out the upper crust of society and their ability to attract the favor of foreign visitors into their homes. The Judge lived in North Bend about seven miles down stream from Cincinnati,[18] a place Ashe would pass on his journey to New Orleans in the Spring of 1806. Ashe says the Judge had no children to call his own, yet he and his second wife (Mary Halstead), were living with Susan Livingston. Ashe says the Judge and his wife doted over Susan like she was one of the family on "whom they fix their affections."[19] Ashe devotes almost a page to the fine amenities of Miss Livingston. This kind of treatment was usually allocated to Dulcinea type bar-maids and other low life women met along the road. Curiously, it seems the Judge was actually married to Livingston and had been since 1804.[20] My question is, who was this "other" woman that Ashe says the Judge was living with at that time?

The first wife of John Symmes was Mary Tuthill (   -1776) and they had two daughters, Maria (a.k.a. Mary, 1763-1801) and Anna (1775-1864). Anna married the future president of the United States, William Henry Harrison (1773-1841), while Maria married Peyton Short.[21] Peyton was an unsuccessful speculator in Ohio and Kentucky lands and is suspected to be the possible renter of the mummy cave called Short Cave.[22] This family alliance produced a close-knit clan of Symmes, Short, Wilkins, Ridgely, and Edmund families. The death of one spouse did not end family ties.

Peyton Short certainly deserved better rewards as a land speculator than his actual efforts showed for his labors. He was not a good manager of his money nor his properties. He squandered his lands as an inept horse trader with visions of big rewards rather than small profits that could grow with wise investments. William Short (his older brother) chose the latter and died a wealthy man, leaving the bulk of his enormous fortune to his favorite nephew (Peyton's son), Charles Wilkins Short, M.D. (1793-1863), the botanist.

Peyton borrowed large sums of money from family and friends using worthless land as collateral. He owed tens of thousands of hard currency dollars to Colonel William Croghan (1752-1822), and his brothers-in-laws: Frederick Ridgely, M.D. (1757-1824), and Charles Wilkins. He pledged his home estate, Greenfield near Versailles, Kentucky, and numerous slaves as collateral to secure some of these loans to Wilkins and Ridgely.[23] Ridgely and Wilkins after much tolerance, demanded payment on the debt. Peyton was unable to pay even the interest. Through the courts, Peyton's brother-in-laws obtained power of attorney and seized all his assets. The Court Order became effective on October 24, 1809. One of his financial assets is suspected (with good reason) to have been the Short Cave.

Wilkins had been speculating in saltpeter since 1808. By January 1, 1810, he and Fleming Gatewood of Louisville, Kentucky, purchased Mammoth Cave. As many as seventy slaves worked the cave for saltpeter.[24]

The only reason Wilkins had any right to be on the land containing Short Cave in 1811 was his administrative credentials of power of attorney.

There were only two things Peyton did really well. He liked to go off and explore far away places, such as Florida; and he was an accomplished raconteur of the fabulous! Charles Wilkins Short recalls his fathers traits:

> Those who knew him, say that he had a wonderful talent for conversation, which with his fine education and mental culture made him a most agreeable companion; that in his happy days his wit and humor were unbounded and "could have passed muster with Swift and Poe, and the "brilliants" of their day."[25]

The correspondence of Peyton Short does not reveal any of the finer characteristics of his story telling. Instead they tell of a grovelling, excuse-making apologies to his brother William for his failure to administer their properties. There is not a word about pre-1811 Indian mummies in any of the letters of: William and Peyton Short, Charles Wilkins, and Judge John Cleves Symmes. For decades, these people were writing one another on a weekly or monthly basis. With only a small sampling of their manuscripts, there may still be the key documentation in collections not yet found or catalogued.

One main reason for not writing about mummies from Short Cave is that all the principals knew about the find. Enquiries about relatives, health and financial matters took precedence over work-a-day chit-chat. Even Mammoth Cave is rarely mentioned in Wilkins' correspondence. Besides the family correspondence, these people frequently visited one another. The newspapers at Lexington and Cincinnati serviced a small population. The towns people knew what was going on and it would serve the papers not to print what everyone already knew. Common knowledge is not news, during an era when rag paper was scarce and at a premium.

The authenticity of the Lexington Catacomb as attributed by Thomas Ashe has long been considered to be pure fiction, principally because the tale is based upon the unsubstantiated written word of Thomas Ashe. The locality for the Lexington Catacomb has been lost since 1806. There are no corroborating persons that have seen Ashe's Catacomb at or near Lexington. Ashe is the only witness. Historians consider Ashe to be an unreliable source, and it becomes difficult to use his book to frame historical events without corroborative evidence. Ashe reports the discovery of Indian mummies in a cave, four years before the discovery at Big Bone Cave, Tennessee, and five years before the child was discovered in Short Cave, Kentucky. The notion of a hoax is remote, because Ashe had discovered a verbal Indian mummy model to work from and the Lexington Catacomb is the result of his labors. Ashe's source is probably William Goforth, M.D., who had the necessary interest and grasp of Midwest antiquities. Goforth's source would have been Judge John Cleves Symmes, who may have received an already embellished story from family member Peyton Short.

A close reading of the Catacomb story along with a genetic comparison with substantiated mummy sites from Big Bone and Short caves, strongly suggest a significant portion of the Catacomb story rests firmly on a legitimate mummy discovery that probably occurred in 1805 in Short Cave.

It is well known that Ashe exercised a great deal of literary license with real historic events and it was one of these that gave rise to the Lexington Catacomb. He was constantly on the lookout for fantastic frontier tales. When he found one, he remodeled it to fit the travel context of his western visit. It is doubtful Ashe ever saw a real Indian mummy, and as a result fell into the same predicament faced by 20th century visitors to Mammoth Cave. With the image of an Egyptian mummy or the Boris Karloff cinematic model to work from, tourists became somewhat surprised when they saw Lost John, without his linen encasing strips.[26]

Mining in caves occasionally uncovered vertebrate remains of extinct animals. Naturalist had been greatly puzzled what animal they represented and how long ago they lived. Wood engraving from L. Simonin, *Les Merveilles du Monde Souterrain*, 1878.

Early in the eighteen hundreds, the documentation of Indian mummy sites is very sparse. Published notices came into print long after the initial discovery. Because of the widespread distribution of *Travels* with its stupendous account of the Catacomb and hundreds of Indian mummies. His book received harsh criticism; especially over the Irishman's dishonest procurement of the William Goforth Pleistocene bone collection. The Lexington Catacomb on the Western frontier momentarily obscured the authenticity of the Big Bone and Short caves mummy sites. Certain elements from the Catacomb story were even grafted to these discoveries, especially their mode of discovery and the mummies being embalmed prior to burial. Fawn Hoof's reputation grew as the Queen of the Caves and Little Al became the Egyptian Mummy of Salts Cave.

The finding of a dried out human body by saltpeter miners or by a contemporary archeologist is an uncommon event. All of the complete mummies were discovered during the saltpeter mining era prior to 1815. Short Cave is the only cave where documented mummy burials have been discovered in Kentucky. Desiccated cadavers have been found in Mammoth and in Salts caves, but these bodies were not buried nor were they accompanied by grave goods. In those early times when the mummies were openly exhibited at Mammoth Cave, all of the mummies were considered to have been embalmed in a manner similar to the Egyptian.[27] Ashe is directly responsible for fathering the misconception that Native American Indians embalmed their dead prior to interment. This theory was believed well into the 20th century and has only recently been debunked by researchers who found Indian cave mummy burials are actually simple burials in which the cadaver becomes desiccated by the dry atmosphere, constant temperature, and soil conditions in the cave environment.[28]

As fantastic as finding mummies in caves sounds, I can only conclude based on all comparative and circumstantial evidence from Ashe's account of the Lexington Catacomb that its location is not in Fayette County, but rather his tale is the earliest physical description of the Short Cave, Edmonson County, Kentucky, site.

The Catacomb is the high point of Ashe's journey of adventure and discovery — thus making the story an easy target for criticism. Kentucky backwoodsmen and river boatmen were noted for spinning yarns and telling tall tales, but the Irishman exceeded their expectations and surpassed his own Cave-In-Rock fantasy. Little did Thomas Ashe know that his Catacomb, augmented with a full measure of mummies would still be a subject of controversy today. If he had left the story unaltered from his oral source, the Catacomb tale would still be just as incredible and just as dubious, only because it originated from the pen of Thomas Ashe, world fireside traveler and story teller — *par excellence.*

Entrance to Big Bone Cave in Tennessee.

# CHAPTER NINE

# COPPERAS CAVE OF MUMMIES

*The vast limestone cavern in Tennessee . . .*
Timothy Flint (1826)

During the pioneer era, caves out of economic necessity were exploited for saltpeter, alum, Epsom salts, copperas, and gypsum. In the course of soil excavation, giant Pleistocene bones, Indian skeletons, mummies, and artifacts were accidentally unearthed. Never again would discoveries of this nature, in so great a frequency, and in this quantity be made in caves of the Midwest. One of these Indian mummy caves "was the vast limestone cavern in Tennessee" called Copperas Cave.[1] The cave produced the first of two sets of Indian mummies on September 2, 1810. By about the same time the following year, "many human Bodies have also been found in the Nitre Caves of the Cumberland Mountains similar to that of the Child" mummy just discovered in a similar cave called Short Cave, Kentucky.[2] By 1818, Caleb Atwater (the antiquarian) knew of at least three mummies from the same Tennessee cave.[3] Published text suggest Copperas Cave may have produced as many as six or more mummies prior to 1815.[4]

Archaeologically, this nationally prominent cave is probably one of the most important human burial sites in context with perishable grave goods found during the Speculative Period of archaeology (1661-1847). The cave was so well known, no one bothered to record its exact location. Using comparative geographical logic, experience with pioneer renaming practice, and documentation from near the time period, I showed the identity of Copperas Cave to be the earliest place name for Big Bone Cave, in present day Van Buren County, Tennessee.[5]

Little more than a year after the publication of the American edition of Ashe's *Travels in America*; on September 2, 1810, ferrous sulfate miners working in James Bryant's Copperas Cave dug open two burial crypts containing a male and female mummy in split cane baskets.[6] The cave is located six miles above the Great Falls on the Caney Fork and very near the Black Fox Trail.[7] Position of the trail and physical characteristics of both cave entrances may have been instrumental in the Indian selection of Big Bone Cave as a burial site. The pioneer discovery created a great

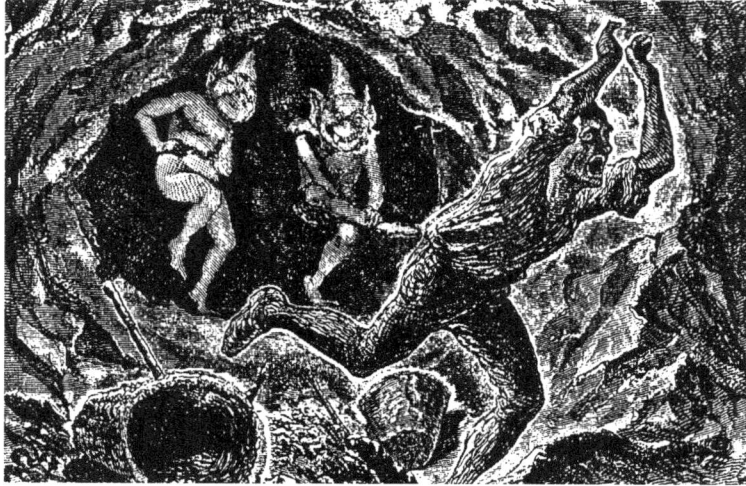

The underworld of mines was believed to be the home of ghosts and infernal beings (thommyknockers). Engraving from *Harpers New Monthly Magazine*, 1873.

amount of skepticism among newspaper editors, laymen, and the scientific community. Here were Indian mummies whose method of burial, discovery, and announcement had all the overtones connected with the mummies from the Lexington Catacomb. The Nashville *Examiner* was the first to carry the late 1810 discovery notice.

Charles Cassedy (1782?-1858?), from his anonymous eye witness, said the preservation was so complete that "the eyes [are] as full and as prominent as if alive."[8] Copies of the newspaper notice reached the eastern sea coast to readers with a full measure of reserve. More than skeptical at first, Pleasant M. Miller gathered what information he could on the Tennessee site. Because he "had some reason to doubt the truth of that statement. Since my return home, I made some enquiry; and I now know that the facts stated in that extract are true."[9] His letter of May 1, 1811, was published in the *Medical Repository* the following year.

Reminiscing eighteen years after the fact, the Indian artifact collector and political commentator, Charles Cassedy recalled events and observations he made in the cave.[10] While in Nashville in January 1811, he was approached by the editor of *The Examiner*. Thomas Easton handed to Cassedy an original, almost illegible manuscript copy for "correctional inspection" and comments on the Copperas Cave mummy discovery.[11] After publication, Cassedy wrote to "Dr. John R. Bedford [M. D., 1782-1827]... and stated to him candidly my opinions." Bedford replied in Cassedy's words "that notwithstanding the state of public opinion, which was often regulated by crude speculations or ignorance, the matter was worthy of further investigation as connected with the aboriginal history of the country...."[12] The last thing Cassedy wanted to happen was to be branded a Tennessee Thomas Ashe. So, Dr. Bedford and Cassedy went to Copperas (Big Bone) Cave in April to establish the validity contained in the original newspaper reports. He reports:

> We found the cavern, if such it might be called, within a few hundred yards of the bank of the Caney Fork of the Cumberland river, in a country remarkable for the ruggedness of its aspect and the lofty and abrupt acclivity of the hills and mountains.....The cavern itself was situated near the top of a gorge or deep ravine, formed by the junction of two lofty and almost impracticable hills, which, approaching each other nearly at right angle, formed a junction at and below the cavern, and opened to the westward. The top of the cave was a projecting flat rock, impervious to water, which rested on the uppermost junction of these hills, and seemed to be incorporated with both. Over the outer edge of this rock, from some fountain which neither the Doctor nor myself had leisure to examine, a small cascade...precipitated itself to the bottom of the ravine, at the opening of the deep valley below, probably a distance of more than one hundred feet. Immediately behind the highest part of this sheet of water, and about six or seven feet below the smooth surface of the projecting rock above, we found the bottom of the cave.[13]

They were informed at the cave that the mummies had been reburied to keep the spirits of the dead from haunting the workers. They found the site without too much trouble and re-excavated the graves. Cassedy makes a careful description of the mummies and associated grave goods.

Cassedy's two letters are our most complete record from the cave and its mummies. He says:

> Unwilling that these monuments of antiquity should only survive in the recollection of two persons, whose authority for representing their existence might even be questioned, I took a sample of the shrouding which immediately enveloped the body of the female, and also another, about a foot square, from the mantle of feathers; then amputating one of the feet at the ankle joint taking care to obtain as large portion of the Tendon of Achilles as could be drawn out without much violence.[14]

Cassedy and Bedford observed the pre-adolescent female mummy had a wound on the right side of her head. There was also a "traverse cut across the abdomen, of some length." Cassedy thought the head wound to be damage marks left by the copperas miners. The male mummy had been initially taken outside the cave where it was mutilated by the miners and began to deteriorate. It was reinterred in the cave. When Cassedy and Bradford dug up the male, it was in such bad condition they decided not to even pull it out of its wicker basket coffin. Pleasant Millers' reports about disarticulation of the legs at the hip joint and the legs were placed over the chest of the mummy.[15] This is a mistaken illusion of Indian burial customs precipitated by the activity of the copperas miners.

The female was in such excellent condition that they amputated both feet at the ankle joint![16] This was done as proof of the existence of Indian mummies in caves. Other extremity body parts may have also been amputated or destroyed. Word of these amputations created outright indignation in scientific journals. Thomas I. Wray said the "illiterate miners...allowed every visitor that wished it, to break off parts either to be totally destroyed on the spot, or taken away."[17] It is not clear if the female was ever reinterned.

These artifacts were carried to Thomas Jefferson at his Monticello residence where they were examined with great interest by him and the "Russian Ambassador," William Short (1759-1849).[18] From there, the artifacts were taken to New York City and deposited in John Scudder's American Museum. Cassedy kept the other foot for his cabinet.

Shortly after Cassedy's excavation, Moses Fisk writes in 1820 about his early visit to the site where he was told of a reburied adult male, and he saw a child between the age of 6 and 8 years old.[19] He recovered its wicker basket for his collection. In the interim, John D. Clifford (1778-1820) acquired this little female mummy for his cabinet in Lexington, Kentucky.[20]

True interest in the mummies only occurred when they were exhibited to the public. The Reverend Timothy Flint (1780-1840) was fortunate to view one of the mummies on or about October 7, 1815.[22] His visit occured during a time when Lexington was celebrating Henry Clay's (1777-1852) return from Belgium after orchestrating the Treaty of Ghent.[21] Numerous tributes and dinner parties were given in Clay's honor.

Flint says two mummies "were found in the vast limestone cavern in Tennessee."[23] He gives a magnificent account of one of the mummies he inspected (the only one then present). Viewing the mummy produced a lasting indelible impression of an incredible petrification from the stuff nightmares are made. The scene was not soon forgotten and it stayed with him all those years:

All that I have seen and heard of the remains of the men, would seem to show, that they were smaller than the men of our times. All the bodies, that have been found in that state of high preservation, in which they were discovered in nitrous caves, were considerably smaller than the present ordinary stature of men. The two bodies, that were found in the vast limestone cavern in Tennessee, one of which I saw at Lexington, were neither of them more than four feet in height. It seemed to me, that this must have been nearly the height of the living person. The teeth and nails did not seem to indicate the shrinking of the flesh from them in the desiccating process by which they were preserved. The teeth were separated by considerable intervals, and were small, long, white, and sharp, reviving the horrible images of nursery tales of orgres' teeth. The hair seemed to have been sandy, or inclining to yellow. It is well known that nothing is so uniform in the present Indian, as his lank black hair. From the pains taken to preserve the bodies, and the great labor of making the funeral robes in which they were folded, they must have been of the "blood royal," or personages of great consideration in their day. The person that I saw had evidently died by a blow on the skull. The blood had coagulated there into a mass of a texture and colour, sufficiently marked to show that it had been blood. The envelope of the body was double. Two splendid blankets, completely woven with the most beautiful feathers of the wild turkey, arranged in regular stripes and compartments, encircled it. The cloth, on which these feathers were woven, was a kind of linen of neat texture, of the same kind with that which is now woven from the fibers of the nettle. The body was evidently that of a female of middle age, and I should suppose, that her majesty weighed, when I saw her, six or eight pounds.[24]

Flint describes a middle aged female mummy (as was Fawn Hoof), four feet high (Fawn Hoof was 5 feet 10 inches; the male Scudder mummy was 5 feet 1/4 inches) and weighed 6 to 8 pounds (14 pounds for Fawn Hoof, and 6 1/2 pounds for the male 1814 Scudder mummy). The 1814 female Peale's Museum mummy showed no damage other than a bullet like hole in the thorax, and her body was larger than the male. I can conclude that Flint is describing a completely different mummy and not the ones from Short Cave, Kentucky.

As a further differentiation of the mummies, Flint observes wide gaps between the mummies small sharp teeth, like "ogres' teeth." Everyone who examined the suite of mummies always remarked about the teeth, but never about the gaps. Flint's chronicle is the only eye witness to mention this characteristic. Flint's "ogres' teeth" description could be an embellishment colored by the passage of time. During mummification, the flesh of the face and lips retract, thereby exposing the teeth in a kind of sardonic smile or sneer. And public viewers may have plucked its teeth to test its authenticity. We know this kind of activity was exercised on Fawn Hoof a year later. Thus Flint says the teeth revived "the horrible images of nursery tales of ogres' teeth."[25] The mummy possessed a skull fracture (with dried blood on the forehead that could only be produced at the time of death; the first female from Big Bone Cave also had a skull fracture). Flint's reference to the "vast limestone cavern in Tennessee" can only be Big Bone Cave. For the sake of future identification, I am calling this individual *the Gapped Tooth Mummy*. As a further differentiation, this mummy was a complete cadaver, with both feet.

An Englishman with the same last name, James Flint, visited Lexington, Kentucky. On December 12, 1818, he saw the mummy in the newly formed Athenaeum (a reading room).[26] One of the second floor rooms was devoted to the Natural History Museum belonging to John D. Clifford. Flint lists some of Clifford's accessions as "a bowl of unglazed earthenware found along with a mummy in a cave in Tennessee." Neither Copperas Cave nor Big Bone Cave are mentioned.

John D. Clifford died on May 8, 1820. All of his collected Indian artifacts, minerals, and fossil vertebrates were deposited with Transylvania University.[27] As the mummy changed hands, so did its discovery location to a new site near Mammoth Cave called White Cave.[28] Here the Gapped Tooth Mummy would take on a role as one of the Mammoth Cave area mummies. A few Mammoth Cave guidebook authors, especially Alexander Bullitt and Horace Martin, mistakenly assigned it to Mammoth Cave.[29] Furthermore, this mummy became confused with one of the mummies found in Short Cave during the year of 1814.[30] This muddied up the picture to no end.

The Gapped Tooth Mummy from Big Bone Cave and antiquarian artifacts were sold in 1824 to Joseph Dorfeuille, the new proprietor of the Western Museum in Cincinnati, Ohio.[31] Under the curatorship of Dorfeuille, Clifford's Megalonyx bones (from Big Bone Cave) and the little mummy were labeled as coming from a saltpeter cave called White Cave, Kentucky.

During or after the summer of 1829, the Big Bone Cave mummy was sold to Albert Koch (1804-1868), a recent German immigrant who arrived in 1826.[32] In January 1834, he opened up his St. Louis Museum.[33] One of his star attractions was the White Cave mummy from a Kentucky saltpeter cave. Broadsides describing this wonder were circulated and are not now known to have survived. Most of the Indian artifacts came from William Clark's Indian Museum in the same city, with almost total transference by 1838.[34] Inspection of Clark and Clark, *Catalogue of Indian Curiosities*, reveals nothing about the mummy. I must presume the mummy was not part of his collection and was instead acquired independently by Koch. Just when Koch acquired the mummy is not definitely known.

In January 1841, Koch sold his museum and most of the exhibits to W. S. McPherson who continued the operation in St. Louis.[35] Chain of custody of the mummy is lost at this point in time. Conceivably this little "female" mummy could still be with us today.

From then on more Indian mummies were dug up by the saltpeter miners within the Caney Fork enclave. Post-1810 newspaper articles establish new caves and dates for additional mummy discoveries. Descriptions consist of various numbers of buried individuals, coupled with age and weight differences, assorted grave goods, and differences in burial practices. From its sketchy nature, Dutch (sic) River could be an obsolete place name or illegible hand script corruption for Rocky River. The small cave entrance and 1811 date of discovery bodes well for the Arch Cave entrance discovery to Big Bone Cave.[36] This 1811 mummy description reads as if it was taken straight out of Ashe's Catacomb, where:

> a large stone was discovered across the mouth of a cave. On entering the cave which appeared natural in a limestone rock, resembling a vault or ancient sepulcher, the bodies of two persons were discovered. They were male and female, and each in a curious wrought basket made of splits of cane. The bodies were in a sitting posture. Around each body was wrapped a kind of large shroud[?] or plain[?] seemingly wrought with the fingures and made of the best of matting resembling wild nettles or Indian hemp. Both bodies and shroud were entire. The Bodies were consolidated. The oldest Cherokee Indians could give no account of ever hearing of the cave or the persons interred.[37]

A different mummy discovery was made in another(?) saltpeter cave. Date of discovery is not known, but probably was prior to 1815. This one is similar to the one above, yet with more description:

> Near the confines of Smith and Wilson counties, on the south side of Cumberland River, about 22 miles above Cairo, on the waters of Smith's Fork, is a cave, the aperture into which is very small. The workmen in the cave enlarged the entrance and went in; and digging in the apartment, next to the entrance, after removing the dirt and using it, they came, upon the same level with the entrance, to another small aperture, which they all entered, and went through, when they came into a narrow room, 25 feet square. Every thing here was neat and smooth. The room seemed to have been carefully preserved for the reception and keeping of the dead. In this room, near about the centre, were found sitting in

baskets made of cane, three human bodies; the flesh being entire, but a little shrivelled, and not much so. The bodies were those of a man, a female and a small child. The complexion of all was very fair, and white, without any intermixture of a copper colour. Their eyes were blue; their hair auburn, and fine. The teeth were very white, their stature was delicate, about the size of the whites of the present day. The man was wrapped in 14 dressed deer skins. The 14 deer skins were wrapped in what those present called blankets. They were made of bark, like those found in the cave in White County [Big Bone Cave]. The form of the baskets which enclosed them, was pyramidal, being larger at the bottom, and declining to the top. The heads of the skeletons, from the neck, were above the summits of the blankets.[38]

This description is no more bizarre than Cassedy's first description of the Copperas (Big Bone) Cave mummy discovery. Apparently these mummies were not subsoil burials, were in a prepared room, yet differed in the method of wrapping and basket design, the skeleton heads protruding above the apex of each basket. This is atypical to all the rest of the known mummy interments. Blue eyed, white Indians surely almost make this discovery worthy of inclusion in the fantastic archaeology section in Chapter Twelve.[39] The last two sites are probably Big Bone Cave locations. Big Bone Cave is near the antique geographic boundary of Smith and Wilson counties.

Note also the Smith Fork site reference could be a typographic error for antique Smith County. The first right hand side passage inside the main entrance to Big Bone Cave might just be the passage mentioned in the undated newspaper article used by John Haywood. Haywood clarifies in part the identity of this mummy cave on Smith Fork. He says:

In White county, on the west side of the Cumberland mountain, in west Tennessee, near the line of Warren county, and about eight miles south or southwest of the spot where were found the two human bodies which will be here after described, is a *cave*, in the spur of the mountain, having a small entry on one side, but on the other a mouth of much larger size. Half a mile from the small entry, the bones of some large animal were found, lying all together.[40]

This refers to the two entrances to Big Bone Cave.

Taking the last two sites at face value gives seven mummies found by Tennessee miners. Only the foot of the Copperas (Big Bone) Cave female mummy and a complete female (Gapped Tooth) mummy are known to have found repose in museums.

# CHAPTER TEN

# MUMMIES FROM SHORT CAVE AND THE MAMMOTH CAVE CONNECTION

*In this small nether subterranean chamber, sat in solemn silence, one of the human species, a female, with her wardrobe and ornaments placed at her side.*

Ebenezer Meriam (1844)

All the ruckus generated by Ashe's book and reviews in 1809 was still strong two years later. The local newspapers did not carry any of the Tennessee mummy discoveries nor did they print notices when mummies started to be dug up in a saltpeter cave near Mammoth Cave. Charles Wilkins (c. 1763-1827), part owner of Mammoth Cave, was one of the chief suppliers of refined saltpeter to the E. I. DuPont Company, in Wilmington, Delaware. His saltpeter mining venture would play a pivotal role that would launch Mammoth Cave to world wide fame.

Infrequently, Wilkins would journey to Mammoth Cave to look over his investment and to escape the "sickly season" about the town of Lexington. While at the cave in August of 1811, he was notified about an amazing discovery just dug up in another saltpeter cave. It was a mummy! He rushed to his brother-in-laws (Peyton Short) cave to see and collect it from the saltpeter miners. When he returned to his Lexington home with news of this exciting find, one of the people he told the story to was the naturalist and merchant John D. Clifford, who in turn wrote a letter to Benjamin S. Barton on September 4, 1811.[1] The letter contained nothing of Lexington Catacomb mummies (something Barton was already interested in), but described something almost as unbelievable as Ashe's original tale, the discovery of a real Indian mummy from a saltpeter cave in the Barrens of Kentucky! This was Short Cave.[2] Without the slightest of incredulous overtones, Clifford makes his report to Barton:

> The Atmosphere of these nitre Caves prevents all putrefaction. Dead bodies have been found when first seen, were apparently as perfect as at the period when deposited there. - A Child was lately dug up in a Cave adjoining that of Mr. Wilkins, wrapped up in a Cloth described as resembling Canvas, this was again enveloped in a Deer Skin - the Corps appeared as if newly Dead but upon

75

Entrance to Mammoth Cave shows saltpeter pipes and evaporation furnaces in the background. Rocks in the lower right hand corner are illustrated over saltpeter kettles in earlier renderings. Lithograph from *American Monthly Magazine*, 1837.

> exposure to the open atmosphere it in a few hours Crumbled into its natural Dust. Many human Bodies have also been found in the Nitre Caves of the Cumberland Mountains similar to that of the Child. tho they were wrapped up in garments made from the outer Surfaces of the Cane intermingling with feathers.[3]

With a skull remaining intact, Clifford hoped Wilkins could recover it and the robe for study. I sensed a certain amount of vindication in this letter over the harsh treatment given to Barton just a few years before by the editors of the *Kentucky Gazette*, and the *Kentucky Reporter*.

The Copperas (Big Bone) Cave mummies were by that time well known to Clifford and his eastern counterparts (or at least those that "believed" Indian mummies had been found in caves). He may have known of one or two other sites in Tennessee. Thus Clifford's account of "many bodies have been found in the Nitre Caves of the Cumberland Mountains," starts to have real meaning for events happening prior to September 1811.[4] It was also clear that he did not yet have possession of the Gapped Tooth Mummy found in the Spring of 1811 from Big Bone Cave.

Responding to a request from the American Antiquarian Society, Charles Wilkins reports in 1817 of another mummy from Short Cave. This was a female associated with a great amount of grave goods.[5] Years later, the "Mammoth Cave mummy" or "Kentucky's posthumous belle" would be named Fawn Hoof by Nathaniel Parker Willis in 1852.[6] Wilkins supplies significant information about the infant mummy thereby supporting what Clifford had already said. Wilkins letter of October 2, 1817, is not exact enough to ascertain an approximate date of discovery. He establishes the female was found about a month after the child was dug up in the cave. Using the Clifford letter as an anchor base gives a late September 1811 date of discovery for Fawn Hoof. Wilkins reports:

> I received information, that an infant, of nine or twelve months old, was discovered in a saltpetre Cave in Warren county, about four miles from the Mammoth Cave, in a perfect state of preservation. I hastened to the place; but to my mortification, found that, upon its being exposed to the atmosphere, it had fallen into dust, and that its remains, except the skull, with all its clothing, had been thrown into the furnace. I regretted this much, and promised the labourers to reward them, if they would preserve the next subject for me. About a month afterwards, the present one was discovered, and information given to our agent at the Mammoth Cave, who sent immediately for it, and brought and placed it there, where it remained for twelve months. It appeared to be the exsiccated body of a female. The account which I received of its discovery, was simply this. It was found at the depth of about ten feet from the surface of the Cave, bedded in clay, strongly impregnated with nitre, placed in a sitting posture, incased in broad stones, standing on their edges, with a flat stone covering the whole. It was enveloped in coarse clothes, (a specimen of which accompanied it) the whole wrapped in deer skins, the hair of which was shaved off in the manner in which the Indians prepare them for market. Enclosed in the stone coffin, were the working utensils, beads, feathers, and other ornaments of dress, which belonged to her. The body was in a state of much higher perfection, when first discovered, and continued so, as long as it remained in the Mammoth Cave, than it is at present, except the depredations committed upon its arms and thighs by the rats, many of which inhabit the Cave. After it was brought to Lexington, and became the subject of great curiosity, being much exposed to the atmosphere, it gradually began to decay; its muscles to contract, and the teeth to drop out, and much of its hair was plucked from its head by wanton visitants. As to the manner of its being embalmed, or whether the nitrous earth and atmosphere had a tendency to preserve it, must be left to the speculations of the learned.

> The Cave in which the Mummy was found, is not of great extent, not being more than three quarters of a mile in length; its surface, covered with loose limestone, from four to six feet deep, before you enter the clay impregnated with nitre. It is of easy access, being about twenty feet wide, and six feet high, at the mouth or entrance. It is enlarged to about fifty feet wide, and ten feet high, almost as soon as you enter it. This place had evident marks of having once been the residence of the aborigines of the

country, from the quantity of ashes, and the remains of fuel, and torches made of the reed, &c. which were found in it.

These excavations in the earth, or rather in the limestone rock, in which this country abounds, are subjects of great curiosity, and worthy the attention of chemist and naturalist.[7]

Fawn Hoof was removed from Short Cave and placed inside the Rotunda of Mammoth Cave.

A fledgling naturalist by the name of John Hay Farnham (1791-1833) explored Mammoth Cave just before the great New Madrid earthquakes devastated the Midwest and wrecked the saltpeter works inside the cave.[8] His cave description appears in an undated letter and only found its way into print nine years after the event. Interpreting his description of Mammoth Cave, with silence about earthquakes, and what we know of the female mummy discovery would place him in Mammoth Cave in late November or early December and definitely prior to the quakes.[9] The first of four devastating earthquakes would strike at 2 O'Clock in the morning on December 11, 1811. Saltpeter mining in Mammoth Cave would never be the same again.

Farnham's guide recited the circumstances surrounding the Short Cave mummy. It was a female "found three months since, under some rocks in a neighbouring Cave, by the workmen."[10] This would place the discovery of Fawn Hoof in September 1811. He makes an indirect reference to the account by Ashe, in which he reports:

> the greatest curiosity, however, remains to be described. It was, in the language of the people, an "Indian Mummy." Mummies, however, or embalmed bodies, have never been found in America; and the art, in its ancient perfection, was, I believe, confined to the Egyptians, with perhaps the exception of their Asiatick neighbours.[11]

Mummies became a lively topic with the scientific community. Samuel Latham Mitchell's (1764-1831) communication to Samuel M. Burnside was quick to separate catacomb burials from subsoil burials. His August 24, 1815, letter reports:

> In exploring a calcareous chamber [Short Cave] in the neighbourhood of Glasgow, for saltpeter, several human bodies were found enwrapped carefully in skin and cloths. They were inhumed below the floor of the cave; *inhumed*, and not lodged in catacombs.[12]

Tourist trail in Main Cave near entrance to the Methodist Church. Wood engraving from *The Illustrated London News*, October 21, 1876.

It is clear Pleasant Miller, Charles Cassedy and Samuel L. Mitchell were familiar and quite skeptical of Ashe's *Travels* and especially mummy burials in catacombs. It is Mitchell who differentiates between subsoil burials and lodgement in catacombs. He also discounts the notion the American Indians used herbs and spices to prepare their dead for burial. Regardless, herbs and spices would become a staple story with guide patter on the Mammoth Cave mummies. Mitchell needed to separate the notion of Egyptian embalming practices using herbal additives to contradict Ashe's description of sweet smelling odors produced when the Catacomb mummies were cremated. Yet, Ashe is certain the American Indian *did not* use herbs, spices, palm wine, or any other chemical to prepare the body for burial. In those early days, Mammoth Cave was "the largest cave now known," and explored "six or seven miles" from its only known entrance.[13] The antique length was only off by about thirty percent from what we know of early pioneer exploration in the cave. By 1814, the cave length was inflated to be "ten or eleven miles" in "the celebrated Mammoth Cave."[14] It was the greatest cave then and still is today. The cave became a yardstick to which all other caves were compared. The cave is rich in artifacts with evidence of Indian exploration and pre-Columbian mining in over five actual miles of the classic known cave. By 2013, over a half a million visitors each year would see the marvels of this underground empire of over 400 miles,[15] truly the longest cave on earth and the mammoth of all caves.

From September 1811 to perhaps the first quarter of 1816, one of the transplanted mummies (Fawn Hoof) from Short Cave was witnessed by a few visitors to Mammoth Cave. Only a small handful bothered to publish their subterranean adventures. This mummy by July 5, 1814 was intended to be presented to Peale's Museum in Philadelphia.[16] Shortly thereafter, three more mummies were dug up from Short Cave.[17] A male and female mummy were taken to the County Seat at Glasgow. James H. Rice said "the third which bodies sent to Peal's Museum Phil" and "these three are all that have been found discovered in this Cave."[18] Rice makes no mention and was probably unaware of the Child mummy nor Fawn Hoof in the Rotunda of Mammoth Cave. The third mummy had already been sent to Peale's Museum. The physician, James H. Rice observes the two mummies in Glasgow, and gives the first detailed forensic description of the cadavers.[19]

These three mummies were probably discovered in the late summer of 1814, after Hyman Gratz's Mammoth Cave visit. The female mummy was sent by Judge Thomas B. Monroe of Glasgow, to Scudder's American Museum in New York City.[20] It was displayed on a pedestal beside the glass case containing the foot of the female mummy from Copperas (Big Bone) Cave. Constantine S. Rafinesque (1783-1840) made a full body rendering of the Short Cave female about 1816.[21] The museum burned to the ground in 1865 under the ownership of showman Phineas Taylor Barnum (1810-1891).[22]

The final repository of the female mummy was Peale's Museum. An early travelogue records two Indian mummies on display.[23] Harold Meloy thought Daniel Drake, M. D. acquired the mummy from Short Cave, and deposited her in the Western Museum in Cincinnati after 1814.[24] There was no museum in Cincinnati at this time period. Letton's Cincinnati Museum opened its doors in 1818.[25] Mammoth Cave guidebooks record the museum housing the mummy was destroyed by fire prior to 1844.[26] The three earliest museums in Cincinnati were Letton's, Western, and much later Frank's. The most famous museum was Drake's brain child, the Western Museum. It was often called the Cincinnati Museum. Under the proprietorship of Joseph Dorfeuille, the Gapped Tooth Mummy from the John D. Clifford collection would find residence there in 1824. This mummy is believed to be the one reported in Mammoth Cave guidebooks as coming from the cave. The Western Museum was not destroyed by fire. Rather, numerous changes in ownership, declining visitation, and dilapidated exhibits, forced the museum to be sold at auction in 1869.[27]

INDIAN MUMMY.

Scale of one Foot.

A                    B

Constatine S. Rafinesque rendering of a female mummy found in Short Cave in the year 1814. The mummy was on display in Scudder's American Museum, New York City. Wood engraving from *Medical Repository*, 1815.

One of Mammoth Cave's underground travelogues was so well written that it enjoyed wide reprinting and catapulted the cavern to international attention. This is the "Wonders of Nature" by Nahum Ward (1785-1860), who exaggerated the length of the cave and inflated the size of the rooms and passages.[28] He produced a fanciful map of the cave showing eleven miles of passage.

What really captivated the public interest was Ward's description of the Indian mummy dug up about three miles from the entrance of Mammoth Cave. He initially neglected to say the mummy was from Short Cave.[29] Ward stated, "my friend Mr. Wilkins, gave me the mummy, which I brought away, together with her apparel, jewels, music, &c."[30] The mummy was taken to Lexington where it created much excitement.[31] Fawn Hoof would join the Gapped Tooth Mummy (from Big Bone Cave) already attracting much admiration and study by the curious public in John D. Clifford's cabinet.

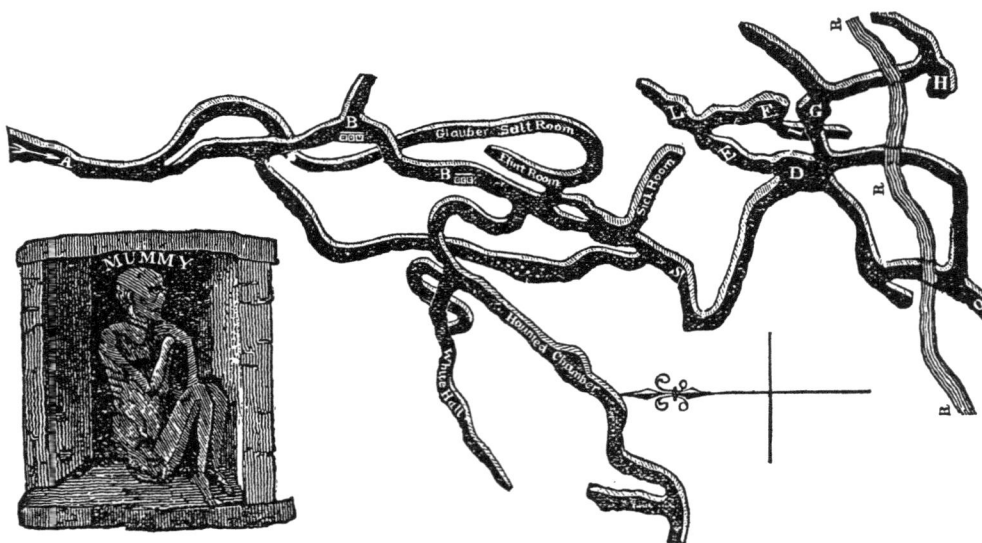

Plan of the Mammoth Cave of Kentucky; with Mummy, now in the American Museum, New York.

Reproduction of Nahum Ward's famous map of Mammoth Cave. Ward's original manuscript map depicted in the insert, a mummy (Fawn Hoof) seated inside a rock sarcophagus (Gordon Smith colection). For the time period, Fawn Hoof resided in the Museum of the American Antiquarian Society, Worcester, Massachusetts. Ward's map and mummy insert was reprinted much later. The mummy in the box grave is renamed the Scudder Mummy. The Scudder Mummy was on display in Scudder's American Museum, New York City. Wood engraving from *The Wonders of the World*, 1877.

# CHAPTER ELEVEN

# ADVENTURES OF NAHUM WARD'S FAWN HOOF AND THE AMERICAN ANTIQUARIAN SOCIETY

*"But, for the children!"*

Michael Caine (as Lawrence Jamison),
in Frank Oz's film
Dirty Rotten Scoundrels (1988)

The mummy named Fawn Hoof would make Mammoth Cave the paramount international show cave. In those early days, few American caves could claim title as "extensive." Only the Indiana Saltpeter Cave (Dr. Adams' Cave, or Wyandotte Cave) and Copperas Cave (Big Bone Cave) had enough known passage to be in the same league. Each of these caves became famous in their own right. Mammoth is the second oldest commercial cave in America, and Wyandotte is the fourth oldest. Big Bone was never commercialized for tourists, yet produced a rich history as a source for saltpeter in two wars, and as a repository of exceptional Indian and paleontological artifacts.

Until now, the story of Nahum Ward and his exploits with Fawn Hoof has never been fully told. Spelean history has not been kind to this man. He is "generally considered the villain of the story;"[1] the villain who made Mammoth Cave famous; the villain who stole Fawn Hoof from Charles Wilkins; the villain who exhibited the mummy in a traveling freak show; the villain who refused to turn the mummy over to the American Antiquarian Society; the villain who tried to sell the mummy to rival institutions; and the villain who was a saint in his hometown, Marietta, Ohio.

Ward's biographic sketch in *History of Washington County*, by Williams in 1881, presents a completely different picture.[2] Williams treats him as a: civic mined pillar of the community, mayor, principal stockholder in the Ohio Company (land speculation), and merchant. With $25,000 of his own money, he built the Unitarian Church in Marietta. Benevolence would have been his middle name; his charitable contributions were boundless to the homeless and unfortunate. Are we talking about the same man here? No villain was he. Rather, his actions relative to Mammoth Cave make him an unsung hero of Kafka-esque circumstances without the gloom.

Before Nahum Ward made his epic visit to Mammoth Cave, few notices about the cave had ever been printed. "The Subterranean Voyage," second hand notes by the ornithologist Alexander Wilson, Benjamin Davies' geographical descriptions and "Green River or Mammoth Cave," are a sampling of the few available published references.[3] Pre-Ward correspondences of a few scientists, intellectual institutions (American Philosophical Society) and industrialists (especially, E. I. du Pont) recorded the existence of Mammoth Cave. But to the man on the street, the only mammoth was the one on display in Peale's Museum in Philadelphia.

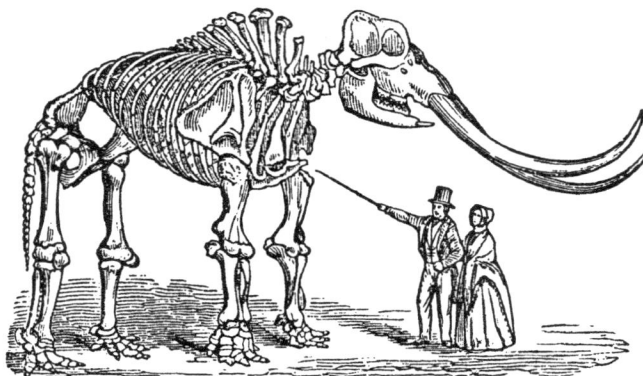

Reconstructed Mammoth skeleton in Peale's Museum.
Wood engraving from *The Elements of Geology*, 1862.

Mammoth Cave, like so many of its cousins, only appeared in court records and private correspondence. The average person took these caves for granted and never realized their potential worth nor the role they played in the history of our nation. All that came later.

Nahum Ward was an early antiquarian with enough free time to delve into the wonders of nature. He was one of the early members of the American Antiquarian Society in Worcester, Massachusetts. In Marietta, Ohio, he operated a general store and speculated in land at a place already noted for Indian fortifications and mounds.[4]

Fresh from exploring Mammoth Cave, tradition has Ward and Fawn Hoof traveling to Lexington, Kentucky. While in town, the mummy was exhibited to the curious public, who plucked her teeth and hair in order to test her genuineness.[5] Fawn Hoof was the largest and best preserved of all of the mummies, and Wilkins had slated her for sale to the American Antiquarian Society.[6] Ward was given the task of ferrying her to this eastern museum. On the road, he changed his mind and decided to exhibit the mummy as the Queen of the caves. The mummy first toured

Cincinnati, Marietta (Ward's home), Boston, Philadelphia, New York, and finally Worcester.[7] While in Marietta, Ward composed the first great classic Mammoth Cave description on the 4th of April 1816.[8] His narrative adventure of the mummy would be published first in the *Worcester Spy* and reprinted numerous times. His article would make Mammoth Cave a household name and world class cave on both sides of the Atlantic.[9] Ward, Mammoth Cave, and the mummy became synonymous. In the course of the road show, Ward refused to turn over the mummy to the American Antiquarian Society. Instead, he tried to sell the mummy to Peale's Museum in Philadelphia, and then to the New England Linnaen Society in Boston.[10] Word of these negotiations circulated in newspapers and finally reached Charles Wilkins, Hyman Gratz (co-owners of Mammoth Cave), and the American Antiquarian Society (the intended buyer). This was their mummy and Ward was trying to sell her to someone else. The owners thought of Ward as possessing excessive gall in fostering the sale of the mummy to rival institutions. His nerve, audacity, and brazenness became a thorn of contention with the Wilkins group. William Blane sums up the feelings of the times:

> Mr. Ward does not blush to affirm, that he himself found it in a recess of the Mammoth Cave, though he received it from Mr. [Archibald] Miller on the express condition of his presenting it to the Boston Museum. This he took care not to do, until he had made a sum of money by exhibiting it, and was only prevented from selling it by threats of the proprietors of the cavern.[11]

Faced with the real prospect of legal prosecution, Ward turned the mummy over to the American Antiquarian Society. The mummy became their most famous exhibit of the time.[12] This is tradition spattered with a few facts. Discovery of Nahum Ward's and Charles Wilkins's correspondence in the files of the American Antiquarian Society cast new light on the early history of Mammoth Cave and the travels of Fawn Hoof.

In November 1815, a business trip brought Ward to Charles Wilkins' general store in Lexington, Kentucky. Putting aside their business transactions, the conversation turned to Mammoth Cave and the resident mummy. It was one of the rarest artifacts that one could find and Wilkins had one in his cave. Perhaps thought Ward, what a boon for science this mummy could make! Wilkins considered it "was of no value," but, after some persuasion, he agreed that some institution should be selected and the mummy sent there for study and preservation.[13] Ward emphasized the mummy was too valuable to be kept in the cave - the whole world must know about the artifact and the early people it represents. Ward gives us insight to these early events:

> I shall state a few facts. In Nov last, when in Lexington, I called on Mr. Wilkins, who, after some conversation on the subject of the *Mummy*, said he once had in contemplation to give it [to] the Philadelphia Society of Phild. But it had gone to decay, as he had been informed by his overseer, he had abandoned the idea. Nothing more was said upon the subject, at that time, as I concluded from what has been said by W. That it had been destroyed by the moisture of the cave. I traveled after this into the Barrens of Ky, and visited the cave - fancied the Mummy an Exication, in much better order that I suspected. I asked one of my guides to bring it out, which he did, or it would have been there to this day. And requested the overseer to place it in his upper chamber, until he receives word from Mr W. On my return to Lexington I told W. what I had done, and suggested he would give it [to] me, to be presented [to] some Society at the Northward[?] and named to him the Antiquarian S. and the N.E.L.S. in Boston. He said to me "leave me your address and perhaps I will send it [to] you;" I did so - and in the month of June, just as I was on the eve of my deportation for Mass, this box containing the M. arrived.[14]

A number of new points are made in this letter. Contrary to tradition, Ward did not walk away with the mummy from Mammoth Cave nor did Archibald Miller give it to him. Rather, Charles Wilkins notified Miller (his overseer at the cave) who sent it to Lexington with a future wagon load of saltpeter. Mammoth Cave ceased producing saltpeter at the end of 1813 or shortly thereafter. The saltpeter shipment may have come from other caves where Wilkins had supply contracts. We now know the month of Ward's visit was November and not October 1815.[15] After Wilkins exhibited the mummy in his home town of Lexington, he sent it on to Marietta. Seven months after Ward's visit to Mammoth Cave, the mummy arrived on his door step in June 1816.

There is enough information in this letter to determine the mummy was stored in the damp Rotunda of Mammoth Cave. This is consistent with the Bogert map indication for the location of the mummy.[16] Ward makes a conscientious effort to stabilize the deterioration of the mummy by having her moved from the damp atmosphere of the First Hoppers to dryer conditions in the Haunted Chambers (Gothic Avenue).

Tradition recalls the presence of the mummy caused the superstitious slave work force to go on strike. Work resumed only when the mummy was moved to the Haunted Chambers (Gothic Avenue). This place already had a reputation for ghost and devils, and what better abode for one of Charon's pledges. She was placed in a recessed niche on a ledge near the entrance to this passage, a place still known as The Mummy's Seat.

The slave workers' strike over the presence of the mummy in the Rotunda and its removal to Gothic Avenue is now shown to be a fractured

Photo-card view of Fawn Hoof was distributed by Nahum's son, William S. Ward. From *The Courier-Journal*, March 4, 1928.

tradition.[17] This tradition does possess two elements of truth that in time were combined into one event. It was Ward, not the slave strikers, who was instrumental in moving the mummy to Gothic Avenue. There were slave strikes after each major earthquake during the 1811 and 1812 time period.[18] Two dissimilar events became intertwined and formed a core folklore of Mammoth Cave that is still told today.

On April 4, 1816, Ward finished writing his epic description of Mammoth Cave. He sent the "Wonders of Nature" to the *Worcester Spy* for publication. Over night, Mammoth Cave became publicly famous and Fawn Hoof would forever be the Mammoth Cave Mummy. While in Woodford County, Kentucky, he composed another Mammoth Cave travelogue in July 1816, entitled the "Kentucky Mammoth Cave," which probably first appeared in the *Worcester Spy* and was reprinted everywhere with typographical errors.[19] He also produced the first White Cave description from his Woodford County vantage point.[20]

GREEN RIVER, OR MAMMOTH CAVE.

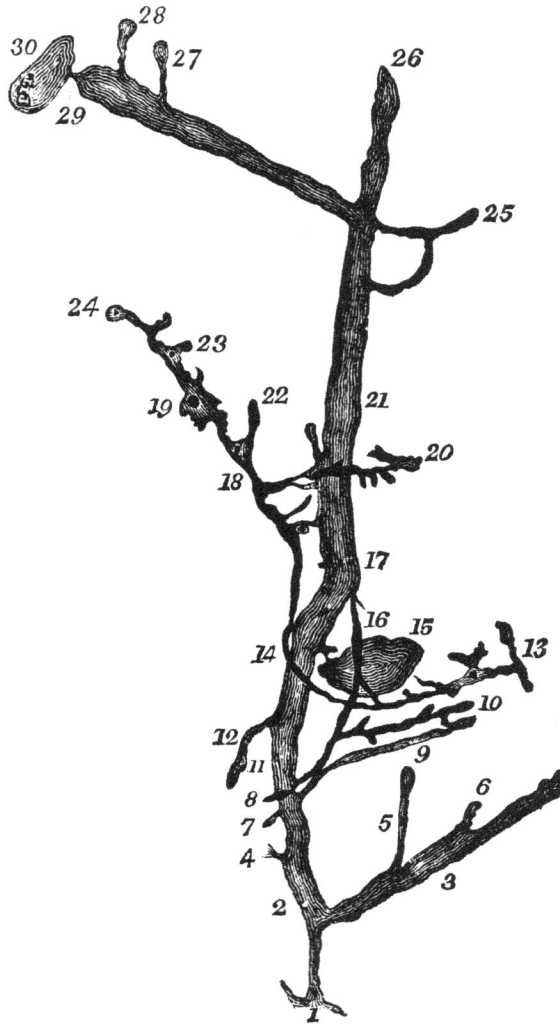

Bogert map of Mammoth Cave. Wood engraving from the *Medical Repository*, 1815.

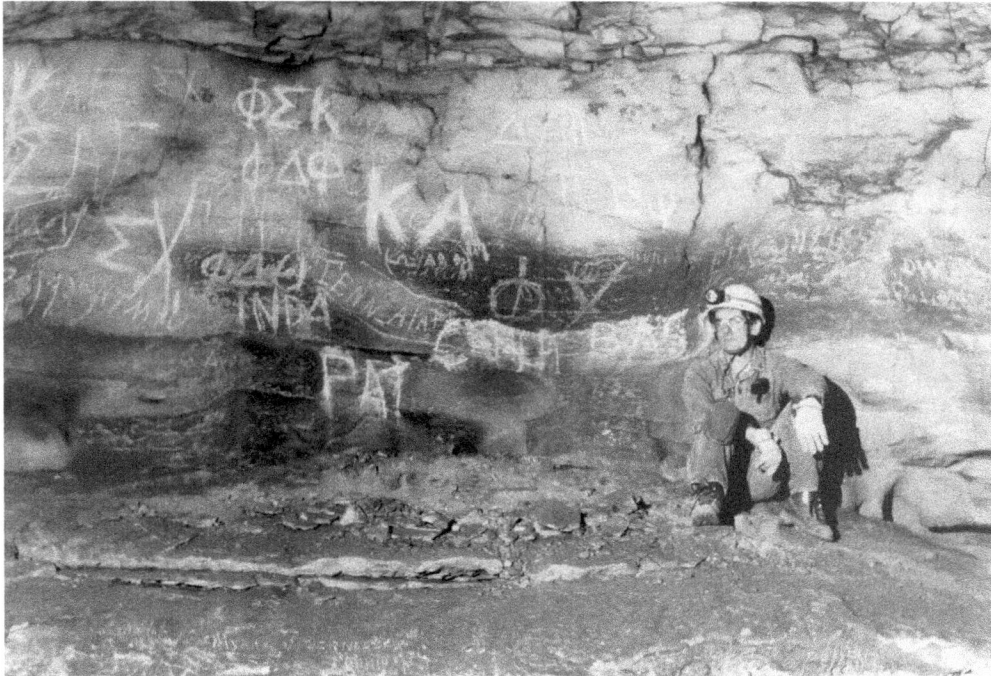

Mummy's Seat in entrance to Gothic Avenue. Fawn Hoof and perhaps the skull of an infant were displayed here from 1811 to 1816. Photograph by Diana Emerson George.

Ward continues his correspondence to his father.

> I was anxious it should go safe to Mass, and therefore arranged for its transportation on springs to Worcester and not in a common wagon. The [ ? ] to pay was $100 for the use of the Bible Society for the privilege of exhibiting of it on the way. And what Society is injured by this public exhibition of it? or nothing whose Society it was benefited by it when the money is given for destitute paupers?
>
> I had nothing from Mr. Wilkins, neither verbally or written - directly or indirectly, when at his house or at this place, advising me what was his wishes relative to the disposition of it. I considered he had given it into my hands to be disposed of as I should think best.[21]

Essentially, Ward considered he had *carte blanche to dispose of the mummy as he saw fit.* They had no written contract, apparently because Wilkins did not think the mummy had any monetary value. To see the mummy safely to Worcester, Ward rented the Bible Society's spring board wagon for one hundred dollars. He left Marietta in June, and probably arrived in Worcester later in the month. In town, he presented his credentials to officials of the American Antiquarian Society. They inspected the mummy and Mr. Ward in great detail. Their conclusion stated the

89

mummy was a fabrication and Messrs. Ward and Wilkins nothing but common charlatans out to dupe them and the public. The Society rejected the gift of the mummy and sent Ward, bags in hand, out the door.

Mortified and challenged as to his and Wilkins's veracity, Ward opted to take matters into his own hands and handle the situation. According to Ward, "the A. S. [Antiquarian Society] said with regards to its being an impostation [sic] and a hoax and by W. [Wilkins] too. Would I give it there? No, Sir, by all that is sacred, if they have it not at this time, they never shall."[22] At the moment, Ward did not inform Wilkins of this misfortune or what the Society thought of Wilkins and his gift, because his business trip up east was not long enough to wait for return correspondence from Wilkins' hand. Such a delay could mean a five week layover for new directions to arrive. This is why Ward decided to handle the situation himself and in his own way. He took the mummy to Boston for further exhibition and obtained the services of Samuel Small as his agent to oversee the exhibit. Small, in turn, commissioned Ethan Allen Greenwood to show the mummy from town to town. Greenwood's contract ran for ninety days.[23] He exhibited Fawn Hoof in Boston, Worcester, Philadelphia, and New York City. There may have also been exhibitions in smaller communities.

For twenty-five cents, the curious could enter her boudoir and view a "thousand year old" person they could identify with.[24] This was no skeleton in a house of horrors that would typify later exhibits in the Western Museum at Cincinnati or Koch's St. Louis Museum (and all of its imitators that would follow). The mummy brought the pioneers closer to an Indian culture that had long since vanished. Here was an actual flesh and blood person, a time traveler so to speak, showing there was not much difference between them and the contemporary viewer. A narrow window had opened for a brief glimpse of an extinct culture with exotic burial customs and apparel that was completely different from that practised by the present Indians.[25] Unknown to the pioneers, the present Indians were the direct descendants of a culture that used caves for their homes and work places for more than three thousand years. The common public loved the excitement of the exhibit, newspapers heralded its arrival, and the intelligentsia detested it.

Rejected by the Antiquarian Society, Ward wrote to George Haywood (president) of the New England Linnaean Society at Boston and offered the mummy to their museum.[26] Ward notified Wilkins of this planned institutional change on the 30th of October.[27] Haywood was requested "to call upon E. A. Greenwood for the mummy, and in my name present it [to] the N.E.L. Society. My letter to him, that is to G.H. was dated Nov. 10 or there abouts."[28] The New England Linnaean Society was definitely more receptive of the gift than was the American Antiquarian Society. Ward said, "I have determined to present it [to] the N.E.L.S. and have written

Haywood to that offer, and Greenwood also.[29] Ward's intention was to *sell* the mummy to the Boston museum.[30]

To the embarrassment of the American Antiquarian Society, evidence began to mount that the Mammoth Cave mummy was authentic. One of the Short Cave mummies along with the foot of the female mummy from Copperas (Big Bone) Cave were already on exhibition in Scudder's Museum of New York City. Samuel L. Mitchell, M.D., said "they are some of the most memorable of the antiquities that North America contains."[31] The Society had in their possession a detail letter from Mitchell to Samuel M. Burnside, Secretary of the Antiquarian Society on this 1814 Short Cave mummy in the Scudder Museum.[32] Mitchell's announcement and a rendering by Constantine Rafinesque had appeared in the *Medical Repository*.[33] It was now time for the Antiquarian Society to reconsider their rejection. The Society then made efforts to intercept Ward and acquire possession of the mummy. For:

> as soon as the Sub-Council learned of this, steps were immediately taken to obtain possession of it, and in July, 1816, Dr. Bancroft, Francis Blake, Rejoice Nelson and Dr. Oliver Fiske were appointed a committee to wait on Mr. Ward. Their efforts were futile for some time, during which the mummy was even exhibited in Worcester.[34]

Isaiah Thomas requested Benjamin Russell in Boston to view the mummy and see what it would take to have the mummy returned to the Antiquarian Society.[35] The Society was prepared to purchase the mummy from the Linnaean Society. Russell and Samuel G. Snelling met with E. A. Greenwood about the return of the mummy to its rightful owners. Greenwood had a ninety day exhibition contract and would not release it before the time of expiration. There were sound legal questions pending. Russell did not have at his disposal any written proof from Ward or Wilkins that the mummy was actually the property of the Antiquarian Society. Lack of which "the holder might have a good action of damage against the A.S."[36]

The excitement displayed by the press and those that viewed her under the care of Ward and Greenwood, fell on cold hands in the American Antiquarian Society. The somewhat wrathful Benjamin Russell submits:

> Very few persons attend to see the skeleton; as those who do, universally express their disgust at it. For myself, I cannot perceive how the cause of science, history or antiquarianism is to be benefitted by the preservation of those dried up particles. I have seen a dead cat, which accidently was inclosed in an oven, and found some months afterwards, in as good a state of mummy preservation as this skeleton. The best thing in my opinion which could be done with it would be to give it to some anatomical school or bury it in the cemetery.[37]

There was more to the public perception of the mummy exhibit than past chroniclers have recorded. Ward reveals in more depth the aristocratic rejection of the mummy from Mammoth Cave. Ward records:

> It is a fact that the majorityship of the lookers generally, and in this case in Worcester, has imitated the generous [ ? ] of the Virginian [,] Mr Wilkins. If there have not been a spirit of envy among the *little souls* of Worcester this transaction might have gone by without disgracing the name of my Native Country. But where is the man who was willing to comfort and defend me. So when the mummy reached them not one solitary devil of them ever, impressed an opinion favorable toward it. Nay, those of the higher class would not even go into the room to look at it. But were doing all in their power to injure me in the public opinion, as an imposter, and some of them say pretended [ ? ]. Silas Brooks, who by the way knows no more about antiquity than my horse, said all he could say to [ ? ] [ ? ] both at Worcester and Boston.[38]

Lack of intellectual acceptance of the mummy as authentic, and calling Ward an imposter became one of the low point in his life. He laments, "not a solitary soul in W.[orcester], less Doct Parker[?]...gave a favorable opinion of it.[39] Isaiah Thomas was still anxious to obtain possession, despite all of the negative publicity and the subcouncils negative report on the subject. Despite the intellectual boycott of the exhibit, the local gentry and the press found it wonderful.

Sometime in July 1816, Ward returned to Versailles in Woodford County, Kentucky. Thereupon he made another eastern trip and arrived in Worcester on or about the 1st of October. While there he wrote a letter nominating Charles Wilkins to membership in the American Antiquarian Society.[40] The Versailles respite was the calm before the storm in Nahum Ward's life.

Apparently Russell had read Ward's publications and letters on the cave and mummy. The subject of who actually owned the mummy was still another question. Charles Wilkins had an altogether different story and he was none too happy about what Ward had done with the mummy.

During the initial Lexington meetings between Wilkins and Ward in November 1815, the first seeds of misunderstanding took place. Wilkins writes to Ward:

> When you applied to me for the mummy in question. I considered you as a member of the Antiquarian Society or engaged in collecting curiosities for it. You represented it as being among the most [ ? ] & respectable society of its kind institution in the United States. Under this impression I forwarded the M[ummy] to be presented accordingly. I did not write to you deeming it

unnecessary as I supposed this subject to be understood between us at the last interview we had. That the business rested until I discovered from the newspapers that the mummy was exhibited in Baltimore Phila etc for pecurniary purposes.[41]

To exhibit the mummy and *charge money* to see her was not Wilkins' intention. Furthermore, Ward did not notify Wilkins as to how he was exhibiting the mummy. This served as additional irritation to Wilkins. But what rankled Wilkins's senses even more was when he:

> wrote to Mr. [Harrison Gray] Otis whom this subject under an impression the confidence [ ? ] in you had been abused. Which added to my mortification & served to irritate me a little, my friends were laughing at me for the "Yankee trick" that had been played upon me....[42]

Wilkins was the laughing stock of Lexington with wounded ego and self-worth greatly diminished. This alone would determine his future action in this matter. If Ward had returned to Lexington; Wilkins had every right to demand satisfaction on the field of honor. Wilkins was not one to actually choose the field to settle disputes. He favored the stinging aim of the courts over ball and shot. This method he often used to settle old differences and accounts overdue. Wilkins letter to Ward continues:

> Had you written to me previous to finding the mummy forward[?], I should certantly have been opposed to exhibiting it in the manner it was done. I should have supposed the Antiquarian Society would not defray the expenses of transportation to Boston I would have made some other disposition of it. It was never my wish to make money from this subject or I would have accepted your offer to purchase it from me & several subsequent ones.[43]

Wilkins had his say and now offers his reconciliation on the subject.

> It now affords me much gratification to state to you that your explanation has given me the most perfect satisfaction as to the course pursued by you, in relation to the mummy. I [ ? ] approve of your refusal to deliver it to the Antiquarian Society since they have treated the offer with so much contempt.
>
> Mr. Hyman Gratz is now here, who is partner with me in the cave and has equal claim with me to the mummy. It is his wish that it be sent to Philadelphia addressed to Simon Gratz & Brothers. Please to direct it to be packed up carefully. Any expense attending the packing, transportation etc will be paid by them. It is our intention to present it to some public institution in Phila[.] You have the goodness to order the conveyance as soon as possible and any advances made by you will be cheerfully paid by myself as soon as the amount is known.

I regret extremely that any misunderstanding has happened between us with the subject in question. Ours were were the same, that is to benefit some public institution by depositing what we both thought an object of curiosity for the benefit of the learned & curious to investigate. I am sorry that it should have given rise to any insinuation of dishonorable motives & [ ? ] I flatter myself that where we are respectively known it cannot have this effect.[44]

After writing this letter, he then had second thoughts and continued to fume over the incident and especially the idea of being duped by Ward. Shortly thereafter, a letter from Rejoice Newton opened this old wound.[45] He gives Newton additional information on the mummy and legal licence to obtain the mummy from Ward. Wilkins adds:

in the meantime I wish such measures to be taken as will enable you to obtain it from the person who has it in his possession. To enable you to understand this business, I will briefly detail the manner in which Mr. ward became in possession of it.

Mr. Ward saw this mummy in a Salt Petre Cave belonging to Mr. Hyman Gratz of Phila. and myself - Upon his arrival he applied to me for it. I told him that it was my intention to send it to some public institution in Phila. Upon his representation of the respectability of the "Antiquarian Society," of Boston [,] I promised that he should have it, if I concluded not to send it to Phila. - Mr. Ward addressed a letter to me on the 18th Apl. last, which determined me to transmit the Mummy thro him to the "Antiquarian Society" & sent it accordingly [ ? ] his letter inclosed/ Hearing that he was exhibiting for money. I addressed a letter to the Hon. H. G. Otis. I rcd no answer from Mr. Otis. But one from Mr. Ward of the 30th Oct last (inclosed) informing me that his father had written to him that my letter was just to Mr. Thomas - Upon the rect. of this letter, I wrote to Mr. Ward expressing my approbation of the course pursued by him and requested him to forward it to Mr. Gratz of Phila. previous to the rect of my letter, he had written to me on the 10th Nov (inclosed). The last letter recd from him was dated 10th Dec (inclosed) - If you will take the trouble of perusing these letters you will at once discover the manner by which I have been duped. These letters will I hope establish the right of the Antiquarian Society to the mummy & I hope you will adopt such measures as will enable you to obtain it. I shall not write to Mr. Ward until I think you are in possession of this information, least he should secret it.

Mr. Hyman Gratz is now here who has an equal claim with myself to this mummy. He request you will accept it as a joint present to you institution.

Be pleased to retain these letters (inclosed) until I shall have occasion for them. If he shall not be disposed to do justice to the institution I will prosecute him for this breach of Trust.[46]

From then on Nahum Ward's life with the mummy became a nightmare. The misunderstanding of intent between Wilkins and Ward reached a fever pitch of accusation in November. Wilkins initially wanted to donate the mummy to some institution in Boston. He used Ward's knowledge of these places to target the Antiquarian Society as the best place to deposit the artifact. Wilkins was no novice when it came to placing Indian artifacts in public institutions. He had already shipped a mummy to Scudder's Museum in New York City and probably two to Peale's Museum in Philadelphia.[47]

Nahum's pitiful hand wringing over his involvement with the mummy and Wilkins legal Breach of Trust threats made his life miserable. He said relative to Charles Wilkins:

> Why in the name of all that is good - did he not send it direct to the Society himself and spare me the trouble and expense at transportation? If that [was his] expectation - as you say, Sir, why did he [select(?)] the Society that he presented it at that time?[48]

Receipts from ticket sales and presumably the proceeds from Fawn Hoof's sale to the New England Linnaean Society would be given to the poor destitute children of Worcester — a noble gesture from a man considered to be an imposter in pawning off on the public a fake Indian artifact. Nahum says:

> I had given all the monies collected for the exhibition of this curiosity for charitable purposes, so far as they had come into my hands, and that what ever monies come hereafter should go the same way.[49]

He is convinced he has done nothing wrong in the promotion and sale of the mummy. He says, "I have done that which was honorable and fair."[50]

Within the first few weeks of the New Year, the Antiquarian Society was probably in possession of the December 20th Wilkins Breach of Trust communication. This instrument established the legal transference of the mummy from Wilkins and Gratz to the Society. It was now time for the Antiquarian Society to execute a restraining order to compel Ward to give up the mummy.

> The *"Mummy,"* lately discovered in a cave in *Kentucky*, was at New-York a few days since, and the person who has the care of her is under bond of 5000 dollars penalty, to deliver her safe and sound in *Boston*. She may be daily expected there or at Worcester.[51]

The mummy in her stone box crypt in Short Cave. Wood engraving from broadside, *Plan and Description of the Great and Wonderful Cave, in Warren County, Kentucky*, n.d.

This only made Ward that much more resolute to not give up the mummy. The pressure continued to mount, for Ward was now faced with having to pay 5000 dollars in real money at a time when most of the economy used barter as a means of payment. More serious than the loss of 5000 dollars, Ward had to explain to his father these circumstances. I envision Thomas W. Ward as a righteous unyielding parent who lived his Old Testament convictions. "Vengeance is Mine" had great meaning in the Ward family. Nahum had something else to worry about with his father. Thomas Ward was high Sheriff of Worcester County![52] It would be his duty to arrest his son on the Breach of Trust agreement. Nahum's confessions of his actions were best issued at the time rather than wait for the legal system and the law (his father) to catch up with him. Isaiah Thomas wrote to Thomas Ward in hopes of exerting family pressure for the surrender of the mummy to the Antiquarian Society.[53] Admission of guilt is good for the soul. Nahum apologized to his father for any transgressions:

> Yet I may be mistaken, and if I am I will acknowledge I have done that which I ought to have done - I should not have given it to the L. Soc. neither should the A. Soc. have had it, after treating it with so much contempt as they did.
>
> Wilkins said to me, and to many others, that the M. was of no value he gave it into my hands at my request, and upon my reputation of the A. Soc. Wilkins knew no more of any Soc of the worth than I do of the inhabitants of the Moon. My impression ever has been and now is that the M. was given to me to be placed in the archives of any Society I pleased to place it. Wilkins in answer to my letter of Nov. last acknowledges he is perfectly

satisfied with my explanation of the M. He says "our intentions were the same; that was intended it for [ ? ] Soc that the learned and curious might investigate it."

How can he have been duped by me when he says to me that he is well satisfied with my statement. And I copy the A. Soc. to show that the statement is incorrect.

"as our intentions were the same," what mighty difference could it make to W. if it was placed in the hands of one of the first Societies in Boston, in preference to the A.S. who treated it with contempt!

Was the public giving me applause which W's accused me? and not only W but many of my brethren the Yankees. If W. considered it of no value why should he threaten me with a prosecution for breach of trust, after he had said he was satisfied with what I had done?

If Wilkins had considered it handled mainly, past, he would have written me instead of Otis, and asked for an explanation of my conduct, but instead of that he has been flattering in his letter, and no sooner sealed and of, then he writes the A.S. that I had duped him and threatened[?] prosecution. And for that too which he says [it] is of no value. He is threatening me in the docks for that which to my face he approves. I am at a loss what to think of this man who has been condensending to [ ? ] my reputation for that which he said was of no value, and which was disposed of by me agreeable to his wishes; "as some institution wanted the same."[54]

Nahum Ward capitulated sometime in the spring of 1817.[55] When the mummy was delivered to Worcester, "the church bells were tolled an *indefinite* number of times for the age of the deceased."[56] Home again in Marietta, Ohio, Ward put all this mummy controversy behind him. To help heal these battle wounds, he purchased in 1817, "the largest and most elegant residence in Marietta."[57]

From then on, the travel-worn Fawn Hoof found a home with less enlightened surroundings and care. Yet, this was minor compared to what the Smithsonian Institution did to her late in the century.

Despite Russell's near-sighted view, Fawn Hoof would be exhibited in two World Fairs of 1876 and 1893 as the Mammoth Cave mummy.[58] From 1876 on, the mummy was under the care of the Smithsonian Institution. The Antiquarian Society traded her for some other specimens in the National Museum.[59] Sometime after 1896, she was taken off public display, dissected, and the bones cleaned for storage and placed in a box as accession number 4789.[60] Alexander Wetmore, Assistant Secretary of the National Museum said, "the skeleton of the mummy...was considered of more scientific value as a determinant of race than the mummy."[61] Benjamin Russell got his wish by relegating her to a grave with a box number on it. Soon thereafter, the public memory of Fawn Hoof faded. By

G. Browne Goode photograph of Fawn Hoof from the collections of the Smithsonian Institution. From Horace C. Hovey and Richard E. Call, *Mammoth Cave of Kentucky,* 1912.

1900, her legacy was largely folklore with a smattering of history recited by the guides at Mammoth Cave. In time, even her special berth in the box at the Smithsonian Institution was forgotten.

Since about 1905 there had been talk about making Mammoth Cave into a National Park.[62] A number of private individuals formed the Mammoth Cave National Park Association. Its goal was simple. Purchase the cave and all of the surrounding land. For 1924, that was easier said than done. By 1926, the last original Croghan heir had died. The way was clear for Serena Croghan Rogers' appointed trustees (William E. Wyatt and Violet Blair Janin) and in turn Violet Blair and Mary J. Sitgreaves to form a joint venture with the Mammoth Cave National Parks Association on January 1, 1929.[63] Mammoth Cave National Park become a reality on July 1, 1941.

To generate subscriptions and donations to buy land for the proposed National Park, civic groups, school children, and especially newspapers championed the cause needed to generate a million and a half dollars. Numerous articles ran in the *Courier-Journal* and others across Kentucky. To garner favorable publicity, the Mammoth Cave Parks Association hired Ted Giles as publicity director.[64] One of his duties was to generate stories about Mammoth Cave and its pioneer history. Fawn Hoof was one of those staple stories, although by this time many people doubted her prior existence. If she ever existed, no one knew the present disposition of the Indian mummy. If she could be located, what were the chances that she could be returned to Mammoth Cave for display in the cave? Giles began a correspondence search in all of the major museums of the world in November 1926.[65] Little more than three months and many return letters in foreign languages. Persistance paid off, she was rediscovered at her Smithsonian Institution box number.[66]

The legacy of all of the Mammoth Cave area mummies was researched by Harold Meloy, a lawyer from Shelbyville, Indiana. He was the paramount authority on the history connected with the Mammoth Cave National Park. No one since Horace C. Hovey knew more about the cave than he. After more than ten years of investigation, he published his *Mummies of Mammoth Cave* in 1968. It went through two editions and a number of reprintings. The book presents a marvelous road map about the mummies, their history, and original references.

Fawn Hoof is still doing well at her old box number in the Smithsonian. Even though she was dissected and the bones cleaned for storage, some mummified flesh still adheres to articular surfaces. There is some mummy left in her after all.

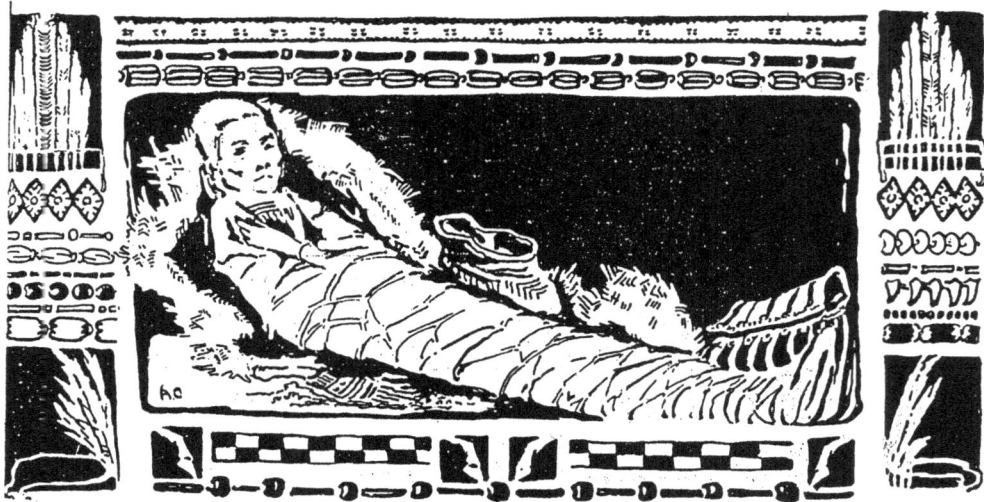

Artistic embellishment of Fawn Hoof into the role of the Mammoth Cave Egyptian Mummy. Courtesy of Charles Hayes, Jr., editor of the *Kentucky Explorer*, 1990, p. 35. *The Mammoth Cave Magazine*, October 1912, Vol. 1, No. 1, p. 4.

# CHAPTER TWELVE

# MARCH OF THE CONTENDERS AND THE SEARCH FOR OLD WORLD ROOTS IN AMERICA

*Why not allow the authors of the antiquated works about Lexington, together with the immense catacomb, to have been, indeed, an Egyptian Colony.*

Josiah Priest (1834)

The specter of fantastic archaeology resurfaces with elements of the Lexington Catacomb tale being incorporated into cave guide presentation stories at Mammoth Cave. This had great entertainment value. No longer did the mummies come from Short Cave. Rather, the locale was changed to the far distant regions of the vast Mammoth Cave. Fawn Hoof, through the promotions of Nahum Ward's agent, was advertised as a Queen of some importance.[1] A Mammoth Cave guide informed Blane that the Indian mummy was *embalmed* with "gum and aromatic herbs."[2] Fawn Hoof is elevated to Queen of the Caves and Little Al is touted as The Egyptian Mummy found in Salts Cave.[3] Visualized renderings from the early 20th century show Fawn Hoof dressed in tight bandages and housed in a straw-like sarcophagus. Another rendering shows the pioneer discovery of Fawn Hoof in a supine position and wrapped in tight linen bandages in Ted Giles book, *Fawn Hoof is Lost*. Such artistic and promotional misconceptions helped to shape the publics image of Egyptian burials in mid-America caves. Even the word "mummy" produces visions of Pharaonic Egypt.

In 1823, the antiquarian and historian, John Haywood put together the *Natural and Aboriginal History of Tennessee*. For the first time all of the significant archaeological discoveries in the state and surrounding area were placed under one cover. His biggest problem was his inability to identify one cave site from another. His documentation was poor and his references practically nonexistent. With less critical evaluation, he championed Caleb Atwater's "Hindoo" colonization of America, accompanied by hordes of aboriginal pygmies in the Midwest. Under the heading of published scholarly research, this book claims a prominent place as the first great American example of fantastic archaeology.[4] He was hampered by a lack of field work and an archaeological frame of reference in which to place events and cultures. Research of this nature would start over twenty years later with the epic field work and publication of E. G. Squire and E. H. Davis, *Ancient Monuments of the Mississippi Valley* in 1848.

Haywood reports from a number of cave sites yielding Indian mummies. One of the descriptions has a high degree of strangeness coupled with out-of-cultural-context artifacts. He says:

> It is stated to have been affirmed by Captain Daniel Williams, a man of undoubted truth, that several years ago, in a cave five or six miles above Carthage, on Cumberland river, in which cave workmen were collecting dirt for saltpetre, were many human skeletons, one of which was a female in a state of preservation, with yellow hair, and the flesh shrivelled. Around the wrist was a silver clasp, with letters resembling those of the Greek alphabet. The body was replaced in the spot whence they had taken it.[5]

It's now time to bring in Josiah Priest (1788-1851), who did more to muddy up the archaeological waters than Ashe ever envisioned. If Egyptian mummies sounded good, why not add Scandinavian mummies from Kentucky caves? Priest was on a roll!

Josiah Priest is an armchair pseudo-natural scientist of the Speculative Period in fantastic archaeology. He accords equal authenticity to both the Short Cave and Lexington Catacomb mummy sites. He was a champion of the "lost race of white men theory," and the discovery and settlement of America by these whites prior to Christopher Columbus in 1492. Priest populates his New World America with a whole raft of Old World voyagers. Never mind historical context! Here was a happy party of Picts, Welsh, Celts, Romans, Egyptians, Scandinavians, Africans, Atlantians, the ten lost tribes of Israel, and all topped off with a hearty band of Greek sailors who were new in town. America definitely was crowded in days of old. From the master ground work constructed by Thomas Ashe, Priest boldly asserts:

> why not allow the *authors* of the antiquated works about Lexington, (together with the immense catacomb as evidence), to have been, indeed, an *Egyptian colony*; seeing the art of embalming, which is *peculiarly characteristic* of that people, was found there in a state of *perfection* not exceeded by the mother country itself.[6]

> This cavern, indeed, is similar to those found in Egypt....It is probable that the cave where these were found was partly natural

102

and partly artificial. Having found it suitable to their purpose, they had opened a convenient descent, cleared out the stones and rocks, and fitted it with niches for the reception of those they had embalmed.

Catacombs are numerous all over Egypt, vast excavations under ground, with niches in their sides for their embalmed dead, exactly such as the one we have described.[7]

Kentucky itself, where we think we have found the remains of an Egyptian colony, or nation, as in the case of the works and catacomb at Lexington, is in a latitude but five degrees north of Egypt; so that whether they may have visited America on a voyage of exploration, or have been driven on the coast against their will, in either case, it would be perfectly natural that they should have established themselves in that region.

But at Lexington, the traits are too notorious to allow them to be other than pure Egyptian, in full possession of the strongest complexion of their national character, that of embalming, which was connected with their *religion*.[8]

Without naming Short Cave, Priest asserts yet another trans-atlantic voyager to the heartland of America, the Scandinavians. He espouses:

notwithstanding the celebrity, founded on the great erudition and critical research of Professor Mitchell, we cannot subscribe to this opinion respecting the red-headed mummy now in the New-York Museum, found in a saltpetre cave in Kentucky. It is well known fact, that invariably all the nations of the earth, who are of the swarthy or black complexion, have black eyes, together with black hair, either straight or curled.

But those nations belonging to the white class, have a great variety of colour in their eyes; as blue, light blue, dark blue, gray, black, and reddish, with many shades of variations, more than we have terms to express. Where this is so, the same variety exist respecting the colour of the hair; black, white, auburn, and red. We are sure this is a characteristic of the two classes of mankind, the dark and the white. If so, then the Kentucky body, found in the cave, is not of Malay origin, but of Scandinavian; of whom, as a nation, it is said that the predominant colour of the hair of the head was red.[9]

Hyperboreans in Kentucky who buried their dead in caves! Hyperborean red-headed mummies![10] The plot thickens with great battles between two fierce hyper-diffusionistic bands of New World settlers. The land hungry Tartars from Asia wiped out the Malays by driving them into Midwest caves. With an actual body count of about seventeen, the New World became less crowded and a much safer place to live. Priest adds:

> In their course, these Asian colonist probably exterminated the Malays, who had penetrated along the Ohio and its streams, or drove them to caverns abounding in saltpetre and copperas, in Kentucky and Tennessee; where their bodies, accompanied with cloths and ornaments of their peculiar manufacture, have been repeatedly disinterred and examined by the members of the American Antiquarian Society.
>
> Having achieved this conquest, the Tartars and their descendants, had, probably, a much harder task to perform. This was to subdue the more ferocious and warlike Europeans colonist, who had intrenched and fortified themselves in the country, after the arrival of the Tartars, or Indians, as they are now called, in the particular parts they had settled themselves in, along the region of the Atlantic.[11]

It probably never occurred to Priest that the hyperborean Scandinavian mummies and the Malay mummies were one and the same and restricted to two caves, Short Cave and Big Bone (Copperas) Cave. None of these caves have identifiable European grave goods. There are no European artifacts in context with any of the mummies, let along the myriad of mounds and graves excavated prior to Priest and up to the present time. Contextual cultural evidence of a European nature is completely wanting in America. But that would wreck a perfectly good story.

Priest's book became immensely popular when it was first published in 1833. Demand for the best seller was so great that it ran through ten editions or printings, ending with the great tome of 1841.[12] There were major text changes with each edition or printing. This consisted of expanded discussions on antiquities (including the Catacomb) and deletions of contested material at the request of Constantine S. Rafinesque.[13] *American Antiquities* had a profound impact on the reading public. Priest's vision of the Lexington Catacomb seems to have given wide spread birth to other catacombs in the Midwest. People started looking for the fantastic and "found" examples in plowed farm fields and in caves. It is the caves that offered the best collection of Old World travelers and their assorted baggage. America was a great place to visit and some stayed and died during their journey. These were no ordinary visitors, for some were Free and Accepted Masons from Egypt and others consisted of Old Testament giants from Israel.

The Great Laurel Ridge Cave over in Hamilton County, Tennessee, produced two mummies and a petrified dog in 1837. Seated on a rock was one mummy, while the other stood erect, holding a spear. The American

Gothic came complete with a dog in repose, ready as if to leap up at a moments notice.[14]

Lovell (Shutt's) Cave, Muhlenberg County, Kentucky, is the site of two fabulous mummy discoveries. About August 1853, a petrified monkey was discovered in the cave.[15] Almost two decades later, in October, 1872, four human mummies were found.[16] These consisted of a "man and women dressed in Roman costume, and each holding in their arms a child - the man one of 10 years, and the women a babe of 1 to 2 years." A family that caves together, stays together.

Responding to the actual discovery of a real Indian mummy (Little Al, a.k.a. The American Mummy, or Little Alice) in Grand Avenue (Long) Cave on July 23, 1875, even more mummies were found in nearby Grand Crystal Cave.[17] The twenty-three mile long cave was discovered in 1878 near Park City, Kentucky (then called Glasgow Junction). Far from the entrance, down rivers and wide corridors, a repository of mummies was found. In that:

> several mummified remains have been discovered in one of the large rooms. They were reposing in stone coffins rudely constructed, and from appearance may have been in this cave centuries. They present every appearance of Egyptian mummies.[18]

Three of the mummies was purchased by Edwin Mortimore of Louisville, Kentucky. George M. Procter purchased the rest from the cave owner, Thomas Kelly. At this time, Procter was in fact exhibiting a real Indian mummy, Little Al in Grand Avenue (Wright's, or Long) Cave. There are many parallels with the hype of Grand Crystal Cave, and the real Grand Avenue Cave. *Scientific American* reprinted the story because it had an air of authenticity, especially since Procter's name was mentioned.[19] More will be said of the Grand Crystal Cave hoax in the next chapter.

The Giants are coming! The Giants are coming! True to Old Testament script, one of the ten lost tribes of Israel made it to an American cave.[20] Perhaps the cave site is located in northeastern Adams County, Ohio, on what was then known as the old Smith farm. Deep in a limestone cave, explorers in early January 1880, discovered a party of nine foot tall giants stored in a mausoleum carved out of solid rock. The walls of the crypt were decorated with *bas-relief* carvings representing the four seasons of mans life; the style of which is "equal to the Greecian school of sculpture." At one end of the room were tablets written in Hebraic script, a mute memorial to those here interred. Even a book filled with a hundred thin copper pages (*laminae*) was discovered. The room had gigantic vases and carved pyramidal columns with Doric caps stood in each corner. One of the giant mummies lay on a raised carved slab of rock in the middle of the room. His face was that of a "Hebrew from the Middle East." From the wall, one of the horizontal niches was opened up to examine another nine foot mummy wonder decked out with an assortment of metal grave goods. *The Weekly News* of Charleston, South Carolina, sums up the story in their subtitle, "the Cardiff Hero Nowhere." A direct reference to the Cardiff Giant, a well known fake discovered in 1869.[21] The Cave of Giants is the most inventive of all the late 19th Century mummy discoveries. Complete with Biblical revelations, and metaphorical allusions to Joseph Smith's discovery of the *Book of Mormon*.

Blitzing back to Litchfield, Kentucky, another cave of mummies is discovered in 1882.[22] The cave possessed Masonic emblems, pyramids, and "several tablets with queer hieroglyphics," associated with bronze and copper vases. A mound was opened up inside the cave. The interior possessed six complete mummies, radiating outward from a common center. Close examination revealed them to be Free and Accepted Masons from Egypt.

A "true" Kentucky Wonder was discovered on the farm of J. Allen near Bloomfield, Kentucky.[23] Perhaps discovered in 1888, this Nelson County cave contained a niche stacked with "numerous mummified bodies. Three of them have been removed to the town and excit great curiosity." Many relics in the form of bronze, copper, and pottery were also discovered.

The march down the hallway of fantastic archaeology is needed to bring authenticated Midwest Indian mummies face to face with their usurpers. Knowing how to identify the characteristics of fake mummy tales is important. They all share a number of inbred individual patterns. Motifs from these tales of fantasy has been grafted into authentic discoveries. Thereby making it harder to separate truth from fiction.

Exterior events shaped the substance of these mummy hoaxes. All use a thin prototype model of the Mammoth Cave and Big Bone Cave area mummies. They borrow the Egyptian motif from Priest and then graft Masonic ritualism to the setting. The Masons are a popular fraternal organization who like to trace their ancestry to Biblical Jerusalem and ancient Greece. Any discovery pointing to their Middle Eastern origin was always welcomed.

Hoax mummy sites never stand the test of close scrutiny. There is only one article in the local papers, and there is usually never any follow up. Discovery is made by one or two people who are unable to produce the cave or the mummy. The story dies on the spot for lack of credible secondary witness. Occasionally a real cave is used as the repository, yet most of the time the cave location is an invention. None of these caves with mummies have ever been elevated to the status of local tradition.

All of the mummy stories have a high degree of strangeness, with a bizarre assortment of voyagers traveling to the New World. Most of the tales describe the discovery of *non-buried* mummies. They are just *sitting* or *standing* there in the cave passage, some reposing in open niches, open stone boxes, or on a raised dais. There is only one story in which the mummies were excavated from a mound in a cave. These are hallmark elements that should flag an impending hoax to the reader. It seems that every fantastic discovery after Priest was inconsistent with the kind of mummy discoveries made by the saltpeter miners prior to 1815. Questions one should ask are: What facts are credible? What elements of the story are fantasy? Are these real American Indian mummies or an imaginary hybrid Egyptian implant? Careful reading and a lot of detective work are often needed to assess the character of out-of-context Indian mummies found in caves.

A non-buried mummy was found in Salts Cave in 1875. The circumstances surrounding Little Al's discovery are enough to flag an element of caution. The next chapter prompts one to initially place the discovery in the fantastic archaeology hall of fame.

The Cardiff Giant created a great amount of public excitement when first discovered. The fake gypsum mummy fooled everyone except geologists. The Giant toured Louisville shortly before Little Al was "discovered" in Long Cave. Wood engraving from *Harper's Weekly*, 1869.

Photograph of Little Al as he looked in the 1920's. Courtesy of the William R. Halliday, M.D., collection of Russell T. Neville photographs and memorabilia.

# CHAPTER THIRTEEN

# THE DUAL NATURE OF LITTLE AL

*She was the daughter of an early settler, who, in some brief jaunt in the woods in search of berries or wild flowers, had been sighted and pursued by a blood-thirsty savage, and had found eternal refuge from his scalping-knife in this desolate chamber of death.*

T. O. Chisholm (1892)

Poor Little Al! He was never who he was supposed to be. From 1875 to 1958, *he* was a *she* called Little Alice — a case of mistaken identity for this "little girl" lost in a central Kentucky cave. It took only a cursory anthropological inspection to determine the true gender . . . eighty-three years later![1] There is no question of the authenticity of Little Al as an Indian mummy. Not knowing the sex of Little Al is only the start in his checkered career as a cave exhibit. Testimony over his discovery is confused, convoluted, and contradictory to the point of a well constructed hoax. The fraud was promoted by a number of individuals who had much to gain financially and even more to lose from possible prosecution by the Mammoth Cave estate.

After the Civil War, Mammoth Cave received thousands of visitors each year. Such an influx sparked the development or improvement of a number of commercial caves, especially Procter family owned: Diamond Caverns, Proctor Cave, and Grand Avenue Cave. The preferred spelling of the family name is Procter, although it is often seen, especially in newspaper articles written as Proctor.

It all began innocent enough with a proposal to build a railroad spur from Glasgow Junction (present day Park City) to Mammoth Cave. The concept was enthusiastically embraced and a stock company was incorporated in 1874. One of its visionaries was the commercial cave and hotel owner, Larkin J. Procter.[2]

By constructing the railroad grade close to Procter-owned caves, visitors could disembark and see an underground selection before arriving at their final Mammoth Cave destination. The railroad concept would channel tourists only to caves owned by this one family. Samuel B. Young was the proprietor of the only other commercial cave in the area, Indian (Osceola) Cave. This important establishment lies on the stage route between Cave City and Mammoth Cave. The proposed railroad from Glasgow Junction to Mammoth Cave would syphon much coveted tourist traffic from Indian Cave.

Project plans were made with great expectations, only to languish twelve long years near death. The concept was revived and construction was initiated on July 3, 1886, four days ahead of formal declaration of the road contract on July 7th. The 8.7 mile spur line was completed and operational on November 8, 1886.[3] A secondary line was built from Diamond Caverns to Grand Avenue Cave prior to 1892.[4]

Major George M. Procter purchased Long (Wright's) Cave from E. H. Wolsey.[5] The name was changed to Grand Avenue Cave in order to attract visitors to a cavern as rival to anything Mammoth Cave could offer. Passages were larger in size than in Mammoth (a true statement), but the actual passage extent fell short of expectations. Grand Avenue was "big," and its floors were level without a lot of breakdown. Dripstone formations were both active and attractive near "ends" of peripheral passages. The interior, dry with gypsum crust and sparkling with selenite in the soils of the trunk cave passage, greeted visitors with spelean delights.

Procter had a number of things going for him in Grand Avenue Cave. He had a big attractive cave with a choice location. The cave required only a minimal amount of physical improvement in terms of trail building. Ladders and steps were built down into some of the deep pits of the cave. A proposed railroad spur would soon bring visitors to his door. With a planned hotel and rail siding, all seemed in order. What Procter didn't have was an *advertising ploy* to make people want to see his cave!

The advertising ploy had its roots in local and regional events occurring in the area. Probably in late 1874, Dr. Frederic Ward Putnam from the Peabody Museum at Cambridge, Massachusetts, visited the cave area. He inventoried Indian artifacts from Mammoth Cave, Salts Cave, Grand Avenue Cave, Short Cave and others. In Salts Cave, he was led to a small cut around where he found twenty-five wove sandals. He did not discover any human remains in the cave, even though he was in the cave where such a discovery would be made in the coming months.[6] His cave guides were William Cutliff and (Thomas?) Lee.[7]

Putnam was then led to Grand Avenue and Short Caves. He made enquiries on the discovery of Fawn Hoof, then more locally know as The American Mummy or the Mammoth Cave Mummy. His guides took him to Short Cave where he was shown the excavation from which the mummy was taken. The seeds as to the importance of the mummy to archaeology and to Mammoth Cave tourism was planted in the minds of Cutliff, Lee, and Procter. By the first quarter of the New Year, "A Wonderful Discovery" of Alaskan cave mummies was announced in January, and the Cardiff Giant had toured Louisville in April.[8]

A local cave explorer by the name of Thomas E. Lee made great strides in pushing the extremities of Grand Avenue Cave. He was one of the best cave explorers of the time and apparently was one of the early guides in the cave.[9] There is not a hint he discovered anything new in the cave that the saltpeter miners did not already know prior to 1815.

The Rotunda in Grand Avenue Cave is formed by the junction of Lee Avenue with Grand Avenue. It is such an impressive place, it is difficult to conceive how Lee Avenue could have been missed all those years. Pre-1815 saltpeter miners knew of this passage and actively mined its saltpeter resources. Highwall excavations on the free face of a fifty-foot deep pit in Lee Avenue shows evidence of saltpeter mining.

Lee Avenue was not a new discovery, but had been known long before Lee ever stepped into the passage. Lee had the habit of recording his conquests on the walls of the caves he explored with signature and usually the date. He reached the point overlooking the first drop-off into Lee Avenue of Grand Avenue Cave on July 12, 1875. He commemorated his penetration on the left hand wall overlooking the abyss. It is not known if the old saltpeter era "banzai" ladders were in place at this time. Even without them, the fifty-foot deep drop into the chasm was well within his technical climbing capabilities.

Lee Avenue became the new discovery that would place Grand Avenue Cave in the public eye. Actually, the passage is only four hundred and forty feet long! It was enough to attract tourist to make the hazardous climb down the abyss and up the other side into walking trunk cave passage. Lateral vertical shafts in this canyon drop into a reported underground river that no one ever saw.

About a week after Lee pushed into his new discovery. Procter traveled to Louisville to promote the new find in Grand Avenue Cave. He had been in Louisville since perhaps the 18th of July, where he took lodging in the Willard Hotel. He issued press releases and presented cave formations to the Graham Museum in the Public Library.[10]

The time was ripe to announce this "unexpected rival of its celebrated neighbor...as one of the most interesting and wonderful of all the caves in the region."[11]

Another announcement was made to the *Louisville Daily Ledger* about the discovery of his great and wonderful cave.

The article reports:

> Major George M. Proctor, of Glasgow Junction, proprietor of "Grand Avenue" Cave, is in this city. He called upon us, and tells us that he has found a bonanza in the Grand Avenue, which has but recently been explored. It excels, he assures us, any subterranean wonder yet discovered. Since it has been opened a number of persons have explored the cave, who have expressed themselves delighted with it. A stock company, for the purpose of bringing the cave before the public, will be formed. The cave is located about three miles from the Nashville railroad, near Glasgow Junction.[12]

The history of tourism in Mammoth Cave and Frederic Ward Putnam's visit provided the gist for a plan to make Grand Avenue Cave even more famous. Just south of the entrance was once one of the most famous caves in Kentucky, Short Cave. Prior to 1815, this cave produced at least six Indian mummies.[13] Most were removed and one was temporarily stored in Mammoth Cave. Word of these mummy discoveries and their new abode made Mammoth Cave and Fawn Hoof (the best known mummy) household names. Mammoth Cave tourism grew on the shoulders of Fawn Hoof. There had not been a Mammoth Cave mummy on display since late 1815.[14]

Fawn Hoof would come back into the limelight in the 1876 Philadelphia Exposition or Worlds Fair.[15] If only Procter could get an Indian mummy for his new cave? Indian artifacts of this nature are exceptionally rare and not the sort of thing one could buy off the shelf, or for that matter go out in some cave and dig up! In what seems like a stroke of blind luck, exploration of Lee Avenue produced a female Indian mummy. It was found in full view of its discoverers. An excited announcement is made to the public from Grand Avenue Cave! "An American Mummy" in words used by Putnam, had been found on the evening of July 23, 1875. Procter's secret wishes were realized:

> An exploring party left here yesterday, in charge of Eugene U. Proctor, for the Grand Avenue Cave, and, after many hours' search in Lee's new discovery, they found a perfect mummy, supposed to belong to the mound builders of this portion of the West. It is a female in perfect state, and can now be seen by anyone who may visit this cave. The explorers were Eugene Underwood Proctor, F. W. Wolsey and W. Wage.[16]

To their amazement, they found a totally nude "female" mummy on the floor of the cave.

The circumstances of the mummy find were as follows:

The discovery of a female mummy in Grand Avenue cave, near Glasgow Junction, Barren County, by Eugene U. Proctor, is attracting the attention of the archaeologists of the country. Major George M. Proctor has received a telegram from Spencer F. Baird, of Woods Hole, Massachusetts, inquiring if the mummy can be obtained by the Smithsonian Institution for the purpose of exhibition at the centennial. Major Proctor is considering the proposition. The mummy was discovered the evening of the 23d ult., while Lee's avenue was being explored. It is that of a women four feet and five inches in length. When found it was lying on its left side in a sleeping posture. The left arm was resting on the ground, but the left hand had disappeared. The right arm rests on the bosom with the hand tucked under the chin. The flesh on the arms and lower limbs is shrunken, but the body and head are well preserved. The face is round and full, and a correspondent says, "very beautiful." It is perfectly white, and shows no Indian characteristics in form or feature. The mouth is full and the lips are partly open, exhibiting the front teeth. It shows unmistakable evidence of having been in its present position for an indefinite period of time. Crowds are flocking to see it, but no one has yet been able to tell to what race of human beings it belongs. Will not some one of our Kentucky scientists rise and explain?[17]

Not one scientist is known to have examined the little "female" mummy who had a more than striking resemblance to Fawn Hoof. Elements of a hoax are present at this early date, especially its similarity to Fawn Hoof: it was found in plain view lying in the cave passage; it was a nude "white" female cave explorer; there were no artifacts; and, Spencer F. Baird's inquiry on behalf of the Smithsonian Institution. Hoax mummy finds and requests of this nature are standard fare with this kind of discovery.[18] Learned institutions and their representatives (from all over the world) trek to the cave and authenticate the mummy and discovery. Enthusiastic proclamations by the cave owners or discovers would follow in due time. Already there was a body of published hoax mummy discoveries from caves, and Little Al was in good company (see Chapter Twelve). The reason he was not investigated is because the discovery lacked credibility to direct scientific enquiry as elements of an elaborate deception surfaced in newspapers. Another eighty-three years would elapse before anthropologists and archaeologists would study Little Al.[19]

Three points were established in an August 9, 1875, letter to the editor by Samuel B. Young.[20] It seems that Grand Avenue Cave was a well known local cave named "Long's Cave," and had been for some time. This was a moot point when compared to Young's more serious charges that the mummy found in "Long's Cave" actually had been removed sometime since from neighboring Salts Cave, and the "mummy has been conveyed to its present location for the purpose of imposing upon the public. If this shall be denied I hold myself prepared to prove it."[21] Eugene U. Procter responded in an August 12th letter to the editor.[22] He acknowledges Grand Avenue was known as Long Cave, and that its had been visited numerous times in the past. However, the discovery of Lee Avenue and the mummy were new:

> As to the mummy, we will give your correspondent a chance to prove what he says; if it was transported from Salt's cave to Grand-avenue cave, I wish him to prove it. I simply say that his statement is false, and that I with two other companions did on Friday night, July 23, find said mummy in Grand Avenue, or "Long's Cave," if he so wishes it. Any scientific man will say after examining the mummy, that it has never been moved and that it would not stand handling. Any of your readers who may known the feelings which Cave City has towards Glasgow Junction or its vicinity may well know the reason why such a big effort is made against our little place. Persons not knowing it can, by stopping a few minutes there, become acquainted with the facts. We have the cave, and all can see it without much difficulty or expense.[23]

Tempers became short as charges and counter-charges were exchanged. The mummy became the talk of the day in Glasgow Junction, Cave City, and the county seat at Glasgow. If the mummy was stolen from Salts Cave, the robbers were not acknowledged at this time period. Apparently their activity and identity were locally well known. They had good cause not to come forward with a public disclosure of their crime. Prosecution for trespass and thievery by Salts Cave owners, the Mammoth Cave estate, was probably a real possibility.[24]

Tourism improved for Grand Avenue Cave, as sightseers marveled at this new Kentucky wonder. The controversy brewed as more information trickled out of the Salts Cave mummy discovery, such as Little Al was found with a mummified raccoon by his side, and the prehistoric mummy may or may not be an authentic Indian relic.[25]

Some substance on the motives of George M. Procter begins to emerge:

> A mummy was found, some time since in a cave near Glasgow Junction. The timing was opportune. Some gentlemen destined to establish a popular resort of the cave. Notices of the mummy, and descriptions of the "great subterranean wonder" in which it was found, soon appeared in various county papers. A prehistoric race had deposited the corps there, according to the notices, for, as it was white, it could not be of the Indian race, and the incrustations found about the body showed conclusively(?) that it had lain there - well several thousand years! A correspondent of the Glasgow Times, of Cave City, stepped to the front and declared

that her mummyship had long quietly rested in a neighboring cave, and was secretly removed to the place it now occupies. A newspaper controversy followed, and affidavits are next in order. The controversy has proved a good thing for the cave proprietors, as numbers of visitors are flocking there. Knowing fellows say the whole thing is only an advertising dodge. As to the mummy belonging to a prehistoric race, it may or may not be true; for by its side was found a mummy coon, and, as these animals are not given to embalming bodies, it shows that the bodies were preserved by the salts of the cave.[26]

Procter used the mummy and the generated controversy to bring tourists to his cave. Free advertisement in the press was one of the ways promoters made known their attraction. Few paid tourist cave notices ever appeared in local and regional newspapers. Cave attractions relied on word of mouth, editorial, and letters to the editor to garner visitation. Having a big cave next to the mammoth of all caves was not good enough, even in 1875. People will remember the great and the infamous, and nothing in between. Grand Avenue acquired its commercial fame through the mummy controversy and the infamous way it found a new home.

A correspondent of the *Courier-Journal* using the byline of "Fawn" makes a visit to Salts Cave to verify in part the original repository of Little Al. Some of the mythological past life of Little Al materializes that would form an outline for T. O. Chisholm's mummy history of Grand Avenue Cave. Fawn reports:

That mummy is still the absorbing topic of our community, and is probably creating a greater sensation now than at any time in its life, although it may have been a dark-haired Indian beauty, whose lustrous eyes and pouting lips caused quite a flutter in the hearts of her dusky admirers. Probably she was woed secretly in these sylvan shades by one offensive to her tribe, and, these meetings having been discovered, her lover wounded "unto death," and she herself amenable to the laws of her nation, had sought concealment in this cave, and, unable to trace her steps, had died of starvation. Whatever romance the imagination may weave, matter of fact people about here are contenting themselves by simply finding out in what cave it was actually discovered. Salts Cave, the one from which it is said to have been removed, is three miles from Mammoth Cave and a portion of that property, and on the Munfordville road. It receives its name from the medical salts which are found there in immense deposits on the ceiling, and it is said that on large parties entering the chambers where these deposits are found the air set in motion by their burning torches causes them to fall to the floor in light, feathery flakes like snow. The existence of this cave has long been known, but, on account of the difficulty experienced in entering and the roughness of the avenues leading through it, it has been but little explored. Early in this summer, during one of my visits to Mammoth Cave, a mummy was offered for sale to the proprietor. The owners of it refused to tell where it had been discovered, but described it as a female lying in a sleeping position with one hand laid across the chin, the other extended, but, so nearly decomposed that it would have to be removed with a great deal of care to prevent it falling off. After some deliberation, it was concluded not to make the purchase, and the matter ended. The incident, then, was in a measure forgotten until the recent announcement of the discovery of a mummy in another cave near by revived the subject, while the similarity in every respect to the one which had been found in the summer gave rise to the surmise that the two were one and the same. The intense interest manifested by every one caused some of the more curious to make a visit to Salt's cave a few days since. They found the entrance very difficult, a spring falling directly from the ceiling, causing the explorers to make quite a detour to escape a bath, and even after this precaution they were sprinkled.

The main avenue is supposed to be nine miles in length, in this respect equalling Mammoth Cave, while the specimens, all of which are found upon the floor, are exquisite. Leaving the main avenue you enter a side route, and after climbing over the roughest of roads for a hundred and fifty yards, reach the spot where a mummy was discovered, and from whence it has been recently removed. An indentation in the ground, under a shelving rock, corresponds precisely with that of the disputed mummy, while the mold formed around the body in all these years is still perceptible, with a few locks of its hair, which time has changed to a dark auburn. There can be no doubt that a mummy was here, the dryness of the atmosphere preserving it, as no water is found within the cave excepting at the extreme end of one of the routes. A great many relics of a Prehistoric Race, of which nothing definite as yet has ever been known, were found. Hidden among the crevices of the rocks or concealed beneath the dust on the floor were moccasins so small that they might well excite the envy of a city belle, and skillfully woven out of the bark of trees. They were much worn, the strings, also of bark, showing the knots where they had been tied. A [r]eticule made from the same material, but with more care and much finer fiber, was also found. Remains of torches half burnt and gourds undoubtedly used for culinary purposes were scattered everywhere, and these mute witnesses of ages long past must certainly be of great interest to the scientific world. That this cave formed at one time the home of an aboriginal race there can be no doubt. That they were unacquainted with metallic substances is proven by no remains of anything of this kind being found. The avenues, which are numerous, communicate with one another, so that there is no necessity for retreating your steps to the main cave, this being a decided advantage over Mammoth Cave. The passages however, are exceedingly rough, far worse than any known, requiring crawling in some places for quite a distance, and nothing but the reward obtained in the beautiful specimens found at the end could induce one to try it. The party of explorers spent the whole day in it, and considered themselves well paid for their labor by the curiosities they found. Whether this cave, which has so suddenly sprung into notoriety, will be opened to the public I am not able to say. The difficulties which I have named will probably prevent it ever being much visited, save by those who possess a passion for such explorations, and are fond of ancient relics.[27]

This is one of the first and earliest published description of the discovery site for Little Al. It is also an early description of Salts Cave exploration. This is the cave that William Cutliff and (Thomas?) Lee took Frederic W. Putnam in late 1874 to conduct his archaeological inventory. The manager of the Mammoth Cave and hotel at this time period is William Scott Miller.[28]

With a penchant nearing illiteracy, someone went into Salts Cave and made an inscription on a rock in the passage where the mummy was supposed to have been discovered. The rock is called the "Discovery Stone."[29] The hand script records:

> Sir I have found one of the Grat wonder of the World in this
> cave Whitch is a muma
> Can All Seed hear after found March the 8
> 1875
>
> T. E. lee J. L. lee an W. d. Cutliff dicuvers
> [sic][30]

The inscription with the names: Thomas E. Lee, his brother John L. Lee, and William Cutliff claimed this honor on March 8, 1875. Three months earlier than the newspaper reported discovery in Grand Avenue Cave by Eugene U. Procter, F. W. Wolsey and W. Wage. This inscription is the only admission to the discovery of the mummy and who was involved in Salts Cave. A portion of the "Discovery Stone" statement is curious from an interpretation standpoint. The statement "Can All Seed hear after found March the 8[,] 1875," indicates the mummy was already on display to the public. Clearly, the "Discovery Stone" inscription could have been back dated to establish priority.

One person with a sense of religion and the sanctity of the grave remarked over the removal of the mummy from Salts Cave. A cave explorer by the name of J. M. Smith went about condemning the act with his own inscription on another nearby stone, called the "Damnation Rock."

It reads:

> How are you grave robbers. What is it you would not do. They is
> nothing too mean for you to do. You low down scoundrls. What is
> it you wouldn't do. Just think for a sec of men to steal the dead...
> [illegible, perhaps "Just speculate on it"]. Sir you are worse than
> a murderer. Are you not afraid it will follow you in your paths of a
> day and your bed at night. You low down dirty damed thief of hell
> yours most...[illegible: "respectfully"?]   J M Smith
>      P.S. Call again you honest fellows when you get hard up for a
> few dimes or call at some other grave yard.[31]

This is what is called balanced spelean journalism. Perhaps the
inscriptions were used when the cave was commercialized in the 1920s.[32]
The penmanship on the "Discovery Stone" appears to be consistent for
the 1870s time period. Old timers with the same characteristics of style
could easily extend their hand script into the first quarter of the twentieth
century.

In the interim, a small wood enclosure or hut with pad locked door
was built in the Race Course of Fairy Avenue of Grand Avenue Cave. This
became the abode of the mummy for perhaps the next fifteen years. Much
embellished color to Little Al's discovery is added by Chisholm in 1892.[33]
He produced the first and only guidebook on Grand Avenue Cave, and in
doing so, recited the circumstances surrounding the mummy discovery.
First of all, the date of discovery is changed from 1875 to 1876, apparently
to coincide with the Centennial Exposition. Eugene U. Procter, F. W. Wolsey
and W. Wage are dropped from the picture as co-discoverers. Now it's a new
discoverer by the name of Thomas E. Lee, who found it while exploring a
passage that would bear his name. He found the mummy "lying on a ledge
of rock in a deep chasm."[34] An impressive fifty-foot deep void opens in the
floor of Lee Avenue. Once at the bottom of the canyon is a ledge where
the nude body of a young girl was found. Chisholm describes the mummy
whose "hair, which dropped from the head, lay about it in a dark, fluffy
mass. The length of the body was five feet, seven inches, and the weight
about thirteen pounds."[35] Early pre-Chisholm newspaper announcements
indicate the height of the mummy was four feet, five inches. Fawn Hoof
was five feet, ten inches in height. Apparently the deception worked, no
one ever suspected this mummy was not Fawn Hoof, the real exhibition
piece at the 1876 Worlds Fair.

In 1892, the Grand Avenue Cave mummy was supposed to be in a
Boston museum.[36] Chisholm says, "the body, however, belongs properly to
the Cave, and the present owners are taking steps toward its recovery."[37]
Here is where the history of Fawn Hoof's travels is further meshed with

Mummy Cabin in Long Cave. Photograph by Diana Emerson George.

Little Al to events that transpiring in 1816-1817, and the 1876 Centennial Exhibition in Philadelphia. There was good reason why the mummy was not at Grand Avenue Cave. He was sold about 1890 to Henry C. Ganter and the Mammoth Cave estate.[38] In a few years tourist interest in Procter's Grand Avenue Cave waned. Since he was not willing to place paid advertisements in regional newspapers to attract tourists, the next best thing for Procter to do was to launch another free advertising campaign with a stupendous announcement of even greater cave discoveries.

For Procter, it was easy. Grand Crystal Cave with twenty-three miles of passage (Wyandotte Cave advertised the same length), three deep rivers, and a number of mummies in stone coffins is announced to the *Cincinnati Commercial*.[39] This notice was widely reprinted throughout the nation, including the *Scientific American*.[40]

Major George M. Procter and his Grand Avenue Cave are also mentioned. Procter is supposed to have purchased some of the mummies from Thomas J. Kelley's new cave.[41]

The *Courier-Journal* was quick to point out the *Cincinnati Commercial* was the recipient of a practical joke. The article was written by Orange Blossom who had also written hoax articles on the bones of John Wilkes Booth and a Big Clifty Kentucky yarn.[42]

119

George M. Procter responded that he had received letters from all over the United States enquiring about the Egyptian mummies and the great cave. He said he had retired from the cave business and the Orange Blossom notice was the first he had heard of the discovery. He denies all association with purchasing some of the mummies or any knowledge of the new cave.[43]

Orange Blossom responds to Procter's letter with new proclamations on the cave and some unique hydrology. Whirlpools in Salt River had captured politicians and spitted them out in the subterranean rivers of the Mammoth Cave region. The reported mummies were in effect these very politicians![44] The Grand Crystal Cave discovery went from the serious to the silly in just a few weeks. This announcement is politically motivated and lacks the inventive character and style of the first Orange Blossom article. I suspect there are several "Orange Blossoms" jumping into the subject. I do not think it above Procter's dignity to have submitted the first Orange Blossom letter on the discovery of Grand Crystal Cave. His involvement, advertising, and promotional ploys in the real Grand Avenue Cave make him the strongest candidate with the most to gain financially. This is typical of Procter's underhanded tricks designed to syphon tourist traffic from Mammoth Cave and other area commercial caves. I think this is one of the reasons why newspaper reporters never went to Procter caves to cover the spelean adventure.

Horace C. Hovey in his *Celebrated American Caverns* makes no reference to the Grand Avenue mummy.[45] He had every opportunity to do so in his exhaustive discussion on cave histories. He gives a detailed lineage of Fawn Hoof and several other mummies from Short Cave. He was quick to point out the Grand Crystal Cave hoax, yet was silent on its stock of mummies or the mummy exhibited in Grand Avenue Cave.[46]

In 1897 and 1910, Bennett H. Young adds to the Little Al discovery in Salts Cave. Drawing substance from the advertised subterfuge, he says of Little Al:

> One curious mummy was removed a short time ago from Salts Cave. It is that of a woman about thirty years of age. The red hair upon her head appears still to be unchanged. She had probably died of starvation. She lay upon her face, with her hands clasped beneath her breast. This mummy can be seen now at Glasgow Junction. It has been moved into Gardner's Grotto, at Glasgow Junction, which Mr. Hazen has leased, and in which he proposes to arrange a museum which shall show something of the life of these Kentucky cave-dwellers.[47]

Young says, "a mat about one yard square was discovered several years ago in a chamber of the lower tier of the cavern known as Mummy Valley, so called because there was found there many years ago, by Messrs.

Cutliff and Lee, the body of a young woman of this lost race."[48] This is the earliest published reference to William Cutliff and one of the Lee brothers and their discovery of the mummy in Salts Cave. The "Discovery Stone" predates Young's 1910 archaeological publication.

Then in 1912, Horace C. Hovey and Richard Ellsworth Call further obscures the identity of Little Al with Fawn Hoof.[49] It was now impossible to separate the two mummies using the latest interpretation from the master speleologists. The admirable research conducted on the Short Cave mummies by Hovey in 1882, apparently was not consulted or simply avoided. The lineage of Fawn Hoof became blurred and stretched into this impersonator from Salts Cave. Hovey and Call had the information on Indian mummies at their disposal, yet they did not use any of it. The use of it would expose the real identity of Little Al.

Years later, more discoverers vie for the prize from Salt Cave. The mummy was found in 1874 by Louis Vial and William Cutliff.[50] Vial owned a secret side entrance to Salts Cave, while the Mammoth Cave estate owned the south entrance. The new mummy discovery story unfolds thus, according to M. Carrie Morgan:

> Bill Cutliff was so elated over finding it he told the Lee boys. They hurriedly went into the cave and got it out and sold it to a man named Proctor who owned a cave not far from Glasgow Junction. Proctor showed it in his cave until rats cut holes in it. It was taken to the Philadelphia Exposition in 1876. My father [Louis Vial], visiting the Exposition, recognized it as the same one he had discovered. It was later shown at Mammoth Cave, I think, in 1920 when I was last there at the new makeshift hotel.[51]

Morgan's is the only reference to target William Cutliff and the two Lee brothers as the ones who removed Little Al from Salts Cave and sold him to (George M.) Procter. Morgan's reminiscence is definitely a new twist on an old theme. It's oral family tradition recited fifty four or fifty five years after the fact. She was about twelve years old when the event happened. Glaring inconsistencies in her version, especially the later disposition of Little Al from 1876 onward makes her statements on the discovery and removal suspect to challenge. No documentation has ever been found for Little Al's presence in the Philadelphia Exposition. If Louis Vial was there, he viewed Fawn Hoof and not Little Al. No verifiable documentation from the time period in question has been discovered associating the Lee brothers and Cutliff with stealing Little Al from Salts Cave. We have only the oral traditions that they are the culprits that did the deed.

Archaeologist Patty Jo Watson interviewed Cave City native and Mammoth Cave guide Lewis Lyman Cutliff (1901-1986) on the subject of Little Al. William Cutliff was Lyman's uncle.[52] The oral family tradition unfolds thus: the two Lee brothers and William Cutliff jointly discovered the mummy in Salts Cave. In the interim, the Lees went back into the cave and stole the mummy from its repository. The mummy was sold to Larkin J. Procter for $85.00. "A main theme of the Little Al story as Lyman told it was that his uncle made the discovery but was done out of credit (and cash) by the underhanded behavior of T. E. and J. L. Lee."[53] This is the first reference to Larkin J. Procter's purchase of the mummy. By this point in time, historical events that transpired in 1875 had been forgotten from memory or blurred by the passage of time.

Scant documentation on the date of Little Al's discovery in Salts Cave is subject to evaluation and interpretation. The inscribed veracity on the "Discovery Stone" with a date of March 8, 1875 is good supporting documentation. A fact-finding visit by Fawn from *The Courier-Journal* in September 1875, is the only first hand documentation from that cave. Fawn establishes a find date of "early in the summer" of 1875.[54] This date would place Little Al's discovery in June and not in the late winter month of March. Dates supplied by the Procters, Chisholm, and Morgan are spurious at best.

After the publication of "That Pickled Squaw" by Fawn, the discussion of Indian mummies from Salts and Grand Avenue caves stopped. The hoax had gone on long enough in the public light. About 1890, Little Al was purchased from Procter by Henry C. Ganter and exhibited periodically up to 1958 at Mammoth Cave.[55] Ganter played along with the hoax and added more to the subterfuge. Now he had an actual mummy who could take on the role of The Mammoth Cave Mummy. Spelean-historian, Harold Meloy said Ganter "encouraged her to inherit all of the history, folklore and legends which had formerly belonged to Fawn Hoof."[56] The public did not know and probably did not care to know the difference between the two mummies. Ganter changed the locale of discovery from Grand Avenue back to Salts Cave. I suspect this was made to establish and reinforce propriety of past ownership from a cave Mammoth Cave could call their own.

In the interim, Henry C. Ganter retires from his duties as Mammoth Cave and hotel manager. He takes the mummy with him and stores Little Al in his barn.[57] There the mummy stayed until 1921. George G. Morrison obtained the mummy from Ganter's estate, and exhibited him in the newly opened New Entrance to Mammoth Cave.[58]

New names would be applied to this lone cave explorer. "The lady of the cave" was a white girl who fled and died in Salts Cave rather than submit to torture by Indian pursuers. This cave romance was first offered by Chisholm in 1892. Morrison dubbed this cave lady with a new name, "Little Alice." She stayed at the New Entrance until 1931, when Morrison sold his cave and exhibits to the National Park Commission for the new Mammoth Cave National Park.

From then on, the much traveled and worn out Little "Alice" was exhibited in a small museum at Mammoth Cave until it was finally retired from public service in the late 1950's.[59] By now, Little "Alice" was not the only mummy on display in Mammoth Cave. In 1935, another mummy, Lost John, was discovered deep in Mammoth Cave, and he took "her" place as The Mammoth Cave Mummy.

In 1958, Little "Alice" was moved to a new home in the Anthropology Department, at the University of Kentucky.[60] For the very first time, this visitor from the past was subjected to a detailed anthropological examination. Some haunting questions were answered at this time. Little "Alice" was showed to be a 9 year old little boy! "Her" name was then changed to Little Al.

Little Al's "history" from his 1875 discovery to 1958 is manufactured for publicity purposes to advertise commercial caves. To foster a history where none had existed before, Grand Avenue Cave, Mammoth Cave, Gardners Grotto, and New Entrance to Mammoth Cave all made use of this Indian mummy. It is unsettling to know of four different sets of discoverers associated with just as many dates and in two separate cave sites. I suspect that the four sets of discoverers are not telling the truth (an understatement on my part). Thomas E. Lee, John L. Lee, William Cutliff, and Louis Vial never told their side of the story. The actual persons who removed Little Al from Salts Cave are not definitely known. William S. Miller, the manager of the Mammoth Cave estate knew the culprits with the mummy when they tried to sell it to him and Mammoth Cave. He declined the offer when there was not a clear chain of custody as to where the mummy came from. George M. Procter and probably Samuel B. Young knew their identities too. There was collusion among George M. Procter, Eugene U. Procter, F. W. Wolsey and W. Wage who knew of the mummy subterfuge in Grand Avenue Cave.

Major Procter needed an exhibition piece to display in his cave. He secretly purchased a mummy recently found in Salts Cave and placed it in his own cave. The mummy and the degree of negative advertising it generated made the cave famous. In time, public interest in Grand Avenue Cave waned and the mummy controversy was forgotten. Procter realized that the influx of new tourists resulted from the summer charade added to his pocketbook. Two years later, the Grand Crystal Cave hoax was promoted to garner attention from train loads of tourists flocking to see Mammoth Cave. There was no fabulous Grand Crystal Cave with miles of passage, great rivers, nor a stock of mummies. The next best cave with more than passing similarities was still close by, Grand Avenue Cave, with a real American Mummy.

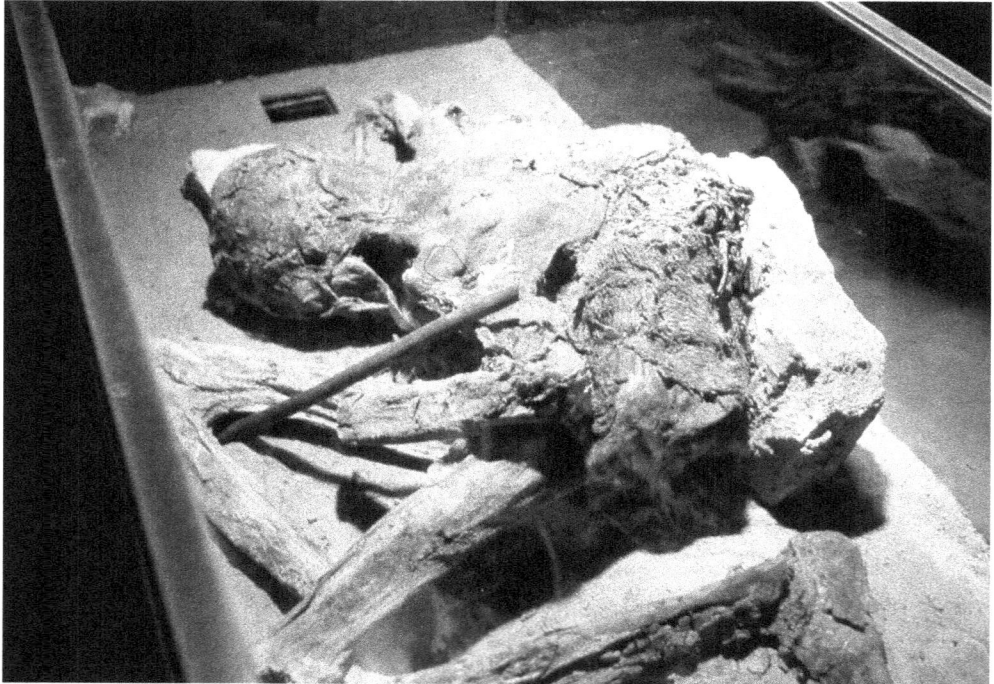

Lost John in Mammoth Cave.

CHAPTER FOURTEEN

# CAUGHT BETWEEN A ROCK AND A HARD PLACE

*"What is it Lyman?"*

*"Gosh! It's a skeleton! No, it's a mummy."*

Lyman Cutliff (1935)

Not since before the War of 1812 had a wooden machine this large and this intricate been built inside the great Kentucky cave. In August 1935, dozens of Civilian Conservation Corps personnel constructed a giant, 30 foot high crane. It was made from 10 x 12 oblong square cut timbers, cross beams, supports of thick ropes, braided steel cables, and all attached to scaffolding and steps. They worked frantically, carrying in all the wood, ropes, and steel cables to a place over two miles from the entrance. A cave rescue was underway, and time was running out. Trapped under an unstable five ton boulder was a forty three year old man. The boulder had every indication its weight was shifting and the man would be completely crushed. He had been caught between a rock and a hard place twenty five centuries ago; and his predicament had only recently been discovered. Lost John was a true American mummy from Mammoth Cave and became the most scientifically studied of all the mummies from the region.

The job of Mammoth Cave guide was a cherished family profession. Children of guides from the time they could talk, heard the lore of the cave spoke at home, chaperoned through the cave, and generally experienced the underground element of Mammoth Cave. In this fashion, the way of the cave, its stories, and traditions was past down from generation to generation. It was natural for the children of cave guides to become one when they grew up. That is the way it always had been until the practice became extinct in 1941, the year Mammoth Cave became a National Park.[1]

Like his father and grandfather, Lyman Cutliff would become a third generation cave guide. Since childhood, Lyman had heard his grandfather's discovery story of Little Al from Salts Cave, the way he was cheated out of the proceed from the sale of the mummy, and generally written out of history for making an epic discovery of profound archaeological importance. Quite naturally, Lyman wanted to find one too. For fifteen

Wire and steel wrapped boulder atop Mummy Ledge in Mammoth Cave. Photograph by Diana Emerson George.

years during off-duty hours, he and Grover Campbell would search Mammoth Cave for vestiges of Indian activity.[2] Cave exploration was in their blood and any opportunity to see more of the cave was eagerly pursued. To find a Mammoth Cave mummy was always Lyman's goal and the cave exploration trip with Grover on June 7, 1935, would yield this sensational discovery. Cutliff said:

> You see, we've always found bits of woven grass, one or two
> sandals, and human refuse in here, and I always argued that men
> worked here. Others said that pack rats carried those things in.
> But I was sure that men had been here long before the white men
> ever came to this country. So we kept after it and found what we
> were looking for.[3]

Mammoth Cave was about to become a National Park. To make the cave ready for added visitation, the U. S. Government stationed a Civilian Conservation Corps camp near the cave. With cheap labor, these CCC men would build new trails, install electric lights in parts of the cave, reforest

126

the surface, and erect new buildings. Experienced cave guides would take these men into the cave and stay with them until they finished their work. It was one of these construction crews that Lyman and Grover were in charge during the building of a new tourist trail through Mammoth Cave. Their duties were to insure the safety of the men, and to protect the interest of the cave management.[4] Work was progressing in Waldach's Dome in the Main Cave near Blue Spring Branch.

This part of the cave is thick with aboriginal remains and evidence of extensive prehistoric selenite mining. From these artifacts it was obvious the Indians had spent time mining in this part of the cave. Remains of wove sandals, antler and stick scrapers, torch material, and climbing pools were everywhere evident. Campbell and Cutliff figured this area was the best place to look for new artifacts. When the CCC workers left the cave for the evening, the two guides went caving.

They climbed up to a ledge thirty feet above the trail work area. Here was the place Campbell had found some mummified bats the day before.[5] He edged along on his belly pushing the gasoline lantern along the way. Cutliff brought up the rear. The ledge crawl descended to a wide sandy plain near a large boulder and the dead bats. Campbell said, "guess I'll crawl down between these rocks. Looks like nobody has ever been down along that sand ledge."[6] Reaching out with his left hand to support himself on a round rock, Campbell moved forward when Lyman said, "That's not a stone"!

Campbell turned to say, "What is it, Lyman?"

"Gosh! it's a skeleton! No, it's a mummy," responded Lyman.[7]

Campbell said, "I felt the hair and wrinkled skin and hollered to Lyman, 'Gosh, this feels like somebody's head.' And sure enough, it was."[8]

Lyman was a proud man. The quest to find a mummy had fulfilled his life long ambition. His family could now boast two mummies in one household. The one discovered in 1875 and now this one in 1935.

At the on-set, Lyman and Campbell decided to keep the discovery secret. They reported their find only to Mammoth Cave Manager, M. L. Charlet; and he agreed secrecy should be maintained until government archaeologist had a chance to study the mummy. Adjusting normal work routines produced an excitement of urgency as the electricity of the moment spread to others who reasoned something wonderful had occured. Harold Meloy collected the tradition that shortly after the secret discovery and plans were being made to bring in government experts. The hotel clerk Arthur Doyle fielded an inquiring question to Charlet, "So you finally found lost John?"[9] We don't know what Charlet's response was, but the name "Lost John" seemed as appropriate a name as one ever needed.[10]

National Park Service representative at the cave was Chief Ranger, Robert P. Holland. He notified the Director of the National Park Service in Washington D. C. Holland then contacted archaeologist Alonzo W. Pond who was conducting field work on Jamestown Island, Virginia.[11] His instructions were to drop everything and immediately come to the cave. Physical anthropologist Georg K. Neumann from Chicago and archaeologist Dr. William S. Webb of the University of Kentucky arrived on the scene too.

By the time archaeologist Alonzo Pond arrived on the scene, the name "Lost John" was already well known. One day as he exited the cave after studying the mummy, one of the guides enquired how long it would be before Lost John would be out of the cave? The name reference was new to him, and asked the guide to explain. The guide responded, it was the name bestowed to the mummy under the rock on Mummy Ledge. Pond later reasoned the name was given by one of the African-American CCC workers who christened him "Lost John."[12] Until now, this was all that was known as to how Lost John received his name.

The name Lost John has its roots in African-American slang and Kentucky folksongs. Robert L. Chapman and Barbara A. Kipfer in their *Dictionary of American Slang* give insight into the derivation of the word *John* from a cultural ethnology standpoint. The name *John* when used in black cultural parlance becomes an identity tag standing for "any man." More explicitly, an average man or Joe. The word matured further in 1946, for any man "regarded as an easy victim."[13] John being a victim dates earlier than Chapman and Kipfer's research.

*Lost John* is one of many folksongs (of the same name) sung largely by southern African-Americans. These songs date from antebellum times with different lyrics and variations on a theme handed down through generations. First quarter 20th century lyrics often revolved around a convict victim who outwits his Bowling Green, Kentucky, captors through stealth and trickery. The African-American Kentucky folksong is variously known as *Long Gone; Lost John; Long John; Long Lost John*; and *John Dean from Bowling Green* to name a few. Lyrics are different in each of these.

In 1920, W. C. Handy, father of the blues, composed a song with words by Chris Smith, and published it as sheet music titled *Long Gone*.[14] This song was based in large part on their collection of idiomatic motifs taken from *Lost John* Kentucky folksongs. A common story line revolves around a prisoner selected from the ranks to be a victim in order to see if he could outrun a pack of new bloodhounds. Lost John outwits the dogs by running faster. Or, he fashions a funny pair of shoes with a heel in front and one in back to obscure his direction of escape. Between 1925 and 1934 more than twelve different Lost John songs appeared as commercial recordings.

The song in its various renditions became a popular work song sung by stoop and pick farmhands, road gangs, laborers, and prisoners. The song helped elevate ones spirits by lightening the load to help make the drudgery of repetitive work tolerable. The cadence song in its numerous renditions was immensely popular in Kentucky for this time period.[15] Especially *Lost John* recorded by the Kentucky dual Richard Burnett and Leonard Rutherford in 1927.

From a folklore standpoint, the story line of the song points toward an antebellum trickster slave named Old John. With the abolishment of slavery, John the slave metamorphosed into an incarcerated prisoner who outwits his captors and escapes.[16] The clever slave is an archetype character in folklore and fairy tales. His lot is a quest for freedom through trickery, stealth and subterfuge. A hero's journey with a bag of tricks designed to slow his pursuers and enable his escape to safe lands.

My thesis is, African-American CCC workers laboring in the vicinity of Lost John developed an attachment with the man under the five ton boulder. The mummy and his predicament reminded them of the plight associated with the protagonist in the song *Lost John*. From their perspective, here was a person they could empathize with. An average man, incarcerated, lost from any hope of rescue and a victim trapped under a giant boulder. It was an easy alliteration to connect everyday African American slang, John in particular with a popular song. The mummy became Lost John in their way of thinking.

To better record body measurements, excavation was made around the mummy to help assess his physical condition, and to inventory any artifacts. Key photographs were made during every aspect of the investigation. The discovery was important because the mummy had not been disturbed in all those years. The site was a snap shot picture of the last day in the life of an Indian selenite miner. Everything was there. His simple tools, loin cloth clothing, torches, and a polished shell gorget necklace were his soul possessions in the cave. He died instantaneously and probably never knew what hit him. Even the digging stick was still in his right hand.[17] Lost John became the oldest known accident fatality in a North America cave.[18] Even in death, Lost John was a survivor. A narrow time portal had opened on the daily life of a man who made part of his living toiling in the selenite mines of Mammoth Cave. Everything seemed in order with a public announcement on June 23, 1935. News reporters and photographers swarmed to the scene. They climbed up to the ledge and generally photographed the mummy from every angle and interviewed everyone in sight. It was headline news that would create even more news copy.

With all this additional foot traffic; sand beneath the five ton boulder began to sift out at an alarming rate. The boulder was now teetering toward the edge of the shelf with the likelihood it would fall off into the Main Cave, and completely crush Lost John. Realizing the boulder was moving, prompted a belated rescue, twenty five centuries too late. After the giant rescue crane was built, the boulder was winched up a few inches from the body of Lost John. Tense moments elapsed as his aged body was pulled from beneath his centuries old tomb. Alonzo Pond summed the feelings of the times when he said, "we consider, this the greatest archeological discovery in Eastern North America."[19]

Once free, Lost John was taken to a work area in Waldach Dome. Pond and Neumann inspected him in even more detail. Then he was taken outside the cave after his final inspection. Shortly after that, a white mold began to grow over his body. No amount of cleaning was successful. Taking him back into the cave was the only solution with constant temperature and humidity. Building a special glass case for Lost John solved the mold problem and presented a new hermetically sealed home for the selenite miner. For over forty years, thousands of visitors to Mammoth Cave viewed the selenite miner from the past.

In July 1976, the National Park Service took the lone selenite miner off public display.[20] After years of exhibition, he was taken to a place in the cave not shown to tourist and rarely visited by cave explorers. This was in keeping with a reverence for the spirit world of Native American Indians.

Lost John is carrying on the tradition as the Mammoth Cave mummy. The legacy of all the mummies made Mammoth Cave what it is today. The majority of the Indian mummies were discovered by illiterate saltpeter miners from a time when little interest existed for their preservation. Their presence languished until the cave's saltpeter manager or the owner collected the remains for preservation and study. Of the dozen or so mummies found prior to 1815 in Kentucky and Tennessee, only Fawn Hoof has partially survived. Two complete mummies were found during cave exploration, Little Al in 1875 and Lost John in 1935. Both mummies became premier exhibition pieces in Mammoth Cave. History and tradition of Mammoth Cave is the travels and exploits of these prehistoric people. The notoriety of the exhibition mummies, especially Fawn Hoof, produced the longevity of this commercial cave and public recognition it now enjoys. The mummies made Mammoth Cave what it is today and insured for all times one of the greatest natural institutions in America.

Climbing to the Mammoth Dome. From *Every Saturday*, May 13 1871.

# END NOTES

## CHAPTER ONE
## INTRODUCTION

1. Pleasant M. Miller, "Account of a Remarkable Preservation of Human Bodies, in a Cave Abounding with Sulphate of Iron Near Caney Fork of Cumberland River, in Tennessee, from a Letter dated May 1, 1811," *Medical Repository*, (1812), Vol. 15, pp. 147-149. Harold Meloy, *Mummies of Mammoth Cave,* (Micron Publishing Co., Shelbyville, Indiana, 1971), 41 p. In 1814, two mummies are said to have been dug up and reburied by the saltpeter miners in Mammoth Cave. Alexander Bullitt, *Rambles in the Mammoth Cave, During the Year 1844 by a Visiter*, (Morton & Griswold, Louisville, Kentucky, 1845), p. 24. Cave guide patter developed to such an extent that all of the Short Cave mummies were said to have been discovered in Mammoth Cave. Bullitt is the only author to report on this new set of mummies. Suspect his guides were actually referring to Scudder's American Museum and Peale's Museum mummies collected in 1814 from Short Cave. Mammoth Cave management problems, latent damage to the cave processing plant during the 1811-1812 earthquakes, and a depleted saltpeter resource forced the cave to close its doors prior to the start of 1814 or shortly thereafter. Angelo I. George and Gary A. O'Dell, "The Saltpeter Works at Mammoth Cave and the New Madrid Earthquake," *The Filson Club History Quarterly*, (1992), Vol. 66, No. 1, p. 22.

2. Harold Meloy, *Mummies of Mammoth Cave*, pp. 6, 22. Thus, the fame of Mammoth Cave, and the exhibition of the mummies in: Clifford's Cabinet, Peale's Museum, American Antiquarian Society Museum, Western Museum, Scudder's American Museum, and St. Louis Museum were enhanced for generations to come.

3. Thomas Ashe, *Travels in America Performed in 1806, for the Purpose of Exploring the Rivers Allegheny, Monongahela, Ohio, and Mississippi, and Ascertaining the Produce and Condition of their Banks and Vicinity*, (Reprinted for Wm. Sawyer & Co. by E. M. Blunt, State Street, Newburyport, London, 1808), 366 p.

4. Francis H. Herrick, "Thomas Ashe and the Authenticity of his *Travels in America*," *Mississippi Valley Historical Review*, (1926), Vol. 13, No. 1, p. 56. Ashe is profiled from his autobiography and other published works by him.

5. Thomas Ashe, *Travels*, p. 196.

6. *Ibid.*, pp. 196-200.

7. *Ibid.*

8. Stephen Williams, *Fantastic Archaeology, the Wild Side of North American Prehistory,* (University of Pennsylvania Press, Philadelphia, 1991), p. 12.

9. Percy G. Adams, *Travelers and Travel Liars*, (University of California Press, Berkeley and Los Angeles, 1962), p. 80.

10. Henry Adams, *History of the United States of America During the Administration of Thomas Jefferson*, (The Library of America, 1986), p. 39.

## CHAPTER TWO
## CHARACTER AND REPUTATION OF THOMAS ASHE

1. Thomas Ashe, *Memoirs and Confessions of Captain Ashe*, (H. Colburn, London, England, 1815), 3 vols.

2. Francis Herrick, "Thomas Ashe and the Authenticity of his *Travels in America*," *Mississippi Valley Historical Review*, 1926, Vol. 13, No. 1, pp. 50-57. *The Dictionary of National Biography*, (Oxford University Press, 1917), p. 641.

3. Eugene H. Conner, M.D., personal oral communication, August 1974.

4. At the present time there is not one iota of evidence for Ashe's first visit to America during this time frame.

5. Ashe's chosen life style is outlined from the immensely popular fireside books of adventure by François Marie René vicomte de Chateaubriand and Michel-Guillaume-Jean de Crèvecoeur. Crèvecoeur changed his name during his residency in America to J. Hector St. John de Crèvecoeur. Of Ashe's old "friend" Jefferson, he says the "gentleman has more theoretical talent than sterling political ability," Thomas Ashe, *Travels*, p. 65.

6. Percy G. Adams, *Travelers and Travel Liars*, p. 158. The book was first published in 1782 and went through many editions. The best and most complete was the 1787 French edition. Travel books by Crèvecoeur were very popular and received wide circulation in America and France. Chateaubriand and Crèvecoeur were French intellectuals who helped shape Europeans views of America "and who powerfully shaped what Americas thought of themselves," Roger G. Kennedy, *Orders from France*, (Alfred A. Knopf, New York, 1989), p. 89.

7. Francis H. Herrick, "Thomas Ashe and the Authenticity of his *Travels in America*," p. 55.

8. Archer B. Hulbert, *The Ohio River*, (G. P. Putnam's Sons, Knickerbocker Press, New York, 1906), pp. 249-250. We have only the testimonial of Thomas Ashe to vouch for his honesty. Let victimized Zadok Cramer and William Goforth attest to Ashe's veracity.

9. Bennett H. Young, *The Prehistoric Men of Kentucky*, Filson Club Pub. No. 25, (John P. Morton & Co., 1910), p. 18. William D. Funkhouser and William S. Webb, *Archaeological Survey of Kentucky*, (University of Kentucky, 1932), Vol. 2, p. 119.

10. Robert Peter, *History of Fayette County*, (O. L. Baskin and Co., Chicago, Illinois, Historical Publication, 1882), p. 221.

11. J. Stoddard Johnson, *First Explorations of Kentucky*, Filson Club Publications, No.13, (John P. Morton and Co., 1898), p. 182.

12. Willard R. Jillson, *Rare Kentucky books 1776-1926*, (The Standard Printing Co., Louisville, 1939), p. 35.

13. Floyd L. McCollum, "Bones from Kentucky Caves," (Unpublished Masters Thesis, University of Kentucky, 1923), type written, pp. 47-48. A hand written copy of these two pages was made for this investigator by Dr. Gary A. O'Dell, Frankfort, Kentucky.

14. Otto A. Rothert, *The Outlaws of Cave-In-Rock*, (Books for Library Press, Freeport, New York, 1924), p. 325.

15. The anonymous reviewer in *The Port Folio* article was thought by Otto A. Rothert, *ibid.*, p. 325, to be Oliver Odlschool. In *Mummies of Short Cave and the Great Catacomb Mystery* by Angelo I. George, (George Publishing Company, Louisville, Kentucky, 1985), p. 23, conjectured the author could have been Benjamin Smith Barton. I felt at that time the connection of Barton's authorship was weak and a little too subjective. Furthermore, the "C." printers mark at the end of the article could be: (1) the editor; (2) abbreviation for the title of the article "Criticism"; or (3) the true author's last name initial. Truly anonymous journal articles are assigned to the editor. The printers mark "C." with the end period is obviously the surname initial of the author. This was standard practice in early publications and is still used in such journals as *Science*. The text is written in a scholarly fashion, overly imperious with deep acerbic cuts into Ashe and his *Travels*. Syntax style is similar to other book reviews by Charles Caldwell, M.D. (1772-1853). See for example Caldwell's review of Daniel Drake's, *Natural and Statistical View, or Picture of Cincinnati*, in *The Port Folio*, January 1816, Vol. 15, pp. 25-38. Caldwell was an irritating authoritative egotistical old cuss in his younger years and impossible to deal with in his twilight years. He took over *The Port Folio* editorship in 1812; and in 1819 became head of the medical department at Transylvania University in Lexington, Kentucky. While there and elsewhere he managed to alienate practically everyone around him through his arrogant unyielding personality. See for example Emmet Field Horine, *Daniel Drake (1785-1852) Pioneer Physician of the Midwest*, (University of Pennsylvania Press, Philadelphia, 1961), pp. 188-191.

16. [Charles Caldwell], "Criticism — for the Port Folio," *The Port Folio*, February 1809, Vol. 1., No. 2, p. 152. Karl Friedrich Hieronymus von Münchhausen (1720-1797), was lionized in a book based upon oral traditions stemming from the Hannover region of Germany, concerning deeds and exploits of this professional soldier. Rudolf Erich Raspe in 1785, published the biography under the title, *Baron Münchausen's Narrative of his Marvelous Travels and Campaigns in Russia*. Münchhausen was a real person, although

his exploits are fictitious in the same vein as Háry János (Hungarian folk hero) or Lieutenant Kije (fictitious Russian military officer). Münchausen stories are still being reprinted in children story books in Europe, and in the 1988 Terry, Gilliam cinema vision of *The Adventures of Baron Muchausen.*

17. [Charles Caldwell], "Criticism," p. 162.

18. *Ibid.*, p. 161.

19. Anonymous, "Ashe's Travels in America," *The Edinburgh Review, or Critical Journal*, January 1810, Vol. 15, No. 30, p. 452.

20. John Melish, *Travels in the United States of America in the Years 1806 & 1807, and 1809, 1810, & 1811*, (Philadelphia, 1812), pp. 197-198. Christian Schultz, *Travels on an Inland Voyage Through the States of New York, Pennsylvania, Virginia, Ohio, Kentucky, and Tennessee, and Through the Territories of Indiana, Louisiana, Mississippi, and New Orleans; Performed in the Years 1807 and 1808; Including a Tour of Nearly Six Thousand Miles*, (New York, 1810).

21. John Bradbury, *Bradbury's Travels in the Interior of America 1809-1811*, Reuben Gold Thwaites, ed., *Early Western Travels 1748-1846*, (AMS Press, Inc., New York, 1966), Vol. V, p. 293.

22. Zadok Cramer, *The Navigator*, (Published by Cramer, Spear and Eichbaum, Robert Ferguson and Co., Pittsburgh, 8th edition, 1814), p. 259.

23. *Ibid.*

24. *Ibid.*

25. *Ibid.*

26. Thomas D. Clark, *Kentucky: Land of Contrast*, (Harper and Row, Publishers, New York, 1968), pp. 62, 78.

27. *Ibid.*, p. 78.

28. Reuben G. Thwaites, *Afloat on the Ohio*, (Doubleday and McClure Co., New York, 1900), pp. 113-114.

29. *Ibid.*, pp. 273-274.

30. *Ibid.*, p. 323.

31. Percy G. Adams, *Travelers and Travel Liars*, p. 192.

32. Jennifer Mossman, ed., *New Pseudonyms and Nicknames*, (Gale Research Company, Book Tower, Detroit, Michigan, 1983), p. 28. While in America, Ashe used: Thomas D'Arville, Thomas Arville, and Mr. Irvills.

33. André François Michaux, M.D., the French botanist adopted buck skins clothes over city dress and pioneer accouterments to get closer to the land. A slower paced life was needed in order to smell the flowers and become one with the land. *Travels to the Westward of the Alleghany Mountains in the States of Ohio, Kentucky, and Tennessee*, (W. Flint for J. Mawman, London, 1805).

34. Daniel Drake, *Pioneer Life in Kentucky: 1785-1800*, Emmet Field Horine, ed., (Henry Schuman, New York, 1948), p. 242.

35. John Melish, *Travels in the United States of America.* Thomas Ashe, *Travels*, pp. 187-188, makes no mention of Ballingal or the breakfast. Ashe's description of the Blue Licks could have been taken from any of a half a dozen sources.

36. Percy G. Adams, *Travelers and Travel Liars.* It is truly amazing the number of travel fakers who published fraudulent trips to the New World. Some of these tricksters covered their tracks so well, it took scholars more than a hundred years to expose their deception. Early adventurers and travel writers would plagiarize the best of these and recycle the hyperbole into their own adventurers. There is nothing like consistency when "borrowing" such "authoritative" works by Chateaubriand and Crèvecoeur. If the travel writers (as in Ashe's case), did not "borrow" their descriptions from recognized "authorities," then the reading public just might suspect some kind of deception.

CHAPTER THREE
# THOMAS ASHE AND THE BIG BONE CAPER

1. Daniel Drake, "Biographical Sketch of Doctor William Goforth," *The Western Spy*, (Cincinnati, Ohio), June 13, 1817, Vol. 2, No. 152, p. 2.

2. Meriwether Lewis to Thomas Jefferson, October 3, 1803, Donald Jackson, ed., *Letters of the Lewis and Clark Expedition with Related Documents 1783-1854*, (University of Illinois Press, Urbana, second edition, 1963), p. 126. Zadok Cramer, *The Navigator*, pp. 259-262. Daniel Drake, "Biographical Sketch of Doctor William Goforth," p. 2. This is possibly Dr. E. Reeder of Cincinnati. Reeder may not have been initially working with Goforth, yet had similar motives of curiosity and perhaps financial reward. The Lewis correspondence clearly indicates Goforth confided to Reeder his objectives in diggings for bones. Reeder took the initiative and launched his own private excavation.

3. Meriwether Lewis, *ibid.*, p. 127.

4. Zadok Cramer, *The Navigator*, (Cramer, Spear and Eichbaum, Pittsburg, 1814), p. 259.

5. Silvio A. Bedini, *Thomas Jefferson Statesman of Science*, (MacMillan Publishing Company, New York, 1990), p. 369. This is at variance with the out right gift by Goforth of part of his collection to Meriwether Lewis to be placed in the hands of Thomas Jefferson.

6. Donald Jackson, ed., *Letters of the Lewis and Clark Expedition with Related Documents 1783-1854*, p. 132.

7. Edward D. Mansfield, *Memoirs of the Life and Services of Daniel Drake, M. D.*, (Applegate and Company, Cincinnati, 1855), p. 51.

8. John Bradbury, *Bradbury's Travels*, pp. 292-293, traveled without a disguise two years later than Ashe's visit. This was at a time period of embargoes and the cry of the War Hawks for war with England. He was always met with kindness and hospitality and never as an aggressor.

9. John Bradford editorial introduction to [John Todd], "Letter from a Young Gentleman of Lexington to General Robert Todd," *The Kentucky Gazette*, April 18, 1809.

10. Zadok Cramer, *The Navigator*, p. 259.

11. *Ibid.*, p. 262.

12. *Ibid.*, p. 259. The original sales destination was New Orleans.

13. Daniel Drake, "Biographical Sketch of William Goforth."

14. There was an undelivered letter in the Cincinnati post office for Thomas Arville advertised in *The Western Spy and Hamilton Gazette*, April 8, 1806, Vol. 7, No. 37, Whole No. 349. Perhaps Ashe had not yet arrived with the bones from Pittsburgh.

15. Samuel Brown to Thomas Jefferson, unpublished, August 24, 1806, Manuscript Department, American Philosophical Society. The exhibited bone collection and Thomas Ashe were seen by Brown's friends: Judge Thomas Rodney, Dr. Frederick Seip, and Col. John Stuart. Stuart was a good judge of the bones, for Ashe had secured a Megalonyx claw, twice the size of the one Stuart recovered from a saltpeter cave in the Greenbrier country of Virginia (believed to be Haynes Cave, West Virginia; Fred Grady, "An Interesting Discovery in Haynes Cave," *D. C. Speleograph*, October 1993, Vol. 49, No. 10, p. 6). Stuart had seen the claw shortly after Goforth excavated it from the Big Bone Lick and frequently viewed it there after. He knew the Goforth claw was the same one in Ashe's possession.

Clearly, the travel dates are spurious. I think these dates are the one from the first river transit in mid-1805. More plausible, because Ashe takes charge of the bones in the winter from Dr. Richardson in Pittsburgh.

Francis H. Herrick, "Thomas Ashe and the Authenticity of his *Travels*," p. 56, said "the indefinite dates of the purely artificial letters of which the narrative is composed precludes the possibility of his [Thomas Ashe] having kept a diary, and he does not mention taking down notes, though it would seem probable that a man of his literary and scientific proclivities would have kept some record of the more important episodes of his travels."

16. Samuel Brown, "Letter." This letter had followed Brown all the way from Kentucky. John Brown had forwarded the letter from Frankfort on the 24th of July. John Brown to Thomas Jefferson, letter dated July 25, 1806, *in* James A. Padgett, "The Letters of

Honorable John Brown to the Presidents of the United States," *Register of the Kentucky Historical Society*, 1937, Vol. 35, No. 110, p. 23.

17. Samuel Brown, "Letter."

18. *Ibid.* John Stuart was a close friend of Brown and an Indian fighter in his own right.

19. William Goforth to Thomas Jefferson, undated letter, in Zadok Cramer, *The Navigator*, pp. 260-262.

20. *Ibid.*, p. 262.

21. Meriwether Lewis, "Letter," p. 127. Ross's agent at the lick was James Colquhoun. Lewis was given a generous collection of bones by Goforth to be shipped to Thomas Jefferson. The bones never made it to Jefferson's hands. The boat sank at the Natchez dock in the Spring of 1804; and most of the cargo was lost in the wreck and the remainder destroyed by curious salvage hands. Donald Jackson, *Letters of Lewis and Clark Expedition*, p. 132.

22. William Goforth, "Letter."

23. Thomas Ashe, *Memoirs*, Vol. 2, p. 201.

24. *Ibid.*, p. 208.

25. Thomas Ashe, *Memoirs of Mammoth, and Various other Extraordinary and Stupendous Bones, or Incognita, or Non-descript Animals Found in the Vicinity of the Ohio*, (Liverpool: G. F. Harris, 1806), 60 p.

26. Willard R. Jillson, *Big Bone Lick*, (Big Bone Lick Association, Pub. No. 1, The Standard Printing Company, 1936), p. 126. Jillson is making direct reference to Ashe's book, *Memoirs of Mammoth*. This book represents the fruits of Ashe's paleontological one-upmanship over his procurement of the William Goforth collection. Outline descriptive data is believed to have come from Goforth. Once Ashe had the bones from the repository of Dr. Andrew Richardson in Pittsburgh; Goforth could not write an accurate description nor did he know the exact number contained in the five ton collection. With Goforth's "eye for anatomy," he reconstructed from memory in part the size, number and body parts of the most significant pieces to Casper Wistar, Jr., and Thomas Jefferson's request of December 1, 1806. William Goforth, "Letter" to Thomas Jefferson, no date, Zadok Cramer, *The Navigator*, pp. 260-262. Ashe's physical anatomical description is thorough, with frequent borrowing from unnamed authorities.

27. Thomas Ashe, *Memoirs*, Vol. 2, pp. 209-210.

28. *Ibid.*, p. 212.

29. *Ibid.*, p. 215. William Bullock was a jeweller, goldsmith, and museum exhibitor. By 1812, he had acquired the collections made by Captain James Cook (1728-1779) from his circumoceanic voyage around the world.

30. [William Newnham Blane], *An Excursion Through the United States and Canada During the Years 1822-1823*, (London: Baldwin, Cradock and Foy, 1824), pp. 132-133.

31. Louis Leonard Tucker, "'Ohio Show-Shop' The Western Museum of Cincinnati 1820-1867," *A Cabinet of Curiosities*, (The University Press of Virginia, Charlottesville, 1967), pp. 81-82.

32. *Ibid.*, p. 74.

33. [William Newnham Blane], *An Excursion Through the United States*, pp. 278, 276 While in Mammoth Cave, he learns of the Indian mummy "preserved with gum and aromatic herbs." He asserted the "accurate" map of the cave and its length made by Nahum Ward's visit in 1815 was from his own observations a gross exaggeration. Blane makes no mention of the Indian mummy in the museum collection nor from any of the other museums in Cincinnati.

34. *Ibid.*, p. 133. This is the only reference signifying the bones never made it out of the country.

35. Daniel Drake, "Biography of William Goforth."

36. William Bullock, letter to William Cooper, dated November 24, 1828, in "Notice of Big-Bone Lick," *The Monthly American Journal of Geology and Natural Sciences*, 1831, Vol. 1, No. 3 pp.158-174, 205-217. Lewis Collins, *Historical Sketches of Kentucky*, (Lewis Collins, Maysville, Ky., and J. A. and U. P. James, Cincinnati, 1847), p. 118.

37. Zadok Cramer, *The Navigator*, p. 259.

38. Silvino A. Bedini, *Thomas Jefferson Statesman of Science*, p. 494.

# CHAPTER FOUR
## EARLY INVESTIGATIONS OF THE CATACOMB STORY

1. [Charles Caldwell], "Criticism — for the Port Folio," *The Port Folio,* February 1809, Vol. 1., No. 2, pp. 150-162.

2. *Ibid.*, p. 160. The review went on deaf ears, for the European intellectual fraternity rarely ever imported American periodicals. They thought the old "Colonies" had nothing to offer of substance from its fledgling science and literature. Robert V. Bruce, *The Launching of Modern American Science,* (Alfred A. Knopf, New York, 1987) p. 12. Import tax on books from overseas was deemed to cost more than the worth of the book.

3. Anonymous, "Travels in America," *The Edinburgh Review*, (1810), Vol. 15, No. 30, pp. 451-452.

4. I have not see this issue of the British *Quarterly Review*, May 1809, Vol. 1: p. 300, as quoted in Percy G. Adams, *Travelers and Travel Liars 1660-1800*, (University of California Press, Berkley and Los Angeles, 1962), p. 192. What is comforting respecting Ashe and his *Travels,* is the *Quarterly Review* had strong anti-American sentiments.

5. Barton was teaching botany, materia medica, and natural history at the University of Pennsylvania in Philadelphia. He taught along side professors Benjamin Rush (1745-1813) and Caspar Wistar, Jr. (1761-1818).

6. [John Todd], "Letter from a Young Gentleman of Lexington to General Robert Todd," *The Kentucky Gazette*, April 18, 1809.

7. John Todd was Daniel Drake's classmate in 1806 (the year Drake graduated), at the University of Pennsylvania. Todd graduated in 1810; is the "second cousin by blood and an uncle by marriage of Mrs. Abraham (Mary Todd) Lincoln; Daniel Drake, *Pioneer Life in Kentucky,* (Emmet Field Horine, ed., Henry Schuman, New York, 1948), p. 91.

8. [John Todd], "Letter." Robert Todd was the brother of Levi Todd (1756-1807), one of the founders of Lexington.

9. See for example the undated *Kentucky Reporter* reprint in Milo M. Quaife, "Thomas Ashe's Travels," *The Mississippi Valley Historical Review*, (1914), Vol. 1, No. 2, pp. 574-575. Reprinted in Angelo I. George, ed., *Prehistoric Mummies from the Mammoth Cave Area: Foundations and Concepts,* (George Publishing Company, 1990), pp. 16-17.

10. [John Todd], "Letter."

11. William A. Leavy, "A Memoir of Lexington and its Vicinity," *The Register of the Kentucky Historical Society,* (1942), Vol.40, No. 131. John Melish, *Travels in the United States of America in the Years 1806 & 1807, and 1809, 1810, & 1811*, (Philadelphia, 1812), pp. 197-198, interview with Mr. Ballingal at the Blue Licks in Kentucky, places Ashe at his breakfast table. Ashe would make no known personal contact south of here in Lexington.

12. Timothy Flint, *The History and Geography of the Mississippi Valley*, (2nd edition, E. H. Flint and L. R. Lincoln, Cincinnati, Ohio, 1832), p. 364.

13. Timothy Flint, *Recollections of the Last Ten Years in the Valley of the Mississippi*, (1823), George R. Brooks, ed., (Southern Illinois University Press, Feffer & Simons, Inc., London, 1968), p. 126.

# CHAPTER FIVE
## LATER INVESTIGATIONS

1. George W. Ranck, *History of Lexington Kentucky*, (Robert Clarke and Company, Cincinnati, 1872), p. 2. Ranck evidently took great pains to substantiate the Lexington Catacomb as reported by Thomas Ashe. He quotes from the John Todd "Letter" to Robert Todd that was published in 1809. Ranck said the subterranean cemetery story had an "improbable air" and that it is a "tradition" of Lexington. Ranck does add some original color that the discoverers were pioneers "most probably from Boonesborough." Ranck received too great a measure of flack over his reporting Indian mummies buried in a catacomb beneath the city of Lexington. He was condemned for this, thereby casting all of his history writings as suspects in shoddy scholarship.

2. William A. Leavy, "A Memoir of Lexington and its Vicinity," *The Register of the Kentucky Historical Society*, 1942, Vol. 40, No. 131, pp. 107-269. Leavy gives short biographical sketches of prominent individuals living in Lexington. He was a contemporary of Charles Wilkins, John D. Clifford, Samuel Brown, and Constantine S. Rafinesque. The *Memoir* was written only for Leavy's edification, it was never intended to be published. The primary documentation does give us valuable insight on how one man thought about the Catacomb.

3. *Ibid.*, p. 114.

4. *Ibid.*, p. 116.

5. *Ibid.* Leavy gives solace that Ashe never visited the city. No Lexingtonian could remember such a character as Ashe or anyone remotely like him ever making a visit to the community. Wherever Ashe visited, he would search out the most prominent individuals in the major cities and towns. He was a social climber and name dropper of the worst sort. In the *Travels* chapter covering the Lexington locality, no names are mentioned. Nor, is there any kind of social interaction with the town's people. Because of these key omissions, I am of the opinion and agree with Leavy that Ashe never went to Lexington. Therefore, he could not have visited the Catacomb. Ashe's autobiography is also silent on his sojourn in Lexington and the Catacomb. Ashe could not have visited the extensive grassland prairie called The Barrens. A feature he would have had to traverse to get to any of the great caves in the region. He would discover the Barrens was not a desert, nor was it devoid of water as pictured by Filson in his *Kentucke*. A place Filson never saw, and a source Ashe quotes when describing this part of Kentucky. The locality was devoid or barren of trees, even in Ashe's time, hence its name.

The local newspapers rarely issued notices of visitors to their city. Only famous politicians and noted war heroes were given this treatment. The tide of European visitors to Lexington never made it to print. The human interest story was a long time in coming to the print media.

6. Joseph Jones, *Explorations of the Aboriginal Remains of Tennessee*, Smithsonian Contributions to Knowledge, (1876), No. 259, p. 5. This is a rewritten account from Timothy Flint, *The History and Geography of the Mississippi Valley*, (2nd edition, E. H. Flint and L. R. Lincoln, Cincinnati, Ohio, 1832), p. 364. Flint's reference to the Gapped Tooth Mummy is from Tennessee and not from Short Cave as it implies.

7. Robert Peter, *History of Fayette County*, (O. L. Baskin and Co., Chicago, Illinois, Historical Publication, 1882), p. 221.

8. *Ibid.*

9. Harold Meloy, *Mummies of Mammoth Cave*, (Micron Publishing Co., Shelbyville, Indiana, 1971), p. 7. Today, Grand Avenue Cave is called Long Cave. Circumstances surrounding the discovery of Little Al is discussed in Chapter Thirteen.

10. See for example Lewis Collins, and Richard H. Collins, *History of Kentucky*, (Covington, 1882), Vol. 2, p. 332.

11. William D. Funkhouser and William S. Webb, *Ancient Life in Kentucky*, Kentucky Geological Survey of Kentucky, (1928), Ser. 6, Vol. 34, p. 140.

12. *Ibid.*

13. Charles D. Hockensmith, "Archaeological Research in Fayette County, Kentucky," *Kentucky Archaeological Association*, Bull. 9 for 1976, (1978), p. 10.

David Ross was the owner of Big Bone Cave and a copious salt spring and lick called Big Bone Lick, Boone County, Kentucky.

14. Don Edwards, "Does Link to Egyptians Lie Beneath Main Street?" *Lexington-Herald-Leader*, (Lexington, Kentucky), June 8, 1987, p. B10.

15. See Chapter Twelve for a complete discussion on this subject.

# CHAPTER SIX
# THE MOUND BUILDERS AND THE CORE OF THE CATACOMB

1. John Filson, *The Discovery, Settlement and Present State of Kentucke*, (James Adams, Wilmington, Del., 1784). Ashe had read the book either from the original or in Gilbert Imley, *A Topographical Description of the Western Territory of North America*,

(J. Debrett, London, 1797, third edition). Imley reprints many natural history papers on North American archaeology, history, geography and exploration. The book is a treasure trove of information under one cover. Ashe, without naming Filson says in *Travels*, p. 36, "The first explorer [Daniel Boone] of Kentucky, hired an author residing in Philadelphia, to write an animated and embellished description of that country....the work possessed every merit except truth." With that revelation, Ashe incorporates much of Filson into his own travelogue without credit, as if it came from his own observations. Zadok Cramer, *The Navigator*, (Cramer, Spear, and Eichbaum, Pittsburgh, 1811), p. 107.

2. John Filson, *ibid.*, p. 33.

3. Anonymous, "Traditional Myth of Catacombs Under City Exploded by Miller; Professor Claims Popular Story Has No Basis of Facts," *Lexington Herald*, (Lexington, Kentucky), November 21, 1920.

4. Thomas Ashe, *Travels in America Performed in 1806, for the Purpose of Exploring the Rivers Allegheny, Monongahela, Ohio, and Mississippi, and Ascertaining the Produce and Condition of their Banks and Vicinity*, (Reprinted for Wm. Sawyer & Co. by E. M. Blunt, State Street, Newburyport, London, 1808), p. 196.

5. *Ibid.*, p. 199.

6. *Ibid.*, p. 198.

7. *Ibid.*

8. John Hay Farnham, "Extract of a Letter from John H. Farnham, Esq. a Member of the American Antiquarian Society, describing the Mammoth Cave, in Kentucky," *Archaeologia Americana, Transactions and Collections of the American Antiquarian Society*, (1820), Vol. 1, p. 359.

9. Thomas Ashe, *Travels*, pp. 234-235.

10. *Ibid.*, p. 207.

11. John P. Campbell, "Of the Aborigines of the Western Country," *The Port Folio*, June 1816, Vol. 1, No. 6, and July 1816, Vol. 2, No. 1.

12. Constantine S. Rafinesque, "Ancient History, or Annals of Kentucky: Introduction to the History Antiquities of the State of Kentucky," *in* Humphrey Marshall, *History of Kentucky*, (Frankfort, 1824).

13. Stephen Williams, *Fantastic Archaeology, the Wild Side of North American Prehistory*, (University of Pennsylvania Press, Philadelphia, 1991).

14. Dana Olson, *Prince Madoc: Founder of Clark County, Indiana*. (Dana Olson, Jeffersonville, Indiana, 1987). Simply an amazing trip into fantastic archaeology.

15. Ephraim G. Squire, and Edward H. Davis, *Ancient Monuments of the Mississippi Valley*, (Washington D. C.: Smithsonian Institution, 1848).

# CHAPTER SEVEN
# CATACOMBS AND SALTPETER CAVES

1. Angelo I. George, "Saltpeter and Gunpowder Manufacturing in Kentucky," *The Filson Club History Quarterly*, (1986), Vol. 60, No. 2, p. 200.

2. *Ibid.*, p. 198.

3. Angelo I. George, "Saltpeter Rock Mining Activity in Dixon Cave, Edmonson County, Kentucky," *Journal of Spelean History*, (1986), Vol. 20, No. 4, p. 92; Angelo I. George, *Mammoth Cave Saltpeter Works*, (H.M.I. Press, 2005), pp.106-133.

4. Thomas Ashe, *Travels in America Performed in 1806, for the Purpose of Exploring the Rivers Allegheny, Monongahela, Ohio, and Mississippi, and Ascertaining the Produce and Condition of their Banks and Vicinity*, (Reprinted for Wm. Sawyer & Co. by E. M. Blunt, State Street, Newburyport, London, 1808), p. 197.

5. Daniel Drake, "XXXIV," *The Daniel Drake Papers of the Draper Manuscripts*, 2 O 30, reprinted in Angelo I. George, ed., *Prehistoric Mummies of the Mammoth Cave Area*, (George Publishing Company, 1990), p. 52. The undated news article used an 1811 date for the discovery of the mummies in Smith County on Dutch River. This is a garbled Copperas (Big Bone) Cave report. The entrance opening is too small relative to the main entrance to Big Bone, but could be the south or Arch Entrance.

6. Anonymous, "Big Bone and Arch Caves," *Village Record*, (West Chester, Pennsylvania), August 8, 1821.

7. *Ibid.*; John Haywood, *The Natural and Aboriginal History of Tennessee*, (Nashville, 1823), pp. 163-164. George M. Crothers, *Final Report on the Survey and Assessment of the Prehistoric and Historic Archaeological Remains in Big Bone Cave, Van Buren County, Tennessee*, (Department of Anthropology, University of Tennessee, Knoxville, Tennessee, 1986), pp. 15, 32.

8. John D. Clifford, "Indian Antiquities, Letter VI," *The Western Review and Miscellaneous Magazine*, February 1820, Vol. 2, No. 1, p. 35-36. After Clifford died in 1820, the bones were sold sometime after 1823 to Joseph Dorfeuille owner and curator of the Western Museum in Cincinnati. Richard R. Harlan, "Description of the Fossil Bones of the Megalonyx, Discovered in "White Cave," Kentucky," *Journal of the Academy of Natural Sciences of Philadelphia*, (1831), Ser. 1, Vol. 6, part 2, p. 1. White Cave should read White County, Tennessee.

9. Timothy Flint, *Recollections of the Last Ten Years in the Valley of the Mississippi*, (1823), George R. Brooks, ed., (Southern Illinois University Press, Feffer & Simons, Inc., London, 1968), p. 126. Anonymous, "Big Bone and Arch Caves," refers to a feathered cape full of Indian bones. D. T. Maddox, "Big Bone Cave," *Niles Weekly Register - Supplement to Volume 5*, pp. 175-176, letter dated August 17, 1813.

10. John D. Clifford, "Indian Antiquities", p. 35. He had been associated with the purchase of saltpeter from this cave since perhaps 1806.

11. George M. Crothers, *Final Report...Big Bone Cave*, pp. 16, 43.

12. Angelo I. George, "Search for the Copperas Cave of Mummies, Tennessee," *Journal of Spelean History*, (1993), Vol. 27, No. 2, pp. 25-30.

13. Thomas Ashe, *Travels*, p. 198.

14. *Ibid.*, p. 197.

15. *Ibid.*, p. 198.

16. Ebenezer Meriam, "Mammoth Cave," *New York Municipal Gazette*, February 21, 1844, Vol. 1, No. 17, p. 318.

17. Moses Fiske, "Conjectures Respecting the Ancient Inhabitants of North America," *Archaeologia Americana, Transactions and Collections of the American Antiquarian Society*, (1820), Vol. 1, p. 303.

18. Timothy Flint, *Recollections*, p. 126.

19. The Linden tree was still called the Linn tree as recently as circa 1900. Its bark was used to make baskets in southern Jefferson and in Green counties, Kentucky. Elmer C. Vance, personal oral communication, December 1974, could remember making and using these baskets on his fathers farm in Green County and later on his own farm in the Wetwoods District of southern Jefferson County, Kentucky.

20. Ebenezer Meriam, "Mammoth Cave," p. 318.

21. John H. Farnham, "Extract of a Letter from John H. Farnham, Esq. a Member of the American Antiquarian Society, Describing the Mammoth Cave, in Kentucky," *Archaeologia Americana, Transactions and Collections of the American Antiquarian Society*, (1820), Vol. 1, p. 360.

22. Dr. James H. Rice to Dr. Daniel Drake, unpublished letter in Draper Manuscripts, 2 0 30 ff, State Historical Library, Madison, Wisconsin, reprinted in Angelo I. George, ed., *Prehistoric Mummies from the Mammoth Cave Area*, p. 85-90.

23. This is probably the oldest Egyptian burial technique now known as desert sand burials.

24. Thomas Ashe, *Travels*, p. 196.

25. [Charles Cassedy] *in* Pleasant M. Miller, "Preservation of Human Bodies in a Cave, in Tennessee," *Medical Repository*, (1812), Third Hexade, Vol. 3, p. 147.

26. Charles Wilkins, "Letter from Charles Wilkins, Esq. A Member of the American Antiquarian Society, to Samuel M. Burnside, Esq., letter dated October 2, 1817," *Archaeologia Americana, Transactions and Collections of the American Antiquarian Society*, (1820), Vol. 1, p. 363. A similar type of excavation is preserved to the right of the Methodist Church over on the other side of the elevated water pipes next to the cave wall

in Mammoth Cave. This excavation through breakdown is testimonial to the industry the saltpeter miners went to in order to reach nitrate impregnated soils.

27. *Ibid.*, p. 362.

28. Thomas Ashe, *Travels*, p. 196.

29. Ebenezer Meriam, "Mammoth Cave," p. 20.

30. Thomas Ashe, *Travels*, p. 197.

31. *Ibid.*

32. Charles Wilkins, "Letter," p. 363.

33. D. T. Maddox, "Big Bone Cave," p. 175.

34. Thomas Ashe, *Travels*, p. 196.

35. John D. Clifford, Letter to Benjamin S. Barton, dated September 4, 1811, *in* Angelo I. George, ed., *Prehistoric Mummies from the Mammoth Cave Area: Foundations and Concepts*, (George Publishing Company, Louisville, Kentucky, 1990), pp. 67-68.

36. Charles Wilkins, "Letter," p. 362.

37. Charles Cassedy, "Western Antiquities," *Nashville Republican & State Gazette*, (Nashville, Tennessee), January 16, 1829, p. 2. Reprinted and condensed in *The Delaware Patron*, (Delaware, Ohio), Vol. 9, No. 24.

38. *Ibid.*

39. Charles Cassedy, *Western Chronicle*, (Columbia, Tennessee), November 17, 1810, p. 2.

40. *Ibid.*

41. Charles Cassedy, "Western Antiquities."

42. Pleasant M. Miller, "Preservation of Human Bodies in a Cave, in Tennessee: in a Letter from Pleasant M. Miller, Esq. of Knoxville, dated May 1st, 1811," *Medical Repository*, (1812), Vol. 3, p. 147.

43. John Haywood, *The Natural and Aboriginal History of Tennessee*, pp. 163-164.

44. Moses Fiske, "Conjectures Respecting the Ancient Inhabitants of North America," pp. 303-304.

45. Anonymous, "XXXIV," Daniel Drake papers of the Draper Manuscripts, 2 O 30, reprinted in Angelo I. George, *Prehistoric Mummies of the Mammoth Cave Region*, p. 52.

46. Thomas I. Wray, "Minerals from Tennessee," *The American Mineralogical Journal*, (1810), Vol. 1, No. 4, pp. 265-266.

47. Harold Meloy, personal oral communication, August 16, 1975. When *Mummies of Short Cave and the Great Catacomb Mystery* was first published in 1986, no contemporary knew of mutilation occurring to the mummies in Big Bone Cave.

48. Thomas Ashe, *Travels*, p. 196.

49. John H. Farnham, "Undated Letter," p. 361.

50. Charles Cassedy, "Western Antiquities."

51. Charles Wilkins, "Letter," p. 362.

# CHAPTER EIGHT
# GEOGRAPHY OF THE CATACOMB

1. Henry C. Mercer, "The Finding of the Remains of the Fossil Sloth at Big Bone Cave, Tennessee," *Proceedings of the American Philosophical Society*, (1896), Vol. 36, No. 154, pp. 9-10. L. E. Ward, "More Subterranean Adventures," *National Speleological Society Bulletin*, (1945), No. 7, pp. 25-27. The George A. White map of Short Cave is only a sketch map with no bar scale. Angelo I. George, "Short Cave Saga: A Historical Field Trip to a Famous Kentucky Cave," *Guidebook to the 1977 Kentucky Speleofest*, (Louisville Speleopress, 1977), pp. 3-1 to 3-11. Brunton, tripod and tape survey of Short Cave by the Louisville Grotto.

2. Thomas Ashe, *Travels in America Performed in 1806, for the Purpose of Exploring the Rivers Allegheny, Monongahela, Ohio, and Mississippi, and Ascertaining the Produce and Condition of their Banks and Vicinity*, (Reprinted for Wm. Sawyer & Co. by E. M. Blunt, State Street, Newburyport, London, 1808), p. 197.

3. Michael Allen, *Western Rivermen*, 1763-1861, (Louisiana State University Press, Baton Rouge, Louisiana, 1990), p. 83.

4. Thomas Ashe, *Travels*, pp. 251-252.

5. Zadok Cramer, *The Navigator*, (Published by Cramer, Spear and Eichbaum, Pittsburgh, 7th edition, 1811), p. 137. All of the earlier editions contain a note on Cave-In-Rock.

6. Thomas Ashe, *Travels*, p. 252.

7. Otto A. Rothert, *The Outlaws of Cave-in-Rock*, (Books for Library Press, Freeport, New York, 1924), p. 19.

8. Charles Wilkins, "Letter from Charles Wilkins, Esq. A Member of the American Antiquarian Society, to Samuel M. Burnside, Esq., letter dated October 2, 1817," *Archaeologia Americana, Transactions and Collections of the American Antiquarian Society*, (1820), Vol. 1, p. 363.

9. Henry C. Mercer, "The Finding of the Remains of the Fossil Sloth at Big Bone Cave, Tennessee," p. 9.

10. Thomas Ashe, *Travels*, p. 200.

11. Salts Cave and Mammoth Cave mummy sites are the result of cave accidents and are not true cave burials.

12. Samuel Brown, "A Description of a Cave on Crooked Creek, with Remarks and Observations on Nitre and Gunpowder," *Transactions of the American Philosophical Society*, (1809), Vol. 6, pp. 235-247.

13. Thomas Ashe, *Travels*, p. 235. When Ashe describes the saline works at Big Bone Lick, he also discusses saltpeter caves in Kentucky. All of which was taken from Cramer's *Navigator* guidebook on the rivers.

14. *Ibid.*, p. 203.

15. *Ibid.*, p. 206.

16. *Ibid.*, p. 213.

17. Israel Ludlow was one of the founders and surveyor of the City of Cincinnati. Ashe is the only one to report about Ludlow's antiquarian interest.

18. Thomas Ashe, *Travels*, p. 213.

19. *Ibid.*, p. 231.

20. Charles Wilkins Short and Mary Churchill Richardson, "A Chronological Record of the Families of Charles Wilkins Short and Mary Henry Churchill," Manuscript Department, University of Louisville Medical Library, (type written, 1979), p. 95.

21. *Ibid.*, pp. 94-95.

22. The actual owners of Short Cave during the time of the child and Fawn Hoof discovery is George and Lenard McLean. They purchased 50 acres from Richard Richardson on September 1, 1810. The parcel of land was surveyed on October 19, 1810. This property along with Long Cave was then sold to John Hann of Lancaster, Kentucky, on January 10, 1812 Stanley D. Sides and Norman Warnell, "Long Cave, Mammoth Cave National Park, Edmonson County, Kentucky," *Proceedings: Mammoth Cave National Park's 10th Research Symposium*, February 14-15, 2013, pp. 139-142.

23. Charles Wilkins Short and Mary Churchill Richardson, "A Chronological Record of the Families of Charles Wilkins Short and Mary Henry Churchill," p. 95.

24. Marsha Mullins, "Mammoth Cave Saltpetre Works," unpublished manuscript, Mammoth Cave Superintendence Office, Historic American Engineering Record, No. KY-13, p. 9. V. T. Rousseau, "Pages from the Past: Boom Times Be-Dazzle Barren County Pioneers," *Glasgow Daily Newspaper*, (Glasgow, Kentucky), February 20, 1939. It is not known if Peyton Short's Greenfield slaves were the ones employed by Wilkins in Mammoth Cave and Short Cave.

25. Charles Wilkins Short and Mary Churchill Richardson, "A Chronological Record of the Families of Charles Wilkins Short and Mary Henry Churchill," p. 122.

26. *The Mummy*, 1932 motion picture in which Boris Karloff played the immortal anguished Imhotep in Karl Freund's classic horror film.

27. Douglas W. Schwartz, *Conceptions of Kentucky Prehistory*, (University of Kentucky Press, 1967), p. 15.

28. Louise M. Robbins, "Prehistoric People of the Mammoth Cave Area," Patty Jo Watson, ed., *Archeology of the Mammoth Cave Area*, (Academic Press, New York, 1974), pp. 159-160. Watson's book is the very best monograph on the archeology of the Mammoth Cave territory.

# CHAPTER NINE
# COPPERAS CAVE OF MUMMIES

1. Timothy Flint, *Recollections of the Last Ten Years in the Valley of the Mississippi*, (1823), George R. Brooks, ed., (Southern Illinois University Press, Feffer & Simons, Inc., London, 1968), p. 126. Anonymous, "Important Discovery," *Farmer's Repository*, (Charlestown, Virginia), October 27, 1809, p. 1. [Charles Cassedy], *Western Chronicle*, (Columbia, Tennessee), November 17, 1810, p. 2, Reprint from the *Review*. Originally published in *The Examiner*, (Nashville, Tennessee), no copies known.

2. John D. Clifford, Letter to Benjamin S. Barton, dated September 4, 1811, in Angelo I. George, ed., *Prehistoric Mummies from the Mammoth Cave Area: Foundations and Concepts*, (George Publishing Company, Louisville, Kentucky, 1990), pp. 67-68.

3. Caleb Atwater, "Observations on the Remains of Civilization and Population, Extant on the Vast Plains Situated South of the North-American Lakes; Communicated by Caleb Atwater, Esq. of Circleville, Ohio, to the Hon. Samuel L. Mitchill, of New York, in a Letter, dated January 16, 1818," *The American Monthly Magazine and Critical Review*, (1818), Vol. 2, No. 5, p. 335.

4. [Charles Cassedy], 1810; Moses Fiske, "Conjectures Respecting the Ancient Inhabitants of North America," *Archaeologia Americana, Transactions and Collections of the American Antiquarian Society*, (1820), Vol. 1, pp. 303-305, 307; and John Haywood, *The Natural and Aboriginal History of Tennessee*, (Printed by George Wilson, Nashville, Tennessee, 1823), p. 163.

5. Angelo I. George, "Search for the Copperas Cave of Mummies, Tennessee," *Journal of Spelean History*, (1993), Vol. 27, No. 2, pp. 25-30.

6. [Charles Cassedy], *Western Chronicle*.

7. The Indian Black Fox Trail crossed the Caney Fork a few miles up stream from Rock Island. Monroe Seals, *History of White County Tennessee*, (The Reprint Company, Spartanburg, S.C., 1988, reprint of 1935 edition), p. 1.

8. [Charles Cassedy], *Western Chronicle*.

9. Pleasant M. Miller, "Preservation of Human Bodies in a Cave, in Tennessee: in a Letter from Pleasant M. Miller, Esq. of Knoxville, dated May 1st, 1811," *Medical Repository*, (1812), Vol. 3, pp. 147-148.

10. Charles Cassedy, "Western Antiquities," *Nashville Republican & State Gazette*, (Nashville, Tennessee), January 16, 1829, p. 2. Reprinted and condensed in *The Delaware Patron*, (Delaware, Ohio), Vol. 9, No. 24, reprinted from *Nashville Republican*. Cassedy had a lifelong problem with chronic alcoholism. Walter T. Durham, "Charles Cassedy Early Nineteenth Century Tennessee Writer," *Tennessee Historical Quarterly*, (1977), Vol. 36, No. 3, part 1, p. 306; such a condition could blur the substance of events in the past.

11. *Ibid*. Cassedy is in error on this January date.

12. *Ibid*.

13. *Ibid*.

14. *Ibid*.

15. Pleasant M. Miller, "Preservation of Human Bodies in a Cave, in Tennessee," p. 147.

16. Charles Cassedy, "Western Antiquities." First published reference for the amputation of both feet.

17. Thomas I. Wray, "Minerals from Tennessee," *The American Mineralogical Journal*, (1810), Vol. 1, No. 4, p. 266.

18. William Short was the older brother of Peyton Short. William Short produced a distinguished career in the international diplomatic corps. He was Thomas Jefferson's protégé, long time private secretary in France, owned land and a house near Monticello, and generally followed his mentor everywhere he went. In 1809, Short accepted the post of minister to the court of St. Petersburg. He got as far as Paris when the Senate rescinded his Jeffersonian appointment. He arrived back in country in 1810, where he remained until his death. Technically, we had no minister to Russia in 1811. Jefferson is using the term "Russian Ambassador" as an honorarium, much as one is called General, long after retirement from the military. I do not know when Cassedy presented the specimens for Jefferson's and Short's view nor when they were deposited in Scudder's Museum. If

Cassedy's April cave exploration date is correct, then he probably arrived at Jefferson's home sometime in April or May.

19. Moses Fiske, "Conjectures Respecting the Ancient Inhabitants of North America," p. 303. This accounts for three mummies as reported by Caleb Atwater, "Observations on the remains of civilization and population, extant on the vast plains situated south of the North-American Lakes," p. 335.

20. Timothy Flint, *Recollections*, p. 137; James Flint, *Letters from America, Containing Observations on the...Western States*, (1822) in Reuben Gold Thwaites, ed., *Early Western Travels 1748-1846*, (AMS Press, Inc., New York, 1966), Vol. 9, p. 126.

John D. Clifford was a merchant, artifact collector, naturalist, saltpeter speculator, and entrepreneur of the Lexington Museum. With a passion and instinct, he actively acquired Indian artifacts, fossils, minerals, and biological specimens. Thereby gaining the respect and admiration of his very close friend and companion, Constantine S. Rafinesque (1783-1840). Prior to 1813, bones of the Megalonyx were unearthed in Big Bone Cave. Gerard Troost in a letter from Moses "Squire" Fisk (1760-1840) said "a full barrel of newly discovered bones was sent to Mr Clifford. He believes that the saltpetre made there was chiefly sold to Mr Clifford." G. Troost, "On the Localities in Tennessee in Which Bones of the Gigantic Mastodon and Megalonyx jeffersonii are Found," *Transactions of the Geological Society of Pennsylvania*, 1835, Vol. 1, pp. 237-238.

21. Timothy Flint, *Recollections*, p. 58. Henry Clay was the leader of the War Hawks that pushed us into war with Great Britain, as such, he became the peace maker for a truce to end the war.

22. *Kentucky Gazette*, October 9, 1815, n.s., Vol. 1, No. 41, p. 3; *Kentucky Gazette*, October 16, 1815, n.s., Vol. 1, No. 42, p. 3.

23. Timothy Flint, *Recollections*, p. 126. Flint's recollections are after a laps of ten years. According to George R. Brooks, the editor of the 1968 reprint of *Recollections*, mote points of inaccuracies are scattered throughout the book. One should use some latitude because Flint had lost his original notebooks on his travels. The mummy is a female Indian found in 1811. Fawn Hoof would tour Lexington at a later date.

24. *Ibid.*

25. *Ibid.*

26. James Flint, *Letters from America*, p. 137.

27. John Bradford, *The Voice of the Frontier*, Thomas D. Clark, editor (The University Press of Kentucky, 1993), p. 257.

28. White Cave is located about 0.45 miles south-southwest from Mammoth Cave's main entrance. White Cave is our first direct clue as to the identity of the mummy cave. Gerard Troost, "On the Localities in Tennessee in Which Bones of the Gigantic Mastodon and Megalonyx Jeffersonii are Found," *Transactions of the Geological Society of Pennsylvania*, (1835), Vol. 1, pp. 236-237. He identified Clifford's White Cave Megalonyx bone site as Big Bone Cave in then White County, Tennessee. Richard Harlan, "Notice of the Os Ilium of the Megalonyx Laqueatus, from Big Bone Cave, White County, Tennessee," *Transactions of the Geological Society of Pennsylvania*, (1835), Vol. 1, p. 347; concurred with Troost's site identification work. Any perishable artifacts labeled White Cave, Kentucky, from the Clifford collection must be assigned to Big Bone Cave. White Cave should read as White County, Tennessee.

29. Alexander Bullitt, *Rambles in the Mammoth Cave, During the year 1844 by a Visiter*, (Morton and Griswold, Louisville, Kentucky, 1845), p. 24; Horace Martin, *Pictorial Guide to the Mammoth Cave, Kentucky*, (Stringer & Townsend, New York, 1851), p. 27.

30. Harold Meloy, *Mummies of Mammoth Cave*, (Micron Publishing Company, Shelbyville, Indiana, 1971), p. 38.

31. Caleb Atwater, *The Writings of Caleb Atwater*, (Scott and Wright printers, Columbus, Ohio, 1833), p. 6. Gerard Troost, "On the Localities in Tennessee in Which Bones of the Gigantic Mastodon and Megalonyx Jeffersonii are Found," pp. 236-237.

32. John Francis McDermott, "Foreword," Albert C. Kock, *Journey Through a Part of the United States of North America in the Years 1844 to 1846*, translated and edited by Ernst A. Stadler, (Southern Illinois University Press, Feffrer & Simons, Inc., London,

1972), p. xi; and Ernst A. Stadler, p. xviii. John Francis McDermott, "Dr. Koch's Wonderful Fossils," *Missouri Historical Society Bulletin*, (1948), Vol. 4, No. 4, pp. 233-256.

33. Koch was a self taught paleontologist who made significant Pleistocene vertebrate discoveries. He was the first to publish the association of Indian artifacts in situ with Mastodon bones. Suggesting these beast were contemporaries with those that killed it. This belief cast his research as a hoax and his theory was only vindicated in the late twentieth century. John Francis McDermott, "Dr. Koch's Wonderful Fossils," *Missouri Historical Society Bulletin*, (1948), Vol. 4, No. 4, p. 233. *Missouri Republican*, (St. Louis, Missouri), January 27, 1836. The Clifford collection was split up once again and probably sold in the summer of 1829. Koch traveled through America and may have purchased the mummy at that time. The Megalonyx bones went to John Price Wetherill who then gave them to the Academy of Natural Sciences in Philadelphia. Richard Harlan, "Description of the Fossil Bones of the Megalonyx, Discovered in "White Cave," Kentucky," *Journal of the Academy of Natural Sciences of Philadelphia*, (1831), Ser. 1, Vol. 6, part II, p. 1.

In 1829, Albert Koch arrived in America from the Duchy of Saxony, Germany. Little is known of his stay in this country until his arrival in St. Louis in 1836. Ernst A. Stadler, "Introduction," pp. xviii, xix. Koch sold his museum, less his major attraction (the Missourium Pleistocene skeleton) in 1841 to W. S. McPherson in January 1841. John Francis McDermott, "Dr. Koch's Wonderful Fossils," pp. 248-249.

34. John C. Ewers, "William Clark's Indian Museum in St. Louis: 1816-1838," *A Cabinet of Curiosities*, (The University Press of Virginia, Charlottesville, 1967), p. 67. Clark had opened his door soon after April 2, 1816, as the first museum west of the Mississippi River. A few artifacts from the 1803-1806 Missouri expedition were probably displayed as early as 1807 along with his personal collection of Indian artifacts and Mammoth bones from Big Bone Lick and Louisville. *Ibid.*, pp.53-54. Inspection of William Clark and Meriwether Lewis Clark, "Catalogue of Indian Curiosities," Unpublished manuscript, n.d., Missouri Historical Society; does not reveal the mummy as part of the inventory.

35. James McDermott, "Dr. Koch's Wonderful Fossils," p. 249.

36. John Haywood, *Natural and Aboriginal History of Tennessee*, (Printed by George Wilson, Nashville, Tennessee, 1823), p. 60; Anonymous, "Big Bone and Arch Caves," *Village Record*, (Westchester, Pennsylvania), August 8, 1821.

37. Daniel Drake, "XXXIV," *The Daniel Drake Papers of the Draper Manuscripts*, 2 O 30, reprinted in Angelo I. George, ed., *Prehistoric Mummies from the Mammoth Cave Area*, (George Publishing Company, 1990), p. 52. The news article used an 1811 date for the discovery of the mummies in Smith County on Dutch River. This is believed to be a garbled Copperas Cave report. The entrance opening is too small relative to Copperas Cave. This report is the most "Catacomb like" account that I have seen.

38. John Haywood, *Natural and Aboriginal History of Tennessee*, pp. 191-192. See also, Joseph Jones, *Explorations of the Aboriginal Remains of Tennessee*, Smithsonian Contributions to Knowledge, (1876), No. 259, p. 2.

39. *Ibid.*; see also, Joseph Jones, *Exploration of the Aboriginal Remains of Tennessee*, Smithsonian Contributions to Knowledge, (1876), No. 259, p. 2. Blue eyed mummies could be the result of fungal growth in the eye sockets; the white skin is another matter. This is body paint used as part of the burial ceremony.

40. John Haywood, *Natural and Aboriginal History of Tennessee*, pp. 191-192.

# CHAPTER TEN
# MUMMIES FROM SHORT CAVE AND
# THE MAMMOTH CAVE CONNECTION

1. John D. Clifford to Benjamin S. Barton, unpublished letter, September 4, 1811, Manuscript Department, American Philosophical Society Library, reprinted in Angelo I. George, ed., *Prehistoric Mummies from the Mammoth Cave Area*, (George Publishing Company, 1990), pp. 67-68.

2. Short Cave is believed to have been rented by Peyton Short (1761-1825) the younger brother of William Short. Renters often acted as if they owned the place, much

like Dixon Cave was subleased to John and Henry Dixon by Charles S. Morton. The name Dixon Cave did not indicate ownership, but the cave became famous as a place name through the mining efforts of the Dixon brothers. The "Short" in Short Cave is a family name and does not indicate a cave of short lateral extent. The cave was three quarters of a mile long, but recent rock falls largely induced by dynamite blasting has truncated this passage to exploration. Financial irresponsibilities of Peyton Short forced Charles Wilkins and Frederick Ridgely (1757-1824) to obtain power of attorney to administer his land holdings on October 24, 1809; Kentucky Court of Appeals Deed Book, M, p. 444. This power of attorney was of an adversarial nature, designed to strip Peyton of his lands to pay back significant debts owned to Wilkins and Ridgely. Subsequently, prior to July 10, 1811, William Short had also appointed Wilkins and Ridgely as his agent to administer his properties. Unpublished letter to Peyton Short dated July 10, 1811, manuscript collection, The Earl Gregg Swem Library, College of William and Mary. The Shorts had extensive lands in Kentucky and Ohio. The only way Wilkins could "legally" take possession of any of the mummies from Short Cave is through his power of attorney. Wilkins' unpublished correspondence in the Filson Club Manuscript Department, shows him as a cold and very direct to the point person. When he walked onto the Short Cave site in August 1811, he did so as legal administrator in control of the property.

3. John D. Clifford, "Letter."

4. *Ibid*.

5. Charles Wilkins, "Letter from Charles Wilkins, Esq. A Member of the American Antiquarian Society, to Samuel M. Burnside, Esq., letter dated October 2, 1817," *Archæologia Americana, Transactions and Collections of the American Antiquarian Society*, (1820), Vol. 1, pp. 361-364.

6. Nathaniel Parker Willis, *Health Trip to the Tropics*, (Charles Scribner, N. Y., 1853), pp. 203-204. It was a great name and still used today.

7. Charles Wilkins, "Letter," pp. 361-362.

8. John Hay Farnham, "Extract of a Letter from John H. Farnham, Esq. a Member of the American Antiquarian Society, Describing the Mammoth Cave, in Kentucky," *Archæologia Americana, Transactions and Collections of the American Antiquarian Society*, (1820), Vol. 1, p. 359. Farnham just graduated from Harvard in 1811; and went on a western tour into the country he would spend the rest of his life. Sometime after 1812, he became a member of the American Antiquarian Society, newspaper editor, and lawyer. His greatest achievement was in the founding of the Indiana Historical Society in 1830. Angelo I. George and Gary A. O'Dell, "The Saltpeter Works at Mammoth Cave and the New Madrid Earthquake," *The Filson Club History Quarterly*, (1992), Vol. 66, No. 1, p. 22.

9. Angelo I. George, and Gary A. O'Dell, *ibid*., p. 8.

10. John Farnham, "Undated Letter," p. 360.

11. *Ibid*., p. 359. Apparently he is unaware of the mummies from Copperas (Big Bone) Cave, Tennessee.

12. Samuel L. Mitchill, "Letter dated August 24, 1815 to Samuel M. Burnside," *Archæologia Americana, Transactions and Collections of the American Antiquarian Society*, (1820), Vol. 1, p. 318.

13. [Robert Fontaine Slaughter(?)], "The Subterranean Voyage," *The Enquirer*, (Richmond, Virginia), April 20, 1810, Vol. 6, No. 109, reprinted in *Journal Spelean History*, (1970), Vol. 3, No. 3, pp. 59-60.

14. [Hyman Gratz], "Green River, or Mammoth Cave," *Medical Repository*, (1815), Vol. 17, p. 391.

15. Charles Fox, "President's Column," *Cave Research Foundation Quarterly Newsletter*, (2013), Vol. 41, No. 2, p. 3.

16. [Hyman Gratz], "Green River, or Mammoth Cave," p. 391.

17. Dr. James H. Rice to Dr. Daniel Drake, unpublished letter in Draper Manuscripts, 2 0 30 ff, State Historical Library, Madison, Wisconsin, reprinted in Angelo I. George, ed., *Prehistoric Mummies from the Mammoth Cave Area*, (George Publishing Company, 1990), pp. 85-90.

18. *Ibid*.

19. Angelo I. George, ed., *Prehistoric Mummies from the Mammoth Cave Area*, p. 64.

20. Samuel L. Mitchill, "The Original Inhabitants of America Consisted of the Same Races with the Malays of Australasia, and the Tartars of the North," *Medical Repository*, (1815), Vol. 18, p. 187.

21. Constantine S. Rafinesque in Samuel L. Mitchill, *ibid*.

22. Harold Meloy, *Mummies of Mammoth Cave*, (Micron Publishing Company, Shelbyville, Indiana, 1971), p. 38.

23. W[illiam] Faux, *Memorable Days in America...Journal of a Tour to the United States*, (1823) in Reuben Gold Thwaites, Early Western Travels, (AMS Press, Inc., New York, 1966), p. 67.

24. Harold Meloy, *Mummies of Mammoth Cave*, p. 38.

25. Daniel Drake, "Cincinnati in 1826," *The Western Magazine and Review*, (1827), Vol. 1, p. 65.

26. Alexander Bullitt, Rambles in the *Mammoth Cave, During the year 1844 by a Visiter*, (Morton and Griswold, Louisville, Kentucky, 1845), p. 24; Horace Martin, *Pictorial Guide to the Mammoth Cave*, Kentucky, (Stringer & Townsend, New York, 1851), p. 27.

27. Louis Leonard Tucker, "'Ohio Show-Shop' The Western Museum of Cincinnati 1820-1867," *A Cabinet of Curiosities*, (The University Press of Virginia, Charlottesville, 1967), p. 103.

28. Nahum Ward, "Wonders of Nature," *Kentucky Gazette*, (Lexington, Kentucky), September 9, 1816, n.s., Vol. 2, No. 37, p. 2.

29. [Nahum Ward], "Kentucky Mammoth Cave," *Georgetown Patriot*, (Georgetown, Kentucky), August 24, 1816. This article clarifies the site of the mummy find to a neighboring cave near Mammoth Cave.

30. *Ibid*.

31. Charles Wilkins, "Letter," p. 363.

# CHAPTER ELEVEN
# ADVENTURES OF NAHUM WARD'S FAWN HOOF AND THE AMERICAN ANTIQUARIAN SOCIETY

1. William R. Halliday, "The American Antiquarian Society's Version of the Fawn Hoof Story," *Journal of Spelean History*, (1973), Vol. 6, No. 3, p. 65.

2. *Williams History of Washington County*, 1881, in *Journal Spelean History*, (1973), Vol. 6, No. 3, pp. 66-69.

3. [Robert Fontain Slaughter(?)], "The Subterrane Voyage, or the Mammoth Cave, Partially Explored," *The Enquirer*, (Richmond, Virginia), Vol. 6, No. 109, April 20, 1810; Alexander Wilson, "Correspondence - For the Port Folio," *The Port Folio*, (1810), Ser. 2, Vol. 4, pp. 310-321; Benjamin Davies, *A New System of Modern Geography*, (Johnson, Warner, Bennett, Walton, Thomas, Bradford, Buzby, and Longstreth, Philadelphia, 1813), p. 377. [Hyman Gratz], "Green River or Mammoth Cave," *Medical Repository*, (1815), Vol. 17, pp. 391-393.

4. *Williams History of Washington County*, pp. 66-67.

5. Charles Wilkins, "Letter from Charles Wilkins, Esq. A Member of the American Antiquarian Society, to Samuel M. Burnside, Esq., letter dated October 2, 1817," *Archaeologia Americana, Transactions and Collections of the American Antiquarian Society*, (1820), Vol. 1, p. 5.

6. Wilkins was an artifact collector and early member of the American Antiquarian Society. The Society was founded in 1812 by Isaiah Thomas. Nahum Ward nominated Charles Wilkins to membership into this Society; in Nahum Ward to Isaiah Thomas, unpublished correspondence, October 1, 1816, Manuscript Department, American Antiquarian Society.

7. No early time period evidence exist for the Cincinnati and Marietta, Ohio, exhibitions. Horace Carter Hovey and Richard Ellsworth Call, *Mammoth Cave of Kentucky*, (John P. Morton & Company, Louisville, Kentucky, 1912), p. 33, list Cincinnati as one of these destinations. The two accounts by Bullitt and Martin in early Mammoth Cave guidebooks

is believed to be references to the Big Bone Cave mummy that came from John D. Clifford's collection. This mummy found its way into the Western Museum in 1824.

8. Nahum Ward, "Wonders of Nature," *Kentucky Gazette*, (Lexington, Kentucky), September 9, 1816, Vol. 2, No., 37, n.s., p. 2.

9. Harold Meloy, *Mummies from Mammoth Cave*, (Micron Publishing Company, Shelbyville, Indiana, 1971), p. 30.

10. *Ibid.*, p. 30.

11. A branch chapter of the American Antiquarian Society was in Boston. [William Newnham Blane], *An Excursion Through the United States*, p. 278. Ward never printed the statement that he was the actual discoverer of the mummy in the cave.

12. Clifford K. Shipton, "The Museum of the American Antiquarian Society," in *A Cabinet of Curiosities*, (The University Press of Virginia, 1967), p. 38.

13. Nahum Ward to Thomas W. Ward, unpublished correspondence, May 2, 1817, Manuscript Department, American Antiquarian Society.

14. Nahum Ward to Thomas W. Ward, unpublished correspondence, November 10, 1816, Manuscript Department, American Antiquarian Society.

15. The October 1815 date is from an advertising photograph card of Fawn Hoof printed by Nahum's son William S. Ward.

16. [Hyman Gratz], "Green River or Mammoth Cave," p. 393. John G. Bogert placed the location of the mummy on his map at place name 2.

17. Harold Meloy, *Mummies of Mammoth Cave*, pp. 24-25. Meloy discusses the tradition of the slave workers strike in the cave.

18. Angelo I. George and Gary A. O'Dell, "The Saltpeter Works at Mammoth Cave and the New Madrid Earthquake," *The Filson Club History Quarterly*, (1992), Vol. 66, No. 1, pp. 16-17.

19. [Nahum Ward], "Kentucky Mammoth Cave," *Georgetown Patriot*, (Georgetown, Kentucky), August 24, 1816. Typographic errors in newspaper reprints give a date of "Woodford Co. (K'y.) July, 1815." There is sufficient information in many of these anonymous reprints to target Ward as the author.

20. [Nahum Ward], "The White Cave," *Merrimack Intelligencer*, (Haverhill, Massachusetts), August 10, 1816, Vol. 9, No. 5, p. 1. Gives a letter date of July 1815, clearly a typographical error for 1816.

21. Nahum Ward to Thomas W. Ward, November 10, 1816.

22. *Ibid.* Statement repeated somewhat in Nahum Ward to Thomas W. Ward, unpublished correspondence, November 21, 1816, Manuscript Department, American Antiquarian Society.

23. Nahum Ward to Thomas W. Ward, November 21, 1816; Benjamin Russell to Isaiah Thomas, unpublished correspondence, October 12, 1816, Manuscript Department, American Antiquarian Society. The exhibitor of the mummy was probably Ethan Allen Greenwood (portrait artist). In 1818, he established his own natural history museum, the New England Museum in Boston, Massachusettts.

24. Anonymous, "Great Natural Curiosity to be Seen at Col. Sikes' Hall," *National Aegis of Worcester*, (Worcester, Massachusetts), September 16 or 17, 1816, in William R. Halliday, "The American Antiquarian Society's Version of the Fawn Hoof Story," p. 64.

25. Today the Stone Age Ice Man (also known as "Ötzi," "man from Hauslabjoch," or "the Similaun man.") from the Tyrolean Alps of north Italy, executes the same amount of wonder and investigation. It was found in the autumn of 1991, incased in a melting alpine glacier. This 5200 to 5300 year old man from the ice offers a brief look into the daily life of this Neolithic or Stone Age culture. Horst Seidler, Wolfram Bernhard, Maria Teschler-Nicola, Werner Platzer, Dieter zur Nedden, Rainer Henn, Andreas Oberhauser, Thorstein Sjvold, "Some Anthropological Aspects of the Prehistoric Tyrolean Ice Man," *Science*, (1992), Vol. 258, No. 5081, pp. 455-456.

For a time, the Ice Man was considered to be a fake mummy planted in the ice from a South American site. Analysis of his DNA shows him to be of north European stock rather than South American. Oliva Handt, Martain Richards, Marion Trommsdorff, Christian Kilger, Jaana Simanainen, Oleg Georgiev, Karen Bauer, Anne Stone, Robert Hedges, Walter

Schaffner, Gerd Utermann, Bryan Sykes, and Svante Pääbo, "Molecular Genetic Analysis of the Tyrolean Ice Man," *Science*, (1994), Vol. 264, No. 5166, pp. 1775-1778.

26. Nahum Ward to George Haywood, unlocated unpublished correspondence, November 10, 1816; quoted in Nahum Ward to Thomas W. Ward, November 21, 1816.

27. *Ibid.*

28. *Ibid.*

29. Nahum Ward to Thomas W. Ward, November 10, 1816.

30. Charles Wilkins to Nahum Ward, unpublished correspondence, November 20, 1816, Manuscript Department, American Antiquarian Society.

31. Samuel L. Mitchill, "Zoological Disquisition," *The National Register*, (1816), Vol. 1, No. 2, p. 169, letter dated March 31, 1816.

32. Samuel L. Mitchill, "North American Antiquities," *Analectic Magazine*, September 1815, pp. 260-261, letter dated August 4, 1815.

33. Samuel L. Mitchill, "The Original Inhabitants of America Consisted of the Same Races with the Malays of Australasia, and the Tartars of the North," *Medical Repository*, (1815), Vol. 18, pp. 187-189.

34. Benjamin Thomas Hill, footnote to "Diary of Isaiah Thomas," *Transactions and Collections of the American Antiquarian Society*, (1909), Vol. 9; reprinted in William R. Halliday, "The American Antiquarian Society's Version of the Fawn Hoof Story," *Journal of Spelean History*, (1973), Vol. 6, No. 3, p. 64.

35. Benjamin Russell to Isaiah Thomas, unpublished correspondence, October 12, 1816, Manuscript Department, American Antiquarian Society.

36. *Ibid.*

37. *Ibid.* Published exerts in Clifford K. Shipton, "The Museum of the American Antiquarian Society," *A Cabinet of Curiosities*, (The University Press of Virginia, Charlottesville, 1967), p. 38, incorrectly assigned the authorship to Isaiah Thomas.

38. Nahum Ward to Thomas W. Ward, November 21, 1816.

39. *Ibid.*

40. Nahum Ward to Isaiah Thomas, unpublished correspondence, October 1, 1816, Manuscript Department, American Antiquarian Society.

41. Charles Wilkins to Nahum Ward, November 20, 1816.

42. *Ibid.*

43. *Ibid.*

44. *Ibid.*

45. Rajoice Newton to Charles Wilkins, unlocated unpublished correspondence, October 18, 1816; reported in Charles Wilkins to Rejoice Newton, unpublished correspondence, December 20, 1816, Manuscript Department, American Antiquarian Society.

46. *Ibid.*

47. These were the three mummies dug up from Short Cave in 1814. By 1818, Peale's Museum was exhibiting two Indian mummies, as reported in W[illiam] Faux, *Memorable Days in America...Journal of a Tour to the United States*, in Reuben Gold Thwaites, editor, (AMS Press, Inc., New York, 1966), Vol. 12, p. 67. There is no period documentation this third mummy ever found residence in the Cincinnati Museum as reported in Alexander Bullitt, *Rambles in the Mammoth Cave, During the Year 1844 by a Visiter*, (Morton and Griswold, Louisville, Kentucky, 1845), p. 24; Horace Martin, *Pictorial Guide to the Mammoth Cave, Kentucky*, (Stringer & Townsend, New York, 1851), p. 27, identifies the museum; and Harold Meloy, *Mummies of Mammoth Cave*, p. 38. Reference to the Cincinnati Museum is actually the Western Museum. The third mummy was deposited in Scudder's American Museum in New York City.

The Western Museum was the brain child of Drake. The museum would be formulated on September 15, 1818, and become a reality on June 10, 1820. Review of their early published collections are silent on the mummy from the cave. A condition, I believe is indicative the mummy was not in their possession. Nor did this museum burn to the ground. Excessive debts forced Drake and his stock holders to sell the museum to Joseph Dorfeuille in 1823. Dorfeuille sold out in 1839, and by 1867, the contents and collections were disposed of at auction. Dorfeuille was in possession of a pre-adolescent female mummy from Big Bone Cave and found residence in Cincinnati from 1824 to perhaps 1829.

The fire that destroyed Barnum's American Museum occurred in New York City, where one of the 1814 mummies from Short Cave did reside.

48. Nahum Ward to Thomas W. Ward, November 10, 1816.

49. Nahum Ward to Thomas W. Ward, November 21, 1816.

50. Nahum Ward to Thomas W. Ward, November 10, 1816.

51. "The Mummy," *Hallowell Gazette*, September 4, 1816.

52. Nahum Ward to Thomas W. Ward, November 10, 1816.

53. Nahum Ward to Thomas W. Ward, unpublished correspondence, May 2, 1817, Manuscript Department, American Antiquarian Society. Isaiah Thomas to Thomas W. Ward correspondence has not been located.

54. *Ibid.*

55. Benjamin Thomas Hill, "Diary of Isaiah Thomas."

56. *Ibid.*

57. *William's History of Washington County*, in *Journal Spelean History*, (1973), Vol. 6, No. 3, p. 68.

58. Harold Meloy, *Mummies of Mammoth Cave*, p. 31; Horace C. Hovey, and Elsworth Call, *Mammoth Cave of Kentucky*, p. 33.

59. Anonymous, "The Facts About Fawn Hoof," *The Courier-Journal*, (Louisville, Kentucky), Magazine Sec., March 4, 1926, p. 6.

60. Harold Meloy, *Mummies of Mammoth Cave*, p. 32. Meloy was not successful in locating post mortem results of the mummy dissection.

61. Anonymous, "The Facts About Fawn Hoof."

62. Margaret M. Birdwell, *The Story of Mammoth Cave National Park, Kentucky*, (Margaret M. Birdwell, 11th edition, 1971), p. 44.

63. *Ibid.*, p. 47-49.

64. Ted Giles, *Fawn Hoof is Lost*, (privately published, n.d.).

65. Anonymous, "World-Wide Search Started for Mammoth Cave's Lost Mummy," *The Courier-Journal*, (Louisville, Kentucky), November 7, 1927, p. 1.

66. Anonymous, "Fawn Hoof, Just Old Bones Now, is Found in National Museum," *The Courier-Journal*, (Louisville, Kentucky), February 10, 1928, p. 1.

# CHAPTER TWELVE
# MARCH OF THE CONTENDERS AND THE SEARCH FOR OLD WORLD ROOTS IN AMERICA

1. Nahum Ward, "Wonders of Nature," *Kentucky Gazette*, (Lexington, Kentucky), September 9, 1816, n.s., Vol. 2, No. 37, p. 2; Ward said she, "must have been some personage of high distinction." [Hyman Gratz], "Green River or Mammoth Cave," *Medical Repository*, (1815), Vol. 17, p. 391, labeled her a queen.

2. [William Newnham Blane], *An Excursion Through the United States and Canada During the Years 1822-1823*, (London: Baldwin, Cradock and Foy, 1824), p. 278.

3. M. C. Morgan, "Reminiscences of Mammoth Cave," *Glasgow Times*, (Glasgow, Kentucky), n.d., in Harold Meloy and Patty Jo Watson, "Little Alice of Salts Cave and Other Mummies," Patty Jo Watson, ed., *The Prehistory of Salts Cave, Kentucky*, Illinois State Museum, (1969), Report of Investigation, No. 16, p. 65.

4. Stephen Williams, *Fantastic Archaeology, the Wild Side of North American Prehistory*, (University of Pennsylvania Press, Philadelphia, 1991), p. 50.

5. John Haywood, *Ancient and Aboriginal History of Tennessee*, (Printed by George Wilson, Nashville, Tennessee. 1823), p. 160.

6. Josiah Priest, *American Antiquities and Discoveries in the West*, (Hoffman and White, Albany, New York, 1834), 4th edition, p. 117.

7. *Ibid.*, p. 116.

8. *Ibid.*, p. 119.

9. Josiah Priest, *American Antiquities and Discoveries in the West*, (Hoffman and White, Albany, New York, 1833), 3rd edition, p. 290.

10. This is the mummy found in 1814, a male, and deposited in the John Scudder's American Museum of New York.

11. Josiah Priest, *American Antiquities*, 3 rd. ed., p. 334.

12. Charles Boewe, *Fitzpatrick's Rafinesque: A Sketch of his Life with Bibliography*, (M & S Press, Weston, Massachusetts, 1982), p. 15.

13. *Ibid.*, p. 17.

14. Anonymous, "Remarkable Discovery," *The New Yorker*, (New York, New York), April 1, 1837.

15. Anonymous, "Another Great Cave in Kentucky," *New Albany Daily Ledger*, (New Albany, Indiana), August 17, 1853.

16. Lewis Collins, and Richard H. Collins, *History of Kentucky*, Vol. 2, p. 641. Otto A. Rothert, *A History of Muhlenberg County*, (John P. Morton and Company, Louisville, Kentucky, 1913), p. 429. Rothert verified the mummies in the cave as a hoax. The first reference to the mummified monkey is only three years prior to the discovery of Little Al in Salts Cave, Kentucky.

17. Anonymous, "A New Wonder," *Record of the Times*, (Wilkes-Barre, Pennsylvania), June 25, 1878.

18. *Ibid.*

19. Anonymous, "A New Cave Discovery in Kentucky," *Scientific American*, November 23, 1879, Vol. 39, No. 21, p. 329.

20. Anonymous, "A Cave of Giants," *The Weekly News*, (Charleston, South Carolina), February 4, 1880.

21. Stephen Williams, *Fantastic Archaeology*, p. 87-90.

22. Anonymous, "The Largest Cave on Earth," *Chattanooga Daily Times*, (Chattanooga, Tennessee), March 6, 1882, p. 4.

23. Anonymous, "A Kentucky Wonder," *Women*, April 11, 1888.

## CHAPTER THIRTEEN
## THE DUAL NATURE OF LITTLE AL

1. Louise M. Robbins, "A Woodland 'Mummy' from Salts Cave, Kentucky," *American Antiquity*, (1971), Vol. 36, No. 2, p. 201. Here is a little boy who died of internal hemorrhages from a fall sustained in Salts Cave. He was prepped for burial by Indian companions. Yet, he was never buried. Preparation consisted of tucking his legs tightly up against his rib cage, and placing his arms next to his breast and hands up under his chin. The body was placed on a ledge in a cut around off of Mummy Valley in Salts Cave. His physical attitude is similar to the photograph of Fawn Hoof in Horace C. Hovey and Richard E. Call, *Mammoth Cave of Kentucky*, (John P. Morton & Company, Louisville, Kentucky, 1912), p. 32. Little Al has the honor of being the latest pre-Columbian Early Woodland explorer in the cave! By a lapse of hundreds of years. Date of death is about 30 A. D.

2. Elmer G. Sulzer, "Gay Nineties Rendezvous: the Mammoth Cave Railroad," *Register of the Kentucky Historical Society*, (1959), Vol. 57, No. 2, pp. 131-132. Larkin J. Procter, brother to George M. Procter, leased the Mammoth Cave and the hotel (1856-1861, 1866-1871), lawyer, land speculator and developer. He was also the owner of Proctor Cave (from 1870). Later in life, he would become one of the owners in the Grand Avenue Cave Company.

3. *Ibid.*

4. Margaret M. Birdwell, *The Story of Mammoth Cave National Park*, Kentucky, (Margaret M. Birdwell, 1971), 11th edition, p. 38.

5. T. O. Chisholm, *Grand Avenue Cave*, (Brandon Printing Co., Nashville, Tennessee, 1892), p. 5. George M. Procter possessed good business sense and was owner and exhibitor of Diamond Caverns from 1860, and Grand Avenue Cave from 1875. He became the owner (in 1854) of Bells Tavern through his marriage to widow Maria L. Bell (Gorin) in 1853. He laid out the community of Glasgow Junction (present day Park City), was politically active, and a successful venture capitalist. Eugene was the son of George M. Procter and Maria L. Bell (Gorin). One of his other sons from his first marriage to Anna Maria (Young), John Robert Procter (1844-1903) became the State Geologist of Kentucky in 1880.

3. Frederic Ward Putnam, "Archaeological Researches in Kentucky and Indiana, 1874," *Proceedings of the Boston Society of Natural History*, (1875), Vol. 17, pp. 319-320.

7. Frederic Ward Putnam, "Archaeological Explorations in Kentucky and Indiana," Eight Annual Report, 1875, *Antiquities of the New World - Early Explorations in Archaeology*, Vol. 8, *The Archaeological Reports of Frederic Ward Putnam*, (AMS Press, Inc., New York, 1973), p. 167.

3. Anonymous, "A Wonderful Discovery," *The Courier-Journal*, (Louisville, Kentucky), January 18, 1875, n.s., Vol. 48, No. 2261, p. 1. Anonymous, "The International Circus," *The Courier-Journal*, (Louisville, Kentucky), April 13, 1875, n.s., Vol. 48, No. 2345, p. 4.

9. Thomas E. Lee was possibly the best hard rock cave explorer up to the time of William Floyd Collins (1887-1925). Numerous caves in the vicinity of Mammoth Cave bear his signature of cave conquest. He periodically guided tourist through Mammoth Cave. By local standards, M. Carrie Morgan in her "Reminiscences of Mammoth Cave," *Glasgow Times*, (Glasgow, Kentucky), December 22, 1929, reprinted in *Journal of Spelean History*, (1984), Vol. 18, No. 2, p. 63, considered him "something of a character." By that admission, Lee was believed to be a wild and reckless individual. Despite being a "character;" he pushed the limits of many caves in the region.

10. Anonymous, "Personal," *The Courier-Journal*, (Louisville, Kentucky), July 19, 1875, Vol. 49, n.s., No. 2442, p. 4. Anonymous, "The New Cave," *The Courier Journal*, (Louisville, Kentucky), July 21, 1875, Vol. 49, n.s., No. 2443, p. 4.

11. *Ibid.*, Anonymous, "The New Cave," *The Courier-Journal*, (Louisville, Kentucky), July 21, 1875, n.s., Vol. 49, No. 2443, p. 4.

12. Anonymous, "A New Kentucky Cave," *Covington Journal*, (Covington, Kentucky), July 31, 1875, Vol. 8, No. 25, n.s., p. 1. Reprinted from the *Louisville Daily Ledger*.

13. Angelo I. George, *Mummies of Short Cave and the Great Catacomb Mystery*, (George Publishing Company, Louisville, Kentucky, 1985).

14. Fawn Hoof was since given to the American Antiquarian Society of Worcester, Massachusetts.

15. The person in charge of securing and setting up the natural history display was Spencer F. Baird (1823-1887). A zoologist by training; with duties for the planned Centennial Exhibition was to collect natural history exhibits from all parts of the world. This he did while working as secretary in charge of exhibits for the Smithsonian Institution and as head of the newly created Commission of Fish and Fisheries.

16. Anonymous, "A Female Mummy in a Kentucky Cave," *Kentucky Gazette*, (Lexington, Kentucky), July 28, 1875, Vol. 10, No. 10, p. 2.

17. Anonymous, "That Kentucky Mummy," *The Courier-Journal*, (Louisville, Kentucky), August 4, 1875, Vol. 49, No. 2457, n.s., p. 4. Use of the pronoun "that" by *The Courier-Journal* was their way in saying they did not believe anything connected with the reported mummy discovery. Review of newspaper runs for 1874-1875 and 1880, always used the pronoun "that" in headlines when printing stories possessing a high degree of strangeness associated with a lack of credibility. Obvious practical jokes were treated in this fashion, for example: "That Bride of Stone," discusses mummification by T. Rial O'Bright, M. D., of his favorite nephew using extract of silica from geodes, *The Courier-Journal*, (Louisville, Kentucky), March 20, 1874, Vol. 46, No. 2053, n.s., p. 3; "That Cave Wonder," about the Grand Crystal Cave hoax, *The Courier-Journal*, (Louisville, Kentucky), July 10, 1880, Vol. 55, No. 2472, n.s., p. 4.

18. Angelo I. George, editor, *Prehistoric Mummies from the Mammoth Cave Area*, (George Publishing Company, Louisville, Kentucky, 1990), pp. 35-43.

19. Bennett H. Young (1843-1919) was a lawyer by trade and an archaeologist by advocation. He saw the mummy in 1897, and gave a cryptic description of it in a newspaper article. He did not take time to study the mummy. If he had, certain physical attributes (its genitalia) on the "female" mummy would become apparent as a male child. Bennett H. Young, "Rivals the Mammoth in Grandeur," *The Courier-Journal*, (Louisville, Kentucky), April 15, 1897, Sec. 3, p. 1.

20. S. B. Y. [Samuel B. Young], *The Courier-Journal*, (Louisville, Kentucky), August 12, 1875, Vol. 49, n.s., No. 2465, p. 4, in letter to the editor dated August 9, 1875. Young

was owner of Indian Cave; and had his own vested interest at stake when confronting competitors and potential lost tourist dollars.

21. E. U. Procter, "Those Barren County Holes in the Ground," *The Courier-Journal*, (Louisville, Kentucky), August 16, 1875, Vol. 49, No. 2469, n.s., p. 3.

22. *Ibid*. This is the start of what in later years would be called "the great cave wars." A time period in which cave operators would exchange advertising wits and even mayhem to rival attractions in order to attract tourist to their show caves. Horace C. Hovey (1833-1914), the father of American Speleology, would change railroad cars at Glasgow Junction for Mammoth Cave in March 1893. He said:

> There are said to be five hundred caves in Edmonson County, and several of these are lauded by their owners as rivals to Mammoth Cave. This petty jealousy cropped out in remarks made to us on our arrival at the Glasgow Junction, where we had to change cars, to the effect that Green River had broken into Mammoth Cave so as to make its avenue impassable; that visitors were not admitted at this season; that the hotel was literally dropping to pieces and had been closed; and, in short, that we had better turn our steps in some other cavernous direction. This local jealousy has occasionally even taken the malignant form of wanton injury to the estate and ugly threats of violence to the manager.

H. C. Hovey, "Mammoth Cave in March", *Science,* (1893), Vol. 21, No. 531, pp. 189-190.

23. *Ibid*. This was the time in Kentucky where the interpretation of the cave law of ownership said, he who owns the entrance, owns the cave. The Mammoth Cave estate owned the only known entrance to Salts Cave, even though the majority of the cave extended under Louis Vial's land.

24. Anonymous, "Barren County. The Circus - That Mummy in the Cave - Hydrophobia Among the Hogs, Etc.," *The Courier-Journal*, (Louisville, Kentucky), August 28, 1875, Vol. 49, No. 2481, n.s., p. 3. It was only in 1896, the Mammoth Cave estate discovered they did not have clear title to Salts Cave entrance. Patty Jo Watson, "An Ancient Cave Mummy From Kentucky," *The Dead Tell Tales: Essays in Honor of Jane E. Buikstra*, Monograph 76, (Cotsen Institute of Archaeology Press), (2013), p. 47,

25. *Ibid*.

26. Fawn, "That Pickled Squaw," *The Courier-Journal*, (Louisville, Kentucky), September 27, 1875, Vol. 49, No. 2511, n.s., p. 3. Fawn wrote a number of articles on scenic natural science and archaeology subjects for *The Courier-Journal*. Fawn is a careful observer with a high degree of technical skill. Fawn could be a pseudonym for Bennett H. Young.

27. *Ibid*.

28. Horace C. Hovey, *Celebrated American Caverns*, (Robert Clarke & Company, Cincinnati, Ohio, 1882), p. 71.

29. The inscription was rediscovered in the Spring of 1969, by Cave Research Foundation personnel. Louise M. Robbins, "A Woodland "Mummy" from Salts Cave, Kentucky," p. 201.

30. *Ibid*.

31. Patty Jo Watson, "Observation and Recording in Salts Cave," Patty Jo Watson, editor, *Archeology of the Mammoth Cave Area*, (Academic Press, Inc., New York, 1974), pp. 25-26. Patty Jo Watson, "An Ancient Cave Mummy From Kentucky," p. 47, presents a good argument for J. M. Smith's authorship of the Damnation Rock in mid to late March 1875.

32. *Ibid*., p. 25.

33. T. O. Chisholm, *Grand Avenue Cave*, pp. 31-32.

34. *Ibid*., p. 31.

35. *Ibid*., p. 32.

36. *Ibid*., p. 33.

37. *Ibid*.

38. Harold Meloy, *Mummies of Mammoth Cave*, (Micron Publishing Company, Shelbyville, Indiana, 1971), pp. 8-9.

39. [Orange Blossom], "Another Kentucky Wonder," *The Courier-Journal*, (Louisville, Kentucky), June 24, 1878, Vol. 54, No. 3456, n.s., p. 4, reprinted with *The Courier-Journal* editorial comment from *Cincinnati Commercial*.

40. [Orange Blossom], *Scientific American*, November 23, 1879.

41. [Orange Blossom], "Another Kentucky Wonder."

42. George M. Procter, "That Cave Wonder," *The Courier-Journal*, (Louisville, Kentucky), July 10, 1878, Vol. 55, No. 3472, n.s., p. 4. Hovey establishes the Grand Crystal Cave as a real cave of some three miles in length. Procter reports in his letter that C. P. Wolsey had explored this cave and found "it a very pretty cave." Physical characteristics inside the cave, especially the three rivers is I suspect, Parker Cave. It is located about two miles southwest of Park City.

43. *Ibid.*

44. Orange Blossom, "The Cave Hoax," *The Courier-Journal*, (Louisville, Kentucky), July 12, 1878, Vol. 55, No. 3474, n.s., p. 1.

45. Horace C. Hovey, *Celebrated American Caverns*.

46. *Ibid.*, p. 20, 66. I suspect Hovey considered the American Mummy from Grand Avenue Cave to be part of the concocted and matured Grand Crystal Cave hoax. Especially since George M. Procter was supposed to have acquired some of these purported mummies to exhibit in his cave. Hovey may not have wanted to soil his hands on a possible fake (manufactured) exhibition mummy. Considering how Hovey thought he was treated at Glasgow Junction by Procter business associates; it is clear Hovey wrote them out of his spelean histories, see Note No. 22. As a result, we know less about Diamond Caverns, Proctor Cave, Grand Avenue Cave, Hundred Room Cave, and Hundred Dome Cave.

47. Bennett H. Young, "Rivals the Mammoth in Grandeur." This is the first reference the mummy had red hair. Young is the only person with a penchant for archaeology to view Little Al during this time period. Other than hair color, hand placement, and cave location, he makes no other inspection of the mummy. He did photograph the mummy for his newspaper article.

The location of Gardner's Grotto as leased to L. W. Hazen is not at the present known. Its commercial life was probably short lived. This is the only reference I have seen for this commercial cave. Presence of the mummy at another cave, other than Mammoth Cave suggest Henry C. Ganter did not have the mummy in his possession.

48. Bennett H. Young, *Prehistoric Men from Kentucky*, (Filson Club Publication No. 25, 1910), p. 308.

49. Horace C. Hovey, and Richard E. Call, *Mammoth Cave of Kentucky*, (John P. Morton and Company, Louisville, Kentucky, 1912), p. 33.

50. M. Carrie Morgan, "Reminiscences of Mammoth Cave," p. 63.

51. *Ibid.* No evidence exist for a secret side entrance to Salts Cave. Mammoth Cave estate owned the only known entrance. It was through that portal that cavers, grave robbers, and clandestine surveyors made entrance.

52. Patty Jo Watson, personal written communication, July 6, 1993.

53. *Ibid.*

54. Fawn, "That Pickled Squaw."

55. Harold Meloy, *Mummies of Mammoth Cave*, pp. 8-9.

56. *Ibid.*, p. 9.

57. *Ibid.*, p. 10.

58. *Ibid.*, p. 12.

59. *Ibid.*, pp. 12-13.

60. Louise M. Robbins, "A Woodland "Mummy" From Salts Cave, Kentucky," *American Antiquity*, (1971), Vol. 36, No. 2, p. 201.

# CHAPTER FOURTEEN
# CAUGHT BETWEEN A ROCK AND A HARD PLACE

1. After Mammoth Cave became a national park, the African American guides could only find employment in the domestic service industry. All of the African American guides, the guides for which Mammoth Cave was famous, were discharged to find meaningful

employment elsewhere. A few of the caucasian guides stayed on until they retired. Jeanne C. Schmitzer, "The Sable Guides of Mammoth Cave," *The Filson Club History Quarterly*, (1993), Vol. 67, No. 2, pp. 240-258.

2. Alonzo W. Pond, "Lost John of Mummy Ledge," *Natural History*, (1937), Vol. 39, No. 3, p. 176.

3. *Ibid*.

4. Malcolm Bayley, "Desiccated Body in Mammoth Cave Viewed as Possible Epochal Discovery," *The Courier-Journal*, (Louisville, Kentucky), June 23, 1935, Sec. 1, p. 8.

5. Alonzo Pond, "Lost John of Mummy Ledge."

6. *Ibid*.

7. *Ibid*.

8. Malcolm Bayley, *Ibid*.

9. Harold Meloy, *Mummies of Mammoth Cave*, (Micron Publishing Company, Shelbyville, Indiana, 1971), p. 19.

10. Alonzo W. Pond, "Raising the Tomb Rock from Lost John of Mummy Ledge," *Journal of Spelean History*, (1971), Vol. 4, No. 1, p. 12.

11. Alonzo Pond, "Lost John of Mummy Ledge," p. 176.

12. Alonzo W. Pond, "Raising the Tomb Rock from Lost John of Mummy Ledge," *Journal of Spelean History*, (1971), Vol. 4, No. 1, p. 12.

13. Robert L. Chapman and Barbara Ann Kipfer, *Dictionary of American Slang*, (Harper Collins Publishers, New York, New York, 1995), p. 317.

14. W. C. Handy (music) and Chris Smith (words), *Long Gone / Lost John*, (Pace & Handy Music Co., 1920).

15. The actual song Mellow's Log Cabin is referring to is the one recorded by the Kentucky dual Richard Burnett and Leonard Rutherford, *Lost John* on Columbia record label 15122-D in 1927. Mellow's Log Cabin, "Wayne Raney's Lost John Boogie," http://hillbillycountry.blogspot.com/2011/04/wayne-raneys-lost-john-boogie.html.

16. Lyle Lofgren, "Remembering the Old Songs: Long John Green (Lost John)," *Inside Bluegrass*, (2012), Vol. 38, No. 1.

17. Kenneth B. Tankersley, "Digging Crystals: Prehistoric Gypsum Mining in Mammoth Cave," *CRF Newsletter*, (November 1989), Vol. 17, No. 4, p. 4.

18. Angelo I. George, "Cave Accidents Before 1900," *Journal of Spelean History* (1995), Vol. 29, No. 2, pp. 55-61.

19. Malcolm Bayley, "Desiccated Body in Mammoth Cave Viewed as Possible Epochal Discovery," p. 8.

20. Anonymous, "Mammoth Cave's 'Lost John' 'Mummy' Out of Public View;" *The Courier-Journal*, (Louisville, Kentucky), July 27, 1976, p. B5.

"Arne Saknussemm!" Wood engraving from Jules Verne, *Voyage au Centre de la Terre*, 1867. Riou illustration edition.

# ABOUT THE AUTHOR

Angelo I. George is a professional geologist and spelean historian. He is the author of "Mammoth Cave Saltpeter Works," "The Saltpeter Empires of Great Saltpetre Cave and Mammoth Cave," and "Outer Door to the Auger Hole ... and Beyond, The Exploration of Wyandotte Cave." He is a member of the Cave Research Foundation, Fellow of the National Speleological Society, and a recipient of the Peter M. Hauer Award in Spelean History for outstanding work conducted in the field of cave history.

www.ingramcontent.com/pod-product-compliance
Lightning Source LLC
Chambersburg PA
CBHW080332270325
41927CB000143/3190